W9-AYQ-300

REVOLUTIONARY JEWS FROM MARX TO TROTSKY

REVOLUTIONARY JEWS FROM MARX TO TROTSKY

ROBERT S. WISTRICH

with a foreword by
JAMES JOLL
Stevenson Professor of International History
in the University of London

HARRAP LONDON

FOR
DANIELLA, ANNA AND DOV

First published in Great Britain 1976
by GEORGE G. HARRAP & CO. LTD
182–184 High Holborn, London WC1V 7AX

ISBN 0 245 52785 0

Photoset in 10 on 11 point Baskerville
Printed and bound
in Great Britain by
REDWOOD BURN LIMITED
Trowbridge & Esher

Foreword

by JAMES JOLL

The tragedy of European Jewry in the twentieth century is made all the more poignant when contrasted with the hopes which were raised by the spread of liberal ideas a hundred years earlier. Liberalism meant, among other things, the emancipation of the Jews: they would be freed from discriminatory laws; they would be able to follow a profession of their own choosing; they would become citizens with equal rights, entitled to practise their own religion on the same basis as members of the Christian churches. They would be Germans or Frenchmen or Austrians of the Jewish faith, as the phrase went: or they could become freethinkers with a confidence in the power of science to solve all problems. In any case, they would now be no different from anybody else.

But the reality was quite other. In some countries, notably Russia, the Jews were subjected to recurrent physical violence. Elsewhere, in France at the time of the Dreyfus Affair or in Vienna when Freud and Mahler were struggling to make their careers in the face of anti-Jewish prejudice, they were subjected to verbal abuse of great virulence in the anti-Semitic press and pamphlets. Moreover, by the end of the nineteenth century the spread of a new nationalism, often based on racial theories given a specious currency by the misinterpretation of Darwin's teaching, led some people to stress the rootlessness of the Jews and to demand their exclusion from the allegedly homogeneous national communities in which they were living.

There were still many Jews who thought that this would pass and that the liberal hopes of eventual assimilation would be fulfilled. But for others there seemed two alternative ways out. On the one hand, the Zionist movement launched by Theodor Herzl in 1897 gave the Jews hope of a national state of their own which would enable them to become an independent sovereign people within the community of nations. On the other hand—and this is the theme of Robert Wistrich's important book—those Jews who became socialists envisaged a world in which national differences, including those between Jew and Gentile, would disappear and in which the only significant distinctions would be those between one class and another, until, after the triumph of the inevitable revolution, a classless society would emerge, and thus the Jewish question would be finally resolved.

Robert Wistrich has provided an original and imaginative analysis of what it meant for an assimilated Jew to adopt the Marxist alternative. Starting with Marx himself and his early essay on the Jewish Question, he has studied ten socialist Jews and shows the dilemmas and equivocations inherent in their position. While they declared that their own Jewish origins were irrelevant, they found themselves under attack, sometimes by their revolutionary comrades, precisely on account of these origins. Some of them, with some backing from Marx's own writings, contributed to socialist anti-Semitism by identifying Jewish characteristics as typical of the capitalist class; others were able to point to elements in the Jewish tradition, especially the emphasis on justice, as providing a link between Judaism and socialism.

The people whose ideas and careers are discussed in this book are very varied: the flamboyant Lassalle, the intense and doctrinaire Rosa Luxemburg, the realistic and ironic Viennese Victor Adler, the sensitive intellectual in politics, Léon Blum, trying to reconcile his socialist beliefs with an instinctive sympathy with Zionism. There are also less well-known figures among them, notably the French anarchist, Bernard Lazare, a visionary poised between socialism and Zionism and the subject of one of the most fascinating chapters in this book.

Dr Wistrich points out that in some cases revolutionary Jews, because of their denial of a separate Jewish identity, were less sensitive to the persecution of the Jews than they were to the sufferings of other oppressed minorities. For many of them, like Martov, Trotsky and Rosa Luxemburg, their attitude to anti-Semitism, even in its extreme forms as in the Russian pogroms, was similar to their attitude to war. Both were evils inherent in capitalism and would only vanish when capitalism was abolished. They shared with the liberal assimilationist Jews a failure to perceive and a reluctance to believe in the true nature of anti-Semitism and in the reality of the danger it presented. We have lived in our own day to see the tragic irony of the Marxist position. The attempt to get rid of the Jewish question by analysing society in terms of class antagonisms rather than racial and national divisions has proved vain. And socialist anti-Semitism, which Robert Wistrich has analysed so well, has reinforced the anti-Semitism indigenous in parts of eastern Europe—in Russia and Poland especially—to produce the ironical situation of Jews suffering at the hands of Marxists in spite of the hopes of an older generation of Jewish revolutionaries that socialism alone could solve all their problems.

This book deals with a neglected aspect of the history of Marxist ideas and is an original contribution to European intellectual history in general. It throws light on the psychology of revolutionaries, and especially those who have broken away from the society in which they grew up and have become, so to speak, marginal men. They felt, like so many middle-class revolutionaries, a particular revulsion against the values of the group with which they had been most closely involved. For some Jews, including the young Karl Marx, this could lead to a peculiar form of self-hatred, in which the material values they rejected seemed to have become particularly associated with the role of the Jews in finance and commerce.

This work also helps us to understand something of the background to the discrimination against the Jews in the communist countries of Eastern Europe. But above all it analyses an important aspect of the failure of the nineteenth-century belief in progress and of the assumption that all problems have solutions. By examining with great fairness and insight, but without concealing where his own sympathies lie, the careers and beliefs of these leading socialist Jews, Dr Wistrich has substantially increased our understanding of what has happened to Europe in the last hundred years.

JAMES JOLL

Preface

For many Jews in the nineteenth and twentieth centuries, Socialism and Communism were a path to their social and political emancipation as human beings. Whether they embraced these ideologies as a means of escape from oppression and social exclusion, or through loss of faith in their own national-religious traditions, or out of more general ethical and humanitarian considerations, this represented for many of them the 'Promised Land'. But the price to be paid for this deliverance was a heavy one. If Moses, according to Jewish tradition, led the Children of Israel out of slavery into freedom, then Communism by a strange twist of fate led them back into bondage. In Soviet Russia the 'Promised Land' turned out to be a twentieth-century 'Egypt'. Hence, it is not surprising that Jews should now be looking to their own heritage for spiritual sustenance and survival.

The revolutionary Jews discussed in this book were the heirs of the dream of assimilation first proclaimed by the French Revolution of 1789. Socialism became in a sense their substitute for a Jewish identity they had either lost or wished to cast off. One cannot properly understand the ambiguities and ramifications of their encounter with revolutionary Socialism if one ignores this crucial fact. They pursued the universalist option with all the passion of neophytes who desired a complete dissolution of Jewish group identity. It is my contention that the logic of Marxism inevitably led them into a cul-de-sac with regard to the Jewish problem. My assumption is that there was no theoretical or practical framework within Marxism which could adequately take account of the Jewish reality in all its human, social and political complexity. By examining the Jewish background of Socialists as different as Marx, Lassalle, Rosa Luxemburg, Otto Bauer, Léon Blum, Martov or Trotsky, one can discover a great deal about the reasons for this failure.

Nevertheless, the Jewish encounter with Socialism, which has exercised a great influence on the development of Marxist ideology, should not by any means be dismissed as a negative experience. Individual Jewish revolutionaries played a remarkably dramatic and colourful role in the history of European Socialism, and thereby had a considerable impact on the making of the modern world. As the perennial outsiders of European Christian civilization, the Jews brought to Socialism their own unique intellectual gifts, apocalyptic visions, passion for justice and hatred of oppression. Their peculiar marginality enabled them to expose the masks and hypocrisies of bourgeois society, to devise bold theoretical syntheses, and to act as pathfinders on the road to human emancipation. Nor should one overlook the fact that the State of Israel owes much of its original inspiration to the ideals and goals of modern Socialism.

In this book, however, I am primarily concerned with the psychological challenge which the Jewish problem posed to revolutionaries and Socialists of Jewish origin. To some extent, of course, this problem varied according to the intensity of anti-Semitism and the progress of enlightenment and emancipation in different societies. Hence, for the benefit of the general reader I have prefaced each section of the book with a brief commentary on the position of the Jews in Germany, Austria-Hungary, France and Russia. But in spite of all national and social divergencies, Jewish revolutionaries from Marx to Trotsky tended to display a remarkable similarity in their assessments of the Jewish problem, which in my view reflected their own incomplete, subjective emancipation.

If this book has cast light on what has hitherto been a sadly neglected, almost taboo subject, it will have amply justified its purpose.

January 1976 ROBERT S. WISTRICH

Acknowledgments

I should like to thank my colleagues on the staff of the Wiener Library, London, and its director, Professor Walter Laqueur, for their invaluable assistance to me during my research on this book. I also benefited greatly from using the resources of the British Museum in London, the Bibliothèque Nationale, the Institute of Social History (Amsterdam) and the Austrian National Library in Vienna. I am very grateful to the German Academic Exchange Service for having awarded me a scholarship to work at the Friedrich-Ebert Stiftung in Bonn, and to spend some months in West Germany gathering material for my thesis. My thanks also go to Professor Chimen Abramsky for supervising the doctoral dissertation at University College, London, in which the present book had its origins.

Among those from whose advice and thoughts I derived stimulation I should like to mention the late Julius Braunthal, whose unrivalled knowledge of the Austrian social democracy was very helpful, the late Professor G. Eckert (Braunschweig), Rabbi Dr Arthur Hertzberg, M. Roger Errera (Paris), Dr Susanne Miller (Bonn), Dr Arnold Paucker (London), Dr Eva Reichmann, Boris Sapir (Amsterdam), Nahum Sneh, Professor Karl Stadler (Linz), Robert Weltsch (London), Dr Gerhard Botz (Linz) and the Alliance Israélite Universelle. I must add that the responsibility for any judgments made or errors committed is entirely my own, as are the translations unless otherwise stated.

I am grateful to the Bibliothèque Nationale, Paris, for permission to reproduce the photographs of Bernstein, Lazare and Blum; to the Radio Times Hulton Picture Library for those of Marx, Lassalle, Rosa Luxemburg and Trotsky; and to the Ludwig-Boltzmann-Institut für Geschichte der Arbeiterbewegung, Linz, for the Bauer photograph.

I wish to express my special appreciation to Professor James Joll of the London School of Economics for his encouragement and sympathetic interest in my work, and to Ken Thomson, General Editor at George G. Harrap, for his unswerving confidence in this project. My deepest debt is above all to my wife Daniella, whose patience, criticism and constant support were of inestimable value throughout. Without her this book might never have been written.

Contents

The Jews and Socialism

> **'Every iconoclastic incident, every convulsion, every social challenge has seen, and still sees, Jews in the front line. Whenever a peremptory demand or a clean sweep is made, wherever the idea of governmental metamorphosis is to be translated into action with frenzied zeal, Jews have been and still are the leaders. Jews are the Jacobins of our age.'**
>
> **Jakob Wassermann**

> **'All these great revolutionaries were extremely vulnerable. They were, as Jews, rootless, in a sense; but they were so only in some respects, for they had the deepest roots in intellectual tradition and in the noblest aspirations of their times. Yet whenever religious intolerance or nationalist emotion was on the ascendant, whenever dogmatic narrow-mindedness and fanaticism triumphed they were the first victims.'**
>
> **Isaac Deutscher**

What role did individual Jews play in the European socialist movement of the nineteenth and twentieth centuries and why did some of them become such important catalysts of social change in this period? Was it a mere coincidence that they participated so actively in socialism, and did this have anything to do with their Jewish origins or heritage? Finally, what effect did this participation have on socialist attitudes to the 'Jewish question'? These are the central questions which I propose to examine in this introductory essay about the relationship of Jews to revolutionary socialism—a complex, emotionally charged subject which has yet to be fully elucidated.

In order to avoid any misunderstanding it should be stated at once that socialism was in no sense invented by Jews, indeed many of its most distinguished leaders were not of Jewish origin. None of the utopian socialists—Robert Owen, Charles Fourier or Pierre-Joseph Proudhon—were Jews. Engels was not a Jew. Nor was Karl Kautsky, despite a curiously tenacious myth. The outstanding figures of the Second International, August Bebel and Jean Jaurès, were not Jewish, nor was Lenin. There is no need, however, to belabour this point, or the equally obvious corollary that the majority of Jews were neither socialists nor revolutionaries. What concerns us here is the indisputable fact that Jews have from the outset played a part out of all proportion to their numbers in the development of modern socialism. It is this fact which requires some explanation and analysis if one is to comprehend the individual case-histories discussed later in this book.

Jews in nineteenth-century Germany were the leaders of the early socialist movement. Moses Hess was the first German Communist.

Karl Marx was the creator of scientific socialism and the international Communist movement. Ferdinand Lassalle was the founder of the first German workers' organization, and inspirer of German social democracy. In the latter part of the nineteenth-century Paul Singer was frequently Chairman of the German Socialist Party Congresses, and also at Congresses of the Second International. Eduard Bernstein was the theorist of the reformist wing in German socialism and the founder of 'revisionism'. Rosa Luxemburg was the leader of the German and Polish left-wing socialists and one of the founders of the German Communist Party. Two of the six People's Commissars in the first post-revolutionary Socialist Government in Germany (1918), Hugo Haase and Otto Landsberg, were Jews. At the head of the short-lived Munich Soviet Republic stood Kurt Eisner, and among his closest collaborators were three other Jewish revolutionaries, Gustav Landauer, Ernst Toller and Eugen Leviné.[1] The leaders of Austro-Marxism, both before 1914 and in the inter-war period, were predominantly Jewish—including the founder of the Social Democratic Party Victor Adler, his son Friedrich Adler, his successor Otto Bauer, and a host of other gifted associates. Jewish intellectuals were equally prominent in the Hungarian social democracy, and virtually dominated the inter-war Communist Party leadership. A similar situation existed in Poland. Jews were extremely prominent at the side of Lenin when the October Revolution in 1917 brought into being the Soviet regime. Apart from Leon Trotsky, who planned and executed the armed insurrection, Sverdlov, Kamenev, Zinoviev, Radek, Joffe, Ryazanov, Uritsky and Litvinov were leading figures in the Bolshevik party. Jews were even more important in the defeated Menshevik faction of Russian social democracy, including such personalities as Paul Axelrod, Lev Deutsch, Martov, Dan, Liber and Abramovich.[2] The Bund, an exclusively Jewish section of the pre-war Russian party, also produced leaders of international stature, such as Vladimir Medem, Arkady Kremer and Kossovsky. A neutral observer like the sociologist Robert Michels could remark in his classic study of the European workers' movement before 1914:

> In many countries, in Russia and Rumania for instance, but above all in Hungary and in Poland, the leadership of the working-class parties (the Russian Social Revolutionary Party excepted) is almost exclusively in the hands of Jews, as is plainly apparent from an examination of the personality of the delegates to the international congresses.[3]

This comment could be extended to other countries, periods and radical movements down to the present day, but the central point should already be clear. Jews have unquestionably been a pioneering element, a ferment and a catalyst within modern socialist and revolutionary movements. But why did so many of them become involved in socialism?

All kinds of reasons have in the past motivated individuals to join radical or revolutionary movements. In the case of oppressed and exploited classes or subjugated nationalities the motivations are generally obvious, and need not delay us here—except to note that this factor clearly applied to Russian Jews, a point to which I shall return. But most radical Jews outside the Tsarist Empire who joined the socialist movement did not belong to an exploited class, or indeed to an oppressed 'nationality'—at least, not in the usual sense of the word. They came from comfortable middle-class backgrounds, from a milieu which was not at all favourable to socialism. Were their motivations any different from non-Jews of the bourgeois class who crossed over the social barriers of nineteenth-century European civilization? Were they not prompted by the same human emotions, such as hatred of injustice, youthful enthusiasm for universalist ideas, or the conviction that the future belonged to socialism?

It is of course true that there was nothing specifically Jewish about intellectuals from a 'bourgeois' milieu rejecting their liberal, middle-class and more or less conformist background. Engels, Liebknecht, Jaurès, Guesde, Plekhanov and Lenin—all of them Gentiles—were rebellious sons of the ruling classes or the bourgeoisie, who had made the ideology of class-struggle their own. Indeed, Kautsky and Lenin never tired of stressing that bourgeois intellectuals were the standard-bearers of socialist consciousness to the working classes. Socialists from a bourgeois background often proved, moreover, to be more proletarian than the proletariat—an over-compensation not surprising in view of the widespread anti-bourgeois and anti-intellectual prejudices within the European labour movement.

A similar social psychology might explain the ultra-radicalism of those Jewish revolutionaries who came from a liberal-bourgeois background. It does not, however, explain why these Jewish intellectuals were much more numerous, relative to their overall numbers, in the ranks of the socialist movement. Nor does it tell us anything about the controversial and difficult question as to whether there was a distinct 'Jewish' ingredient in modern socialism. A great deal of speculative nonsense has been written about this subject, and about the alleged affinities between Judaism and Marxian socialism, so I shall begin by clearing away what seem to me to be the most popular myths.

In the first place, the parallel between Jewish and socialist messianism, as it is customarily formulated, should in my view be treated with some scepticism. One of the best expositions of this theory was by the Russian philosopher of history Nicolas Berdyaev (himself an ex-Marxist), who wrote:

But the most important aspect of Marx's teaching concerning the

> proletariat's messianic vocation is the fact that he applied to the proletariat the characteristics of God's chosen people. Marx was a Jew; he had abandoned the faith of his fathers, but the messianic expectation of Israel remained in his subconsciousness. The subconscious is always stronger than the conscious, and for him the proletariat is the new Israel, God's chosen people, the liberator and builder of an earthly kingdom that is to come. His proletarian Communism is a secularized form of the ancient Jewish chiliasm. A Chosen Class takes the place of the chosen people. It was impossible to reach such a notion by means of science. It is an idea of a religious kind. Here we have the very marrow of the Communist religion. For a messianic consciousness is surely always of ancient Hebrew origin.[4]

This passage is quoted at length because it illustrates a popular view of Marxism as a messianic religion, an eschatological outlook somehow related to the Jewish origins of its founder. This viewpoint can also be found in various guises and disguises in such commentators as Toynbee, Künzli, Massiczek and Karl Löwith. It is essentially a theological position, which attributes the universalist messianism of Marxian socialism to an unconscious strain of Hebraic prophetism in its founder. The 'Jewish' component in Marxism becomes its struggle for the concrete realization of social justice in *this* world, and its vision of ultimate human redemption as the culmination of the historical process.[5] But this approach, however interesting, seems to me to distort the general attitude of Marxism to religion and to misunderstand the nature of Jewish messianism.

Marxism transformed the critique of religion into a political issue, making it a reflex of the secular contradictions in civil society. By politicizing religion and deifying human self-consciousness, by reducing spiritual phenomena to a function of impersonal economic laws, Marxism broke completely with the Judaeo-Christian tradition and the teachings of the Hebrew prophets. Nor should the universality of Marxist and traditional Jewish messianism be regarded as comparable.

The universalist thrust of prophetic Judaism always co-existed in a polarized tension with belief in the chosenness of Israel, its particular mission among the nations. Socialist assimilationism, on the other hand, expressly derided this Jewish messianism, which it regarded as a reactionary attempt to preserve the independent existence of a 'chimeric' nationality. Jewish nationalism and Zionism as secular forms of this traditional messianism (though they should also be viewed as a revolt against the quietism of orthodox belief) were treated with disdain and contempt by many Marxists—for reasons to which we shall return. The crucial point, then, is not that there are no affinities between Judaism and socialism, but that within the framework of

Marxist theory there could be no scope for any such rapprochement. In this context it is significant that neither Moses Hess, Bernard Lazare nor Léon Blum—all of whom recognized a parallel between Judaism and socialism—were Marxist in their approach. Hess was philosophically an idealist and politically a Zionist when he discovered the identity of Mosaic and socialist principles; Lazare was a revolutionary anarchist who translated his own principles back into Old Testament prophetism; Léon Blum equated Judaism and socialism through the prism of French rationalism, as two forms of universalism based on the supremacy of reason, science and justice. None of this proves, however, that the Jewish heritage of biblical prophetism favours revolutionism of the Marxian variety. On the contrary, the repudiation of the ancestral faith by Jewish Marxist revolutionaries suggests the opposite conclusion. It was not the Jewish religion which in the nineteenth and twentieth centuries was responsible for Jewish radicalism; rather its tribal-national bias encouraged cultural separatism and its messianic hope promoted if anything political indifference. Both these features of traditional Judaism were of course anathema to Marxists, who naturally disapproved of any form of tribalism or separatism. But this hostility towards Judaism was intensified by the enlightenment principles which Marxism had inherited from the French Revolution. Anti-clericalism was one aspect of this legacy which influenced the negative evaluation of Judaism (and of course Christianity), but still more important was the denial to the Jews, as Jews, of any national rights.

The French Revolution had emancipated the Jews as individuals, not as a group. It offered them freedom, equality and brotherhood at the price of dissociation from their own people. No distinct Jewish identity, no form of cultural particularism, no defence of exclusively Jewish interests was envisaged as being compatible with the ideals of emancipation. The ultimate objective was the assimilation of the Jews, which implied that they must partially or wholly lose their original *national* identity, in order to fuse with the majority. Socialism took over this standpoint as its own, confident in its ability to overcome any residual obstacles in the way of absorbing the Jews.

The forms which this socialist assimilation adopted varied in different societies, depending on their level of development and on the progress already achieved with regard to Jewish emancipation. In Germany before 1848, for example, the Jewish demand for civil rights was closely linked to the liberal struggle for German emancipation.[6] Radical Jews like Boerne, Heine, Moses Hess and Karl Marx supported Jewish emancipation as a progressive step on the road to liberalizing the Prusso-Christian State and transforming Germany into a modern secular society. They were themselves individuals in the process of assimilation, marginal men in transition between different cultures and social groups. Already alienated from their own history and traditional identity, but not yet integrated into Gentile society, their concerns were no longer primarily related to their own community. The ideology of universal human rights proclaimed by the French Revolution and reinforced by socialist principles directed their attention towards non-Jewish horizons. In the case of Karl Marx, the ultimate goal of total human emancipation envisaged in his writings of 1844 clearly presupposed the de-judaization of the Jew and at the same time the abolition of bourgeois society. The standards by which Marx and his radical Jewish disciples judged their former co-religionists were, however, borrowed from the secular enlightenment, itself a product of the Christian society and culture into which they were assimilating. As revolutionaries they were of course committed to overthrowing this society in the name of the messianic universalist ideal of socialism. What is at first sight puzzling is that this same revolutionary outlook could still contain anti-Jewish stereotypes inherited from an earlier period.

The most obvious example of this was the tendency of the early socialists, especially in France, to identify the Jews with capitalism. For French socialists like Fourier, Proudhon and Toussenel the prominence of Jewish bankers in the international economy, in railway-building and in providing Government loans provoked an intensely hostile reaction. The Rothschilds in particular were identified with a kind of neo-feudalism (*la féodalité financière*) in the emerging capitalist society of the 1840s. Marx, Heine and Boerne also regarded the money-power of the Rothschilds as symbolic of the new age. But only Marx went so far as to equate this 'universal dominion' of money with the 'Jewish spirit', and to transform the issue of Jewish emancipation into its dialectical antithesis—the liberation of society from Judaism.

Marx's anti-Judaism was psychologically speaking different from that of early anti-Semitic socialists by virtue of his Jewish descent. This fact reflects the most paradoxical element in the relationship between the Jews and socialism—namely, the role which Jewish self-hatred played in activating latent prejudices in the socialist movement. Since this is a phenomenon to which I shall return in my profiles of leading socialist Jews, it is as well to be clear in what sense I am using this term. Self-hatred can take many forms, and is often difficult to detect, let alone diagnose. Frequently it is hidden from the self-hater himself, and not visible to his closest colleagues. It can exist on the Right as well as the Left, and one cannot say that any particular nationality, social group or type of personality has a monopoly on it. Nevertheless, from the sociological point of view it appears obvious that members of a minority group are likely to be more susceptible to such feelings by virtue of their vulnerable position.[7] Gifted individuals within a minority are particularly exposed to self-hatred, because their abilities give them a greater possibility of recognition within the majority culture. If this majority has a hostile attitude to the minority group in question, then feelings of rejection are bound to arise in the individual who cannot achieve full acceptance by virtue of his origin. When his aggression becomes directed against the members of his own minority, rather than against the discriminating majority, then we are likely to be in the presence of self-hatred of one kind or another.

In the case of the Jews—the classic example of a persecuted minority group—it is not difficult to see that self-hatred has in the modern age been a very common affliction. The origins of this disease go back to the Enlightenment, with its insistence that the Jews must change themselves, repudiate their own identity, if they were to receive full equality. They would have to lose their unattractive characteristics and abandon the professions of commerce, usury and peddling with which they were associated in the Middle Ages. The impact of modern anti-Semitism, with its long catalogue of hateful accusations, inevitably influenced the self-image of the modern Jew. For those Jews who sought to assimilate, and accepted the assumptions of the Enlightenment concerning Jewish 'inferiority', the temptation to harshly criticize or completely reject their co-religionists was very great. This temptation existed no less for enlightened socialist intellectuals than it did for the Jewish upper classes, who sought a different kind of assimilation into the ruling class of Gentile society. A radical Jew who believed in the fashionable nineteenth-century caricature of his co-religionists as being separatist, clannish, parasitic, hostile to culture, money-grabbing etc., was likely to go to extremes in his repudiation of these allegedly 'Jewish' faults. This was particularly evident in the attitude of assimilated socialist intellectuals to the ghetto Jews of Eastern Europe, which often reflected traditional Gentile stereotypes. Jewish self-hatred was in this respect the faithful echo of prejudices in the dominant Christian majority towards the Jewish minority. It was self-hatred where it was primarily directed against the 'Jew' in oneself, against a residual identity which was rejected or denied.[8] It became Jewish anti-Semitism when it was directed against the Jews as a group, who had no right to preserve their identity, to defend themselves against criticism or attack, or to pursue their own interests.

The classic form of this ethnic death-wish was the repeated assertion by assimilated Jewish Marxists (long before the emergence of Israel as an independent state) that the Jewish collectivity should disappear. This demand had of course been implicit in the ideology of emancipation as formulated by the French Revolution, but it was reinforced with a peculiar intensity by many radical Jews. Their specific arguments might vary, but the common denominator always remained the same: any rights accorded to the Jews as a minority or as a national group would merely preserve their 'ghetto' identity, their undesirable 'Jewish' characteristics, and inevitably provoke anti-Semitism. Since the religion of the Jews was considered obsolete, their language (Yiddish) regarded as barbarian, their manners as lacking in tact, and their involvement in capitalism as a legitimate object of popular wrath, the preservation of Jewry might be considered by many socialists as reactionary. But this by itself does not explain the enthusiasm with which radical Jews attacked specifically 'Jewish' interests, and the practices, customs and characteristics of the Jewish group.

The individual psychology of the Jewish revolutionary was in this respect one of the most illuminating examples of the collective neurosis of a persecuted minority in the age of assimilation. Self-hatred became an integral part of that general attitude of negation, iconoclasm, non-conformism, rebellion and questioning of established values which to some observers was a hallmark of the 'Jewish spirit' at the turn of the century. Like most generalizations, this obviously could not apply to the Jews as a whole, but in the paranoid world of anti-Semitic fantasy, it tended to promote fear of the Jew as a subversive, rootless agent of social dissolution.[9] The tragic irony in this situation was that both the Jewish revolutionary and the pathological anti-Semite who feared and hated him, starting from wholly different general premises, desired the ultimate disappearance of the Jew.

This may seem a highly paradoxical assertion to make about individuals who for the most idealistic and humanitarian motives stood in the forefront of a movement for universal human emancipation. But there is in my view nothing in this interpretation which is incompatible with human nature. Why should self-hatred not be a galvanizing, revolutionary stimulus, a motivating factor for Jewish participation in radical movements? The marginality of the assimilated (or semi-assimilated) Jewish intellectual, whose radicalism made him a heretical figure with regard to his minority community and the Gentile world, could encourage both self-hatred and the lofty universalism idealized by writers like Isaac Deutscher.[10] The 'non-Jewish' Jew may well be the heir of a specifically Jewish 'tradition' (though in my view this can hardly be traced further back than Spinoza), he may well have displayed superior powers of intellectual synthesis, but he was also the tragically deluded victim of an imposed situation. It is misleading to argue that he 'transcended' Judaism, when he had no interest in or knowledge of Jewish history, values and culture. It is insufficient to say, as does Deutscher, that he found Jewry 'too narrow, too archaic, and too restricting', when his judgments were based on second-hand, prejudiced stereotypes. What is more to the point is that as a permanent outsider 'on the borderlines of various civilizations, religious and national cultures', the 'non-Jewish Jew' was in a unique position to formulate bold, innovative ideas about the future development of society.

Isaac Deutscher, was right, it seems to me, to point out that Marx, Rosa Luxemburg and Trotsky shared a 'dialectically dramatic vision of the world and of its class-struggles'; that they strove 'for the universal, as against the particularist, and for the internationalist, as against the nationalist solutions to the problems of their time'.[11] Where his own Trotskyist sympathies led him astray was in assuming that this passionate rejection of *all* nationalism was realistic, tenable or even progressive. Far from being the strength of the non-Jewish Jew, this socialist assimilationism was invariably his Achilles heel, the unconscious projection of his self-negation as a Jew. It is significant that social democrats like Eduard Bernstein and Léon Blum, who did not seek to expunge their Jewish identity, did not also share this abstract, utopian brand of internationalism, with its denial of cultural particularism. The revolutionary form of assimilation which Marxism offered the Jews has proved so disastrous precisely because it did not go beyond the negative one-sided view of the Enlightenment with regard to Jewish group-identity. On the contrary socialism reinforced this bias by abstract theorizing which neglected the specific conditions of Jewish existence, which ignored the concrete humanity of the Jews as a collectivity, and the creativity of their culture. This hostility to Jewish group-identity was directly related to the anxiety of so many revolutionary Jewish leaders in the socialist movement, not to be identified as Jews, and to out-trump the anti-Semitism of their Gentile environment by their ostentatious indifference to the Jewish problem. But there is a further aspect of socialist assimilationism which has implications for Marxist attitudes to the Jews in our own day.

In the last analysis, what was destructive about Marxist universalism was its insistence on levelling out group differences, on the assumption that some nations were to be considered more 'progressive' than others. With regard to small, backward peoples this attitude already contained the seeds of future tyranny. Marx and Engels dismissed the South-Slav peasant peoples of South-Eastern Europe as 'history-less nations' whose perpetuation was counter-revolutionary. This pseudo-historical judgement (an offshoot of Hegelian metaphysics) was applied by Otto Bauer, Kautsky, Lenin and Stalin, in a slightly different form to the Jews. They were depicted either as a parasitic 'class' (Marx), a 'caste' (Kautsky/Lenin), a historical fossil (Stalin) or a nation in the process of irreversible dissolution (Otto Bauer). All these definitions served to deny 'scientifically' to the Jews their right to preserve, renew and recreate their identity. The Marxist interpretation of history was and still is being abused in order to pronounce the sentence of death on the legitimacy of a particular human group to choose its own future. Whether this is done in the name of progress, of historical necessity, of dialectical materialism or as a result of an openly racist ideology matters little to the victim. Nor does it matter much that the Left promised everything to the Jews as individuals in the universal classless society of the future, as long as there is a 'Jewish problem', as long as there are Jews who want to live in their own independent state, as long as nationalism is a reality of life—not least, in the Communist world.[12]

Marxist ideology (long before Stalin) was operating with a terminology and assumptions which precluded respect for the culture and national rights of minorities. By interpreting diversity and cultural autonomy as an obstacle to the class struggle, it simply reproduced in heightened form the centralized rigidity of authoritarian structures inherited from the past. Only the Austro-Marxists living in the multinational Austro-Hungarian Empire departed from this levelling model, but here again their respect for national individuality disappeared in the case of the Jews. Why were the Jews an exception? Why was Marxism, reminiscent in this respect of another universalist creed turned imperialist (Christianity!), so insistent on negating their national character?

The pretence that Judaism was only a religion, so stubbornly reiterated by assimilationist groups within Jewry itself throughout the nineteenth century, cannot in my view be taken seriously as a factor. While it was just possible at one time to reduce the denationalized Jews of Western Europe to this category, it never applied at all to the centre of gravity of world Jewry in Russia and Eastern Europe, where Jews clearly constituted a *national* group before 1939. Therefore, however much Marxists might attack Judaism as an obscurantist superstition, this was not central to their argument. The polemics of Lenin, Trotsky, Martov and Rosa Luxemburg against the Bund demonstrate conclusively that the leaders of revolutionary Marxism not only refused to tolerate the Jews as a separate national minority in Russia and Eastern Europe, they not only dismissed the Jewish religion, but they even regarded the preservation of Jewish culture as completely reactionary.

The Bund was the most powerful movement of the Jewish working class before 1939; it had systematically denounced Zionism since the late 1890s as a form of 'bourgeois chauvinism', and its leaders fervently believed that only the proletarian revolution would solve the Jewish problem. Nevertheless, the Bund had already by 1903 come round to the view that only separate organization could ensure its ability to defend the special interests of the Jewish masses and guarantee the survival of Jewish national identity. Its so-called nationalism—for which it was so strongly denounced by Lenin, Trotsky and Martov—was an inevitable outgrowth of its close ties with the Jewish proletariat in Russia. The Russian Marxists (both Bolsheviks and Mensheviks) sought on the other hand to de-nationalize Russian Jewry and its special culture, on the model of Western emancipation. Within this concept there was no room for a separate Jewish 'nationality', as

Lenin explained in 1903:

> The idea of a Jewish "nationality" is definitely reactionary, not only when expounded by its consistent advocates (the Zionists) but likewise on the lips of those who try to combine it with the ideas of Social-Democracy (the Bundists). The idea of a Jewish nationality runs counter to the interests of the Jewish proletariat, for it fosters among them, directly or indirectly, a spirit hostile to assimilation, the spirit of the "ghetto".[13]

Lenin and his colleagues in the Bolshevik party anticipated a universalist pattern of assimilation before 1914 in which after the Revolution there would remain only individuals of Jewish origin. Writing in 1913, Lenin expressed a point of view which was undoubtedly shared by assimilated Jewish revolutionaries such as Martov, Trotsky and Rosa Luxemburg.

> Whoever, directly or indirectly, puts forward the slogan of a Jewish "national culture" is (whatever his good intentions may be) an enemy of the proletariat, a supporter of the *old* and of the *caste* position of the Jews, an accomplice of the rabbis and the bourgeoisie. On the other hand, those Jewish Marxists who join international Marxist organizations, together with the Russian, Lithuanian, Ukrainian and other workers doing their bit (in Russian and in Yiddish) towards the creation of the international culture of the working-class movement—such Jews, despite the separatism of the Bund, uphold the best traditions of the race, by fighting the slogan of "national culture".[14]

This was in the last analysis a translation of French revolutionary doctrine on Jewish emancipation into Russian Marxist language and Russian conditions—i.e., all rights to the Jews as individuals, none to the Jews as a people. Thus although Lenin himself was devoid of any trace of anti-Semitism (which under his Soviet regime indeed became a crime), although he fought sincerely for Jewish civil equality, his teaching already contained the seeds of an irresolvable clash. The negation of Jewish national culture, of the Jewish religion, and of the Zionist movement by the Russian Marxists was bound by the logic of events to produce tragic results. Individual Jewish revolutionaries like Martov, Trotsky and Luxemburg might absorb Russian (or Polish) culture, but the mass of Jews had a culture clearly different from that of the surrounding peoples. They were a nationality apart, however exasperating this fact might be to those revolutionaries who had left the group and regarded their Jewishness as nothing but an accident of birth. The refusal of the Soviet regime consistently to recognize and respect this reality led in the long run to the suppression of Yiddish literature, the erosion of Jewish culture and the resurgence of anti-Semitic discrimination in the Soviet Union.

The ambiguity between Marxist theory and practice on the Jewish question was especially poignant in Soviet Russia, in view of the great hopes which had been placed in the Russian Revolution by Jews all over the world. Before 1917 the Tsarist authorities had persecuted the Jews as dangerous aliens, and this repression had driven many young Jews into the revolutionary ranks. The use of anti-Semitism as a tactical diversion by the regime was so blatant that Russian Marxists and revolutionaries were bound to oppose it resolutely. This opposition was further reinforced by the pogroms of the Russian counter-revolutionaries (Whites) during the Civil War period.[15] Over 200 000 Jews were massacred in the Ukraine alone, and many more made homeless by these pogroms—the worst in Jewish history since those perpetrated by the Cossack bands in 1648–9. After the civil war Bolshevik measures during the period of War Communism brought about the economic ruin of a large mass of Russian Jews concentrated in petty trade and business. Nevertheless, the Soviet Government did make some efforts in the 1920s to improve the situation of the Jewish masses, first by agricultural settlement on the land and later by industrializing the Jewish population. In 1928 it was even decided to set up a special area for Jewish settlement near the Mongolian frontier, called Birobidzhan—with the prospect that it might eventually become an independent Republic and a centre of Jewish culture.[16] For various reasons, which lie outside the scope of this book, the plan proved a fiasco, as did other efforts of the Soviet regime to solve the Jewish problem. This was partly recognized by the exiled Leon Trotsky in the 1930s, who had modified his earlier view that assimilation would provide an automatic answer to the Jewish question. But Trotsky, like other Jewish revolutionaries who remained loyal to the tenets of universalistic Marxism, proved incapable of providing a deeper analysis of the failure of the Russian Revolution with regard to the Jewish 'nationality'. He could still not conceive of any resolution of the Jewish problem short of the world-wide victory of socialism. Not even the rise of Hitlerian fascism with its violent racial anti-Semitism, nor the resurgence of Russian nationalism under Stalin, could shake his convictions on this point. Having sacrificed his Jewish identity on the altar of a utopian Marxist internationalism, he was too deeply committed to re-examine the fundamental premises of his own outlook.

Even those Russian Marxists of Jewish origin like the Mensheviks Axelrod and Martov, who had showed a more sensitive awareness of the strength of anti-Semitism, repressed their insights in order to participate more fully in the revolutionary movement. Axelrod, for example, had been profoundly shaken by the Russian pogroms of 1881, and he drafted a pamphlet which expressed the shock of many

Jewish socialists at the ambivalent attitude of their Gentile comrades. In this pamphlet (which was never published, at the request of his colleagues) Axelrod wrote that

> the pogroms made the Jewish socialist intelligentsia realize that the Jews as a people were in a unique situation in Russia, hated by the most diverse segments of the Christian population; and that they, the Jewish Socialists, had committed an error in overlooking the actual condition of the Jews as a people different from the rest of the population. The Jewish social revolutionaries understood now that they were wrong in forsaking the Jewish masses in the name of cosmopolitanism. The 'native masses' not only lacked cosmopolitan feelings and ideas but they were wanting even in the idea of class solidarity among the poorer classes of Russia's nationalities.[17]

It was precisely this awareness of the depth of prejudice against the Jews among the Russian muzhiks, and the poverty, backwardness and isolation of the Jewish masses in the Tsarist Empire, which gave birth to the separatist Jewish socialism, represented by the Bund, and later by Marxian and Poalei-Zionism, the 'Workers of Zion' party. But assimilated Jewish intellectuals such as Axelrod, Martov and Trotsky deliberately played down 'the actual condition of the Jews as a people different from the rest of the population', in order to promote the cause of an all-Russian revolution. This cosmopolitan socialism was equally characteristic of other revolutionists from the Russo-Polish milieu such as Rosa Luxemburg, Leo Jogiches, Alexander Israel Helphand (Parvus), Karl Radek and Eugen Leviné, who came to play a considerable role in German socialism. Uprooted émigrés who had emerged in one generation from their pariah status in Eastern Europe to the centre of the historical stage, they embraced socialism with all the fervour of a new religion.

In the increasingly rigidified structures of the German Social Democratic Party their ultra-radicalism acted as a galvanizing agent which was not altogether welcome. Reformist trade-union leaders and the moderate Bavarian wing of the German Socialist Party regarded the sharp polemical tone of Parvus and Luxemburg as intolerable. 'Revisionists' like Wolfgang Heine, Richard Fischer and Eduard David who felt sympathetic to the liberal socialism of Bernstein deeply resented the fierce attacks on him by the 'intruders' from the East. A mildly anti-Jewish nuance crept into inner-party polemics surrounding the revisionist controversy of 1900—just as it had briefly surfaced in the mid-1870s, when Dühring attacked the 'Jewish' socialism of Marx and Lassalle. It was essentially a conservative reflex, a distrust of rootless intellectuals, foreigners from the East, ultra-leftists, who seemed to be lacking in proper respect for the organization, discipline and hierarchy of the German Socialist Party.

Not for nothing did Bebel write to Kautsky just before the Party Congress at Lübeck in 1901 about 'the intense animosity among the rank and file against Rosa and Parvus', adding that 'one cannot altogether ignore such prejudices'.[18] Though Bebel and Kautsky were generally philo-Semitic in their attitudes, they did not significantly defend the new recruits 'from the East' against the personal attacks on them by delegates. Wolfgang Heine (a former chairman of the anti-Semitic German student organization) even accused Parvus and Luxemburg of abusing German hospitality, slandering the German people, and thereby making the struggle against anti-Semitism more difficult![19] The Lübeck Congress was perhaps an exceptional episode in German socialist history, where open expressions of anti-Semitism were exceedingly rare. Nevertheless, there is some evidence to suggest that a clandestine form of Judaeophobia continued to exist, which was largely directed at the role of Russian and Polish-born revolutionaries in the German party. As late as 1947, Gustav Noske, a right-wing German socialist and expert on military affairs, could write in his memoirs the following revealing passage:

> The pretension of a number of foreigners from Poland and Russia who behaved like schoolmasters to the German workers was taken amiss. Moreover, the Party was sometimes burdened with very unworldly idealists and *déclassés* from the bourgeoisie. It has nothing to do with anti-Semitism when it is stated that the East European Jewish 'Marxists' possessed a special talent for perfecting socialism into a dogma and transforming platitudes into a confession of faith. They hatched a secret science which has always remained incomprehensible to the German workers.[20]

This brutal, unflattering verdict of a German working-class socialist who became Minister of the Interior in 1918 and crushed the Spartacist revolt is significant because it undoubtedly expresses the feelings of a section of the party against Jewish intellectuals. One has only to read the wartime diaries of Eduard David, another nationalistic socialist, to find confirmation of this state of mind.[21] In the case of David (despite his name, he was not Jewish) a latent anti-Semitism found expression in his growing conviction that the radical Jews in the party were all pacifists, who were sabotaging the German war effort.

Against this one should set the philo-Semitic declarations made by some outstanding leaders of the Second International, about the services of Jewish intellectuals to the revolutionary socialist movement. The French Marxist Paul Lafargue (son-in-law of Karl Marx) wrote in 1886 in *Le Cri du Peuple* 'We regret that there are so few Jews among us in France; because the Jews are able, clever, devoted and indefatigable'.[22] The leading German Marxist theoretician, Karl

Kautsky, in an article published in the English socialist review *Justice* (1904) maintained, 'the Jews, since the time they have entered into European civilization, have given to the world more great thinkers in proportion to their numbers, than perhaps any other nation, and the names of Spinoza, Ricardo and Marx form epochs in the history of thought'.[23]

Kautsky tried to explain the preponderant role of Jews in the European socialist movement by their 'distinctive spiritual physiognomy', which found its expression 'in a splendid power of abstraction and a keen critical intellect'. Jews, moreover, had 'on the whole belonged to the downtrodden classes', and this, according to Kautsky, made them apply their speculative and critical powers to the cause of the oppressed. Kautsky's tribute, like that of Lafargue, appeared in a left-wing paper which had gone rather far in its socialist anti-Semitism—directed primarily against Jewish financiers and cosmopolitan bankers. Both articles, by singling out the services of Jews to the revolutionary movement, seem to have been designed to correct this imbalance, and to serve as a warning against such prejudices in the labour movement. This was also the purpose of Friedrich Engels, when he wrote to an Austrian correspondent in 1890 that 'we owe the Jews much too much'—going on to mention Victor Adler, Paul Singer and Eduard Bernstein (alongside such figures in the past as Heine, Boerne, Lassalle and of course Marx)—' men of whose friendship I am proud, and all of them Jews! I myself have been made a Jew by the "Gartenlaube", and indeed, if I had to choose: then better a Jew than *Herr von* . . .'.[24]

When he wrote these lines Engels must have been well aware of two facts. Firstly, the anti-Semitic movement in Austria-Hungary was 'socialistic' in its propaganda, and sought to identify the Jews with capitalism in the eyes of the masses. Secondly, the labour movement was showing signs of flirting with this anti-capitalist anti-Semitism. Hence, Engels's letter, apart from stressing the importance of Jewish intellectuals to the socialist movement, tried to unmask the reactionary pseudo-socialist character of Judaeophobia in Germany and Austria-Hungary.

The irony of this situation was that the leader of the Austrian Social Democratic Party, Victor Adler, was himself a baptized Jew, with no special sympathy for his former co-religionists. It was, significantly, under Adler's leadership that the motives of bourgeois Jews who sought entrance to the socialist ranks first encountered suspicion and prejudice. Adler's attitude towards anti-Semitism was indeed highly equivocal, like that of many Jewish intellectuals in the labour movement of Central Europe. As a Marxist, of course, he regarded Judaeophobia as a specific product of capitalist society, as a diversion from the class struggle. It could only exist in a class-divided society, and it served primarily to create dissensions within the working class which would favour the interests of the bourgeoisie. Therefore the general struggle against capitalist society was the best method of combating and eliminating Jew-hatred. This was the standard Marxist analysis of anti-Semitism, to be found with some slight variations among the German, Austrian, French, British, Russian and Polish social-democratic parties.

As a Jew, however, Adler had a rather different attitude to the anti-capitalist rhetoric which had emerged in the 1890s as the most popular platform of Karl Lueger's Christian-Social Party. Though Adler scarcely admired Lueger's slick, demagogic exploitation of anti-Semitic propaganda, he did sympathize to some extent with the backlash of petty-bourgeois resentment against Jewish capitalism in Vienna. A marked antipathy to the Jewish establishment, to its importance in the press, in finance, commerce, liberal causes, the universities and cultural life in general, was characteristic of Adler and many of his colleagues in the Austrian Socialist Party. Those comrades who were of Jewish origin felt obliged completely to repudiate their background, which generally linked them in terms of class and culture to the enemies of the proletariat. Victor Adler was after all the son of a real-estate speculator, Heinrich Braun of an industrialist, Otto Bauer of a wealthy textile-manufacturer. A similar reaction had occurred in Germany among those socialists who came from a prosperous, Jewish middle-class background. Marx was the son of a respectable lawyer, Lassalle of a self-made silk merchant, Paul Singer was a highly successful capitalist manufacturer, Karl Höchberg the son of a wealthy Frankfurt banker. The Jewish self-hatred which existed in all of them was in part at least a product of guilt-feelings and of the desire to be rid of the 'Jew' in themselves in order to become new men in the service of the proletariat. Adler's selfless devotion to the cause of the Austrian working class, his humanistic concern for improving their living conditions and educational possibilities, cannot therefore be altogether divorced from his Jewish background. On a conscious level he would have repudiated any attempt to classify him as a 'Jew'—as a member of a middle-class group to which he was openly hostile. Unconsciously, however, he transmitted many liberal bourgeois values to the Austrian labour movement—notably, the emphasis on education (*Bildung*) the humanistic ethos of the medical profession, and his personal skill in negotiation and compromise.

An even more striking contradiction was evident in the case of Otto Bauer, one of the most intellectually gifted of Jewish revolutionaries, and at the same time one of the most original Marxist theorists on the national problem. Few examples illustrate more clearly the distorting effect of an assimilationist outlook on the manner in which some Marxists discussed the 'Jewish question'. It was the Austro-Marxist school in Vienna led by Karl Renner (a Gentile) and Otto Bauer which had promoted the idea of cultural-national autonomy as a solution to the nationality conflict which was threatening to tear the Austro-Hungarian Monarchy asunder. This theory had a considerable impact on the Jewish labour movement in Russia and Eastern Europe—indeed, the Bund became its most persuasive advocate before 1914 in the multi-national Tsarist Empire. Nevertheless, Otto Bauer explicitly denied that his general theories of nationality could be applied to the Jewish people, since this would have entailed conceding to them a measure of national autonomy in the Habsburg lands. Instead he returned to the analysis of Karl Marx on the Jewish question, which exercised such an unfortunate influence on European socialism.

Sixty years after Marx, Otto Bauer portrayed the compact mass of Jews in Russia, Galicia and Lithuania as a non-historical nation in the process of disappearing. This was written, moreover, at a time when the Eastern European Jews were fighting for their social and national liberation, when a remarkable Jewish cultural renaissance was blossoming forth in Yiddish and Hebrew. As a Westernized intellectual trying to apply the methodology of historical materialism to the Jewish national problem, Bauer was faced with an intractable contradiction between theory and reality: according to Marxist economic laws, the Jews should have disappeared long ago, since they lacked all the economic, social and political prerequisites of nationhood. But in Russia and Eastern Europe it was an observable fact of life that the Jews constituted a distinct national-religious community of a special type. This nationality might not fit into the pattern of history evolved by Marx and his disciples, but it was an inescapable everyday reality for the Jewish masses in the East.

It was the cohesive, non-assimilated Jewish communities who were the foundation of the separate Jewish labour movement which first emerged in the Tsarist and Austro-Hungarian Empires and then spread to America, Palestine, England, Argentina and other parts of the globe. The leaders of the Jewish labour movement, whether Zionist or anti-Zionist in orientation, differed from cosmopolitan revolutionary Jews on one fundamental issue: they sought to *reconcile* Marxism and Jewish national identity, to achieve the cultural and national regeneration of the Jewish people through socialism. The Westernized Jewish intelligentsia, with whom I am mainly concerned in this book, tried on the contrary to *dissolve* Jewish identity through socialism. With the exception of Bernard Lazare and Martov (in his youthful phase), both of whom were influenced by the emergence of Jewish nationalism, they did not envisage working within the Jewish community for the realization of their ideals. Apart from Léon Blum and, belatedly, Eduard Bernstein, neither of whom were orthodox Marxists, they would have regarded such an option as intrinsically reactionary and separatist. Moreover, in Western and Central Europe this alternative had little meaning, since the social base of a militant Jewish proletariat did not exist. Hence it was in Russia and the Eastern hinterlands of the Dual Monarchy that this clash between Marxism and Jewish nationalism really came to a head.

In these backward, semi-feudal societies the impact of Marxism as a scientific system, a total *Weltanschauung*, a programme for transforming the world, was enormous. The Russified and Polonized Jewish intelligentsia, though they were only a small minority among the Jewish population as a whole, discovered in Marxism a way of synthesizing a newly acquired Westernized identity with the Russo-Polish environment from which they were alienated. It was a futurist, post-Jewish form of assimilation to the secular messianic ideal of the 'proletarian fatherland'. Marxism had replaced Judaism (with its traditional isolation from the Gentile world) by a gospel of militant activism. *Das Kapital* became the Torah of this intelligentsia, over which they argued with a learning, skill in logical exposition and genius for abstract interpretation reminiscent of their rabbinical and Talmudic ancestors. Divorced from the societies into which they were born, uprooted and driven into exile, revolutionaries like Trotsky, Martov and Rosa Luxemburg believed with passionate intensity in the advent of the classless, international society. Not for nothing could Lenin say in the course of a lecture in 1917 in Switzerland that 'it should be said to their credit that today the Jews provide a relatively high percentage of representatives of internationalism compared to other nations'.[25]

But in what sense can this internationalism be marked down as a specifically 'Jewish' trait? The sociologist Robert Michels, writing in 1913, had little doubt that 'the Jewish intelligence is apt to find a shorter road to socialism than the Gentile', which he partly attributed to the fact that the Jews lacked a homeland. Their cosmopolitan tendencies had been developed

> by the historical experiences of the race, and these combine to push them into the arms of the working-class party. It is owing to these tendencies that the Jews, guided in part by reason and in part by sentimental considerations, so readily disregard the barriers which the bourgeoisie endeavours to erect against the rising tide of the revolution by the accusation that its advocates are *des sans patrie*.[26]

An internationalist like Rosa Luxemburg was for example totally impervious to the charge of being a homeless, intellectual vagrant. Marxism was for her a class-based form of internationalism which completely transcended the framework of the nation-state. With superb disdain she could tell her Prussian prosecutors in 1914 that she had a more genuine homeland, deeper roots than that of the average German citizen and patriotic philistine. 'What other fatherland is there than the great mass of working men and women? What other fatherland is there than the improvement of life, the improvement of morality, the improvement of the intellectual strength of the great masses which constitute a people?'[27] The idea of a national fatherland, of a special cultural home, was as foreign to her as it was to other Jewish revolutionaries such as Leo Jogiches and Karl Radek, who also came from the Polish milieu. Like Trotsky, she regarded nationalist passions and prejudice with loathing, and no Marxist ever went to further extremes in declaring national self-determination to be incompatible with socialism. Like Marx himself, she 'succeeded in transposing her loyalties from *nation* to *class*'—to quote the judicious formulation of her most recent biographer.[28]

It seems difficult to deny that this transposition was easier for Jews than for non-Jews even in the socialist movement—at a time when there was no Jewish State or officially recognized 'Jewish' nationality. Admittedly there were Poles in her socialist party like Julian Marchlewski, Lithuanians like Feliks Dzierżyński, Germans like Karl Liebknecht, and even Russians like Lenin who were as genuinely internationalist as Rosa Luxemburg. But none of them seems to have clung with quite the same fervour to the mystical ideal of a proletarian fatherland beyond the concrete boundaries of geographical space, national groups and cultural differences. As a Polish-speaking Jewess brought up in a Russian environment, who adopted the German language and culture at a Swiss university, she was uniquely well placed to act as a bridge between East and West in the golden age of international socialism. In this respect she epitomized the special mediating function of revolutionary Jews in a period when the internationalist message of Marxian socialism could still be pronounced with enthusiasm and conviction.

It should, however, be emphasized that the Luxemburgist brand of revolutionary internationalism was by no means typical of Jews in the European labour movement. It was essentially an East European phenomenon, much less common in Central and Western Europe, where social democracy had adapted itself to the institutions of the national body-politic. German-speaking Jewish intellectuals like Bernstein, Victor Adler and Hugo Haase, in common with the mainstream of Central European socialism, sought to reconcile social reform with the older revolutionary phraseology of Marxism. They were gradualists who believed in parliamentary democracy and regarded socialism as an extension of equality to the economic sphere. In France it was another Jewish intellectual, Léon Blum, who interpreted Marxian socialism in the spirit of Jaurès, as the heir of republican legality and liberal-bourgeois democracy. For Léon Blum, socialism was a long revolution, a non-violent change towards a collectivist system of production and distribution. Like Bernstein, Adler and Bauer, he regarded it first and foremost as a synthesis between the values of his adopted national tradition and the highest ideals of European humanism—not least, the vindication of the rights of the individual.

With respect to the 'Jewish question' there was, however, one point on which virtually all European socialists, whether they were Jews or Gentiles, revolutionaries or reformists, left or right-wing in tendency, made the same assumption, whatever their other differences. They all appeared to believe that anti-Semitism was an ephemeral, secondary phenomenon, part of a broader syndrome of racism and oppression caused by capitalist society. Only Bernard Lazare among the revolutionaries discussed in this book attempted a deeper, historical analysis of the 'Jewish question' which brought him to very different conclusions. The revolutionary internationalists and the evolutionary socialists for their part clung to the view that anti-Semitism was inconceivable in a socialist society which had abolished class conflict. The one significant difference between them was that the revolutionaries believed that a classless society entailed the complete disappearance of the Jews. Their assimilationism was more extreme because as revolutionaries they had broken more sharply with their Jewish background, their national-religious heritage, culture and tradition. They did not experience this as a loss, for as a result they had been able to become involved in the destinies of millions of people, to become leaders in a large, well-organized, disciplined international movement in whose ultimate victory they fervently believed. As citizens of the world, they no longer regarded themselves as Jews, and any reminder of their origins seemed to disturb, irritate, even exasperate them. They were—or so they appeared to believe—a post-Jewish phenomenon.

For evolutionary socialists like Bernstein or Léon Blum, who were more concerned with the practical goals of social reform than with the final goal of revolution, the messianic goal of *one* mankind was a very remote perspective. Although they took no part in the affairs of the Jewish community, their temperament and outlook on the world did not necessitate any violent rift with their milieu. Hence they were not embarrassed by references to their Jewish descent, and felt a natural sympathy with those of their co-religionists who were persecuted or discriminated against. In moments of intense social crisis such as the Dreyfus Affair, the periodic anti-Semitic eruptions in Germany and Austria, the pogroms in Russia or the rise of Nazism, this sympathy became more evident, and expressed itself in support for the principle of a Jewish national home.

Revolutionary Jews like Marx, Trotsky, Luxemburg, Victor Adler and Otto Bauer do not appear to have had such feelings of attachment, or if they did they systematically repressed them. Marx reduced the Jew to a purely economic figure, a huckstering bourgeois existing in the crevices of civil society. Lassalle could not forgive the Jews their passive acceptance of suffering, and later came to detest in them the servile features of German liberal philistinism. Trotsky and

Luxemburg disapproved harshly of Jewish 'separatism' and mocked at efforts to revive the Jewish nation, even in the name of socialist ideals. Adler and Bauer despised the non-assimilated Jews, with their alien ways, their strange dialect and ghetto traditions, and also attacked the slick, well-heeled representatives of Jewish capitalism in German Austria. Even a Jewish nationalist like Bernard Lazare had to overcome a profound disgust for his non-assimilated brethren before he could realistically diagnose the Jewish problem. The crucible of the Dreyfus Affair, with its paroxysm of nationalist xenophobia in France, enabled him to perceive more clearly the disease of self-hatred which had afflicted the French Jews since their emancipation. This growing awareness led Bernard Lazare to attack not only the assimilationist self-deception of the Jewish bourgeoisie in France but also the various superstitions on the Right and the Left concerning 'Jewish' parasitism. Lazare realized that even socialists had accepted misleading stereotypes equating the Jews with the power of money. Gentiles could in many cases be leading bankers, brokers and middlemen without attracting popular wrath—but the Left in France would invariably single out the Rothschilds for condemnation. Moreover, Lazare understood that anti-Semitism was in fact much older than capitalist society, and could not therefore be regarded as its specific product. What guarantee was there that socialism would solve the Jewish problem, when it could not even come to terms with the Judaeophobia in its own tradition? There could be no substitute for the auto-emancipation of the Jewish masses, and it was for this reason that Lazare turned to Zionism, without abandoning his anarchist convictions. Unlike the other revolutionaries of his time (the Zionist-socialists and the Bund excepted) Lazare regarded the restoration of Jewish national consciousness as the prerequisite for a genuine socialist internationalism. Though French Jewry would have nothing to do with his radical ideas, there was a certain grandeur in Lazare's failure. He had attained a lucid awareness of the inescapability of the Jewish problem which his better-known colleagues in the revolutionary movement preferred to overlook. Jewish participation in other people's revolutions would not solve the pressing needs of the Jewish masses who lacked a homeland, who were forced by persecution and poverty from one exile to another.

This was a lesson singularly ignored by most Jews in the revolutionary and socialist movements, who had already severed their ties with the Jewish community. They may have believed 'in the ultimate solidarity of man', but they all too rarely included the Jews within their universal embrace. Moreover, their optimism about humanity scarcely seems justified by a world which could tolerate Auschwitz. Even Isaac Deutscher had reluctantly to concede that their 'optimism reached heights which it is not easy to ascend in our times'.[29] Unfortunately, he did not ask himself whether their message of universal human emancipation might not also have been a mirage. Instead he affirmed with unshaken conviction that the credo of the non-Jewish Jew had triumphed and would continue to triumph over parochial nationalism.[30] However moving this faith in internationalism, it would appear to offer little consolation to members of oppressed minorities who are unable or unwilling to assimilate, or who are threatened with persecution and discrimination. Historically speaking, the Jews are the classic example of such a people, which is the primary reason why Israel will remain central to their collective survival in the post-Holocaust world.

The Jews could not wait for the Messiah—they had to solve their problems as a people in an imperfect world which had considered them as expendable. The secular religion of the non-Jewish Jew, who became in the twentieth century the idol of a revolutionary mythology and the martyr of a counter-revolutionary backlash, has so far foundered on this intractable reality.

Germany

Karl Marx; Ferdinand Lassalle; Eduard Bernstein; Rosa Luxemburg

'How much of me was German, how much Jewish? Must I then join the ranks of the bigoted and glorify my Jewish blood now, not my German? Pride and love are not the same thing, and if I were asked where I belonged I should answer that a Jewish mother had borne me, that Germany nourished me, that Europe had formed me, that my home was the earth and the world my fatherland.'

Ernst Toller

This anguished expression of the German-Jewish duality by a revolutionary torn between the alternative identities offered by a century of assimilation sums up many of the dilemmas we shall be treating in the following chapters. Marx, Lassalle, Bernstein and Rosa Luxemburg were all in their different ways strongly attached to the German language and culture. At the same time they were socialists who believed in an internationalist form of assimilation. In addition, they were also Jews, even if Marx and Lassalle in particular suffered from the feelings of self-hatred common among the newly emancipated generation in Germany. A brief summary of the historical background may help the reader to understand this point more fully.

In the first half of the nineteenth century the emancipation granted to German Jewry as a result of the French Revolution and the Napoleonic conquests was gradually rescinded. Even the Prussian emancipation edict of 1812 which had given equal rights to the Jews was not observed in practice. The romantic nationalist *Weltanschauung* inspired by the revival of Christian-Teutonic culture in the 1820s made the perpetuation of a distinct Jewish identity in Germany more difficult. The place of the Jews as equal citizens in a Christian-Germanic state like Prussia was made conditional on their acceptance of Christianity. Even a radical Young Hegelian like Bruno Bauer (Karl Marx's first spiritual mentor) argued that Jews had to rid themselves of their Jewishness in order to become citizens. There were many distinguished apostates in this pre-1848 generation of Jews, including the sons and daughters of Moses Mendelsohn, Rachel Varnhagen, Eduard Gans, Heinrich Heine, Ludwig Boerne, Friedrich Julius Stahl and the father of Karl Marx.

The 1848 Revolution temporarily brought equal rights to German Jews, whose socio-economic role made them natural allies of the

German liberals. But following the reaction of the 1850s the Jews had to wait until 1869 before the North German Confederation abolished all civil and political restrictions on their freedom. After the Franco-Prussian war of 1870–1 this was extended to the South German states. In 1871 there were 512 158 Jews in Germany (1·25 per cent of the total population), many of whom were very active in the liberal professions, in the liberal and socialist parties, in banking, industry and commerce. As in France, Italy and other Western countries, the Jews were almost entirely absent from the fields of primary production—that is to say, as agricultural or industrial workers. Their socio-economic structure was overwhelmingly urban and middle-class. The *Ostjuden* (East European Jews) were the only proletarian element in the Jewish economy. By 1910 they numbered 78 746 (12·8 per cent of all Jews in Germany), and it was only this steady influx which prevented an absolute numerical decline in German Jewry.

In the 1880s an important anti-Semitic movement emerged in Germany which challenged the premises of Jewish emancipation. It reached an early peak between 1890 and 1895, but did not succeed in undermining the legal status of the Jews before the First World War. Nevertheless, Jews were excluded from the Prussian officer-corps as well as leading positions in the State and civil service. As a result many German Jews felt that they were second-class citizens, and suffered from feelings of social inferiority.

The political orientation of the German-Jewish community before 1914 was generally progressive, tending towards national-liberalism in the earlier period and later towards the Social Democrats. Until the 1890s the zealous German patriotism of the Jews, their belief in a free market economy, and attachment to religious values, prohibited support for the extra-legal socialist movement. But the need for self-defence against anti-Semitism and the fact that the Social Democrats were the only reliable defenders of Jewish civil equality, made a rapprochement with the Left possible. This was especially true after 1918, when anti-Semitism revived in Germany, and liberalism had become the creed of a minority capitalist class.

The growing socio-economic crises in the 1920s, inflation, unemployment and National Socialist propaganda (which was especially effective among the German middle classes) made the Jews, in spite of their economic interests, more ready to support the Social Democrats. Already in Imperial Germany a significant part of the Jewish intelligentsia had been active in the labour movement. Apart from Marx, Lassalle and Bernstein, many Jewish intellectuals mainly from the middle classes, such as Paul Singer, Leo Arons, Emmanuel Wurm, Bruno Schoenlank, Otto Landsberg, Arthur Stadthagen and Ludwig Frank, had played a leading role as propagandists, journalists, organizers and deputies in the Socialist Party. In 1912 there were 12 Jews out of 110 deputies in the parliamentary Socialist group, most of them lawyers with an indispensable academic training. They were reinforced by an émigré Russian-Jewish element, including such colourful figures as Rosa Luxemburg, Alexander Israel Helphand (Parvus), Leo Jogiches and Karl Radek—not to mention a number of gifted Austrian Jews like Heinrich Braun, Gustav Eckstein and Friedrich Stampfer. During the abortive 1918 Revolution in Germany Jewish intellectuals were especially prominent within the revolutionary government in Bavaria under Kurt Eisner, with which Eugen Leviné, Gustav Landauer and Ernst Toller were also associated. The leadership of the German Communist Party in the early years also included a substantial number of Jews, though by 1930 they had been virtually eliminated. Luxemburg, Jogiches, Eisner, Landauer, Leviné and the moderate socialist Hugo Haase were all either assassinated in 1918–19 or else executed by the military in a counter-revolutionary backlash.

Their tragic fate was a significant prelude to the disasters which later overtook the Weimar Republic. Hatred of the Jews became a central pillar of the Nazi movement which eventually came to power in 1933 and fabricated a fantastic mythology in which capitalism and Marxism were identified with the machinations of world Jewry. After 1933 the National Socialist regime officially branded the Jews as an 'alien race' in Germany and systematically expunged them from all areas of German public life. The anti-Semitism which had been a more or less constant feature of German society and culture for over a century climaxed in the nightmare of the 'Final Solution' during the Second World War.

CHAPTER 1

Karl Marx, the Iconoclast

'In the last analysis, the *emancipation of the Jews* is the emancipation of mankind from *Judaism*.'

Karl Marx

'Besides, we owe so much to the Jews. Not to mention Heine and Börne, Marx was of purely Jewish blood. Lassalle was a Jew. Many of our best people are Jews.'

Friedrich Engels

Karl Marx, the greatest revolutionary thinker of the modern age, was born in 1818, in the small, predominantly Catholic city of Trier, in the Rhineland. His father, Heinrich (Hirschel), was the son of Marx Levi (Mordechai ben Samuel Halevi), the rabbi of Trier. The name Marx itself derives from an abbreviated form of Mordechai, later changed to Markus. On his father's side Karl Marx was the heir and culmination of an extraordinarily rich tradition of learning which can be traced back to the sixteenth century. His grandfather Mordechai was the descendant of a line of rabbinical scholars, and his grandmother Eva (Chaja) Lwow had an equally illustrious ancestry. Eva's father, Moses Lwow, like his predecessors, was also rabbi in Trier and the son of Joshua Heschel Lwow, a famous Talmudic scholar. The Lwow family originally came from the city of Lwow in Poland (known as Lemberg in German); their ancestors included Meir ben Isak Katzenellbogen, rabbi in Padua, who died in 1565. Other offshoots of the Marx family tree had been rabbis in Cracow and Brest-Litovsk.[1]

Although Karl Marx completely rejected his background, that does not mean that it exercised no influence on his revolutionary career.[2] His intransigent hostility to Judaism should not blind one to the role which insecurity about his origins played in shaping the intellectual and moral character of his outlook. Nor should one forget that those adversaries with whom he clashed most violently emphasized his Jewishness in their polemics. Marx did not answer these aspersions, perhaps because he shared their antipathy to Judaism: as a baptized, assimilated Jew of the pre-1848 era in Germany, he could scarcely avoid seeing the Jewish problem through the distorting-glass of endemic Christian Judaeophobia. Although Marx was to give his name to a secular, universalist ideology, as hostile to Christianity as it was to Judaism, he never freed himself from subjective prejudices which reflected the oldest anti-Semitic stereotypes of European Christian society.

The decisive fact which conditioned Marx's attitude towards Judaism was his conversion to the Lutheran faith at the age of six.[3] His father, Heinrich, a knowledgeable, industrious lawyer in the high court of Trier, was responsible for this fateful step. But although Heinrich Marx was, according to his granddaughter Eleanor, a 'true eighteenth-century Frenchman in spirit', immunized against Judaism by his love of Rousseau and Voltaire, he did not voluntarily abandon his religion.

In 1815 he still identified himself sufficiently with his co-religionists to address a memorandum in their name to the Prussian Governor-General, von Sack, requesting the abolition of the Napoleonic ordinances of 1808, restricting Jewish rights in licensing and trade.[4] This Napoleonic legislation was to prove benevolent, however, compared to the Prussian regulations enforced after the annexation of the Rhineland in 1815. The new dispensation obliged Heinrich Marx to choose between his career as a lawyer and his family loyalties to Judaism, if he were to remain in the service of the Prussian State.[5] In 1817 Marx's father was converted to Lutheranism, the minority religion in Catholic Trier, to preserve what Heinrich Heine once called the 'entry-ticket to European civilization'. In 1824, when his numerous children were of school age, Heinrich Marx had them all baptized into the Lutheran religion.

Karl Marx's mother (*née* Henriette Pressburg) delayed her conversion until 1825, when her father, Isaac Pressburg, rabbi in Nijmegen (Holland), died. This deference to Jewish tradition suggests that she felt some respect for family customs, and perhaps a greater affinity for the religion which her husband had cast off.[6] Henriette Marx was also descended from a long line of rabbis, driven by persecutions from Hungary to Holland.[7] Her letters to her Dutch relatives and to her son, written in a clumsy, ungrammatical German, show a warm if somewhat narrow personality. Her relations with her gifted, rebellious son became noticeably cooler during the 'Sturm und Drang' years which Karl Marx spent in the universities of Bonn and Berlin. After the death of her husband the relationship deteriorated still further, leading to a rift in 1843—the year of Karl Marx's marriage to Jenny von Westphalen.

Already in January 1843 Marx had mentioned in a letter to his friend Arnold Ruge that 'as long as my mother lives, I have no right to my inheritance'. Money matters were most probably at the root of this friction, and it is possible that Karl Marx identified his mother with the egoistic, materialistic form of piety which, in 1844 he brutally caricatured as 'Judaism'.[8] There is doubtless something in the story that Henriette Marx (who lived until 1863) disapproved of her son writing so much about Capital, but singularly failing to make a decent living.

But although Marx's strained relations with his mother in the 1840s may have influenced his negative attitude to Judaism, one should not make too much of this. He maintained close ties with his maternal uncle, Lion Philips, a Dutch banker, whose grandson was the founder of the internationally famous electrical concern. In the 1850s and 60s Karl Marx received financial assistance and useful information on economic matters from his uncle, whom, although a banker, he held in high regard. It was to Lion Philips (a fellow-convert) that Marx permitted himself a solitary and indirect reference to his own racial origins. In a letter of 1864 he jokingly identified himself with our 'fellow-Jew' (*unser Stammesgenosse*) Benjamin Disraeli, the English Tory leader who, like Marx, was also a baptized Jew.[9]

Although Marx was the descendant of generations of rabbis, available evidence points to rather diluted Jewish background in the baptized Rhineland household where he grew up. It is true that his uncle Samuel Marx (brother of Heinrich) remained rabbi of Trier until his death in 1827, but Karl Marx was then only eight and a half years old. At the former Jesuit school which the young Marx attended between 1830 and 1835 most of the pupils were Catholic and the instruction was permeated with the humanist ideals of the German Enlightenment. Marx received a firm grounding in Greek and Latin literature, but no education in the Hebrew religion, except through the distorting prism of German Christianity. Later, at the University of Berlin, Marx, like so many of his generation, became an adept of the dominant Hegelian philosophy. He wrote his doctoral dissertation on 'The Difference between the Democritean and the Epicurean Philosophies of Nature', already identifying himself with the Promethean credo of German philosophy—that man's self-consciousness is the highest divinity.[10]

By July 1841, after submission of his thesis, Marx had rejoined his close friend Bruno Bauer, the leader of the politically left Hegelians in Bonn. Both Bauer, a Protestant theologian, and Marx were by this time confirmed atheists and philosophical radicals, opposed to the Christian State and its quasi-medieval restrictions on human rights in Prussia. Moses Hess, the 'communist rabbi' and Young Hegelian who met him at this time, prophetically anticipated that 'Dr Marx . . . will give medieval religion and politics their *coup de grâce*'.[11]

Moses Hess was instrumental among others in recommending Marx for the position of editor of the liberal *Rheinische Zeitung*, which he held until March 1843. It was the period when Marx began to develop the Young Hegelian critique of religion into a more incisive critique of politics. He also became aware for the first time of the agitation for Jewish emancipation in Germany—a movement supported by the Rhineland bourgeoisie, and not surprisingly by the *Rheinische Zeitung*.[12]

As editor of the paper, Marx did not oppose this policy, backed by its managers, by liberal opinion and by most of the journalists on its staff. Marx had no reason to disapprove of a movement which, at least indirectly, might help undermine the repressive Prussian autocracy in the Rhineland. It was this tactical consideration which led Marx to declare his readiness to sign a petition for Jewish civil equality to the Rhineland diet, presented to him by the President of the local Jewish community. On 13th March 1843 he wrote to Ruge, informing him of this decision, and adding, 'We must riddle the Christian State with as many holes as possible and smuggle in the rational as far as we can. The bitterness only grows with every petition rejected amid protests'.[13]

This letter, written a few days before his resignation as editor of the *Rheinische Zeitung*, is an important document, both as to Marx's personal development and to his attitude towards Judaism. In the letter he recounts with some bitterness the hard struggle which he and his future wife, Jenny von Westphalen, had to wage against bigoted in-laws in both families who opposed their marriage. Since the death of Heinrich Marx and of the liberal Baron von Westphalen (who had been something of a spiritual guide to the adolescent Karl Marx), relations between the two families in Trier had evidently deteriorated. Marx's anger seems to have been directed primarily against reactionary in-laws in the Westphalen family, his future wife's 'pietistic-aristocratic relations, for whom the "Lord in heaven" and the "Lord in Berlin" are alike objects of reverence [*Kultusobjekte*]'.[14] Most probably these 'aristocratic relations' objected to the prospect of a son-in-law who was not only a revolutionary but also an atheist and a *Judenstammling* (offspring of Jews).

Marx also hinted at opposition to the marriage within his own family 'in which some parsons [*Pfaffen*] and other enemies of mine have settled'.[15] We do not know who these 'parsons' were, but the term accurately reflects Marx's general aversion to religion and his tendency to subsume Judaism and Christianity under the same loathing. It seems reasonable to suppose from this letter that there was a strong personal element at this time in Marx's hostility to organized religion. This impression is reinforced by Marx's first reference, in the same letter, to the pamphlet of his friend Bruno Bauer on the Jewish question.

Bauer's *Die Judenfrage* (1843) had argued that the Christian State in Prussia could never emancipate the Jews. Only a secular atheistic society might achieve general German emancipation, but Jewish emancipation was, according to Bauer, a selfish, unattainable and undesirable goal.[16] Marx's comment to Ruge on this pamphlet was brief and cryptic: 'Although the Israelite faith is repugnant to me, Bauer's point of view still seems to me too abstract'.[17]

In the autumn and winter of 1843 Marx prepared a more detailed answer to Bauer, which appeared in the *Deutsch-Französischer Jahrbücher* (February 1844), which he edited in Paris, together with Ruge. The article, entitled 'Zur Judenfrage', dealt specifically with Judaism, but also contained an exposition of Marx's theories on civil society and the State, and the meaning of secularization. Before we examine this essay, it is worth recalling the harsh expression which Marx had used in his letter to Ruge, to explain his attitude to the 'Israelite faith'.

Why was it so 'repugnant' (*widerlich*) to this young Rhinelander, steeped in the literature of German classical philosophy? The reason must be sought in a combination of psychological conflicts and intellectual influences which shaped the personality of the 25-year-old Marx. 'Zur Judenfrage' must have been, at least partly, an intensely emotional polemic, a cathartic release for Marx of deep-seated resentments towards an inheritance to which he felt neither sympathy or attachment.

In 1843 he had broken with his family, he had married into the

Prussian aristocracy against considerable opposition, he was without material resources and cut adrift from the land in which he had been born. Was it pure coincidence that under the weight of these personal pressures, perhaps intensified by bitterness against his mother, Marx felt a strong compulsion ostentatiously to throw off the burden of his Jewishness once and for all?

Added to this psychological crisis was the powerful influence of the German philosophy in which the young Marx had steeped himself. Its verdict on his ancestral religion was unceremoniously harsh.[18] It matters little whether Marx took his anti-Judaism directly from Kant and Hegel or only from his Young Hegelian contemporaries, Bruno Bauer and Ludwig Feuerbach. What is clear is that German idealism, preoccupied with the dialectics of immanence and a heady faith in the supremacy of human self-consciousness, regarded Judaism in wholly negative terms. Through Kant, Fichte, Hegel, Feuerbach and Bauer, the antagonism to the Jewish religion undergoes a progressive vulgarization. The culmination of this trend can be found in Marx's essay of 1844, with its depiction of Judaism as a religion in which money is God—and which is therefore the antithesis of human emancipation.

Bruno Bauer's *Die Judenfrage* seems to have been largely a pretext for Marx to settle his accounts with the hated ancestral religion. But it was also a useful vehicle for him in developing that immanent critique of Hegelian philosophy which led him irreversibly toward socialism.

The most significant idea in Marx's 'Zur Judenfrage' which pointed to the future was his theory of human emancipation.[19] The first part of his essay explores this idea in bold fashion, only indirectly hinting at the virulent attack on Judaism which is to follow. Essentially, Marx believed that once man began consciously to organize his social powers for the general good, and overcame the contradiction between his empirical essence as a member of the species (*Gattungswesen*) and his selfish existence in civil society, he would achieve his human emancipation. But in 'Zur Judenfrage' this embryonic expression of Marx's youthful humanism lies buried under his emotionalized antipathy to the Jewish religion. The tenuous link between the two sections of the essay is supplied by the premise that, with the abolition of private property, and hence of man's dualistic existence as *citoyen* and bourgeois in civil society, the secular basis of religion will disappear. Once this happens, the Jewish question would allegedly dissolve into 'the general questions of the age'.

Marxist commentators have frequently seen in this assumption a 'scientific' de-mystification of the Jewish problem.[20] In reality, however, Marx had never scientifically studied 'empirical Jews', let alone Jewish history. His judgments were based on highly subjective projections of hostility, on manifest ignorance and unreliable second-hand sources. Nor can there be any doubt that he was as hostile to Judaism as his erstwhile mentor, Bruno Bauer, whose anti-Semitism even left-wing critics generally concede.[21] Marx's own Judaeophobia is no less transparent, even if his attack was directed not at the Jew as an 'alien' or religious phenomenon, but rather at the metaphysical embodiment of a 'capitalist spirit'.

His image of the Jew was in fact nothing but the classic stereotype of European Christian society, inherited from the Middle Ages and resurrected with new force in the 1840s by reactionaries, radicals and socialists alike.[22]

It was a tragic and fateful paradox that Marx reproduced the deeply rooted anti-Jewish mythology of the bourgeois Christian society which he was seeking to overthrow. In 1844 Marx held that this society was itself 'judaized'—a notion which was to have a disastrous influence on the attitude of other socialists (including the revolutionaries discussed in this book) towards the Jewish problem.

How was it possible that Marx, one of the great iconoclasts in the history of human thought, could arrive at such an amazing, distorted and unoriginal conclusion?

In the first place, Marx accepted the caricature of the Israelite religion given by the Young Hegelians, and specifically Bruno Bauer.[23] Summarizing Bauer's criticism of the Jewish faith, and his analysis of 'the *religious* opposition between Judaism and Christianity', Marx enthusiastically acknowledged that 'He [Bauer] does this with boldness, perception, wit and thoroughness, in language that is as precise as it is vigorous and meaningful'.[24]

One must actually read Bauer's text, with its implacable hostility to Judaism, to fully understand the implications of this warm praise. In fact, despite his repeated claim that he was breaking 'the theological framing of the question', Marx in large measure echoed Bauer's ideas on Judaism, and its relation to the Christian world. Hence he could write, entirely in the Young Hegelian idiom:

> The law of the Jew, lacking all solid foundation, is only the religious caricature of ungrounded and unfounded morality and law in general, of the purely formal rites in which the world of property clothes its transactions.

Continuing in this vein, Marx added:

> Jewish Jesuitry—the same practical Jesuitry which Bauer finds in the Talmud, deals with the wily circumvention by the world of self-interest of the laws that dominate it—and constitutes the principal skill of that world.[25]

For Marx Judaism was 'the religion of practical necessity' which can 'achieve perfection only through practice, because practice is its truth'. Ludwig Feuerbach, in his *Essence of Christianity* (1841), had said much the same thing when he argued that Judaism was a narrow, egoistic cult of utility, based on selfish needs. Equally unoriginal was Marx's assertion, taken from Bruno Bauer, that 'the Christian was from the start the theorizing Jew' and 'the Jew was the practical Christian'—a formulation to be found also in Moses Hess.[26] Marx's contrast between the 'material egoism' of the Jew and the 'spiritual egoism' of the Christian had, however, a nastier edge to it than other Young Hegelian formulations.

> Christianity overcame real Judaism only in appearance. It was too spiritual, too refined to abolish crude practical need other than by raising it into the blue heavens. Christianity is the sublime thought of Judaism, Judaism the everyday vulgar application of Christianity.[27]

Marx departed from Bruno Bauer only in his determination to provide something more than a speculative critique of Jewish emancipation, not in his hostility to Judaism.[28] For Marx the central question was not whether the negation of Christianity or of Judaism would make man more free, but 'what particular social element needs to be overcome in order to abolish Judaism'. Marx's hatred was therefore focused not against Bruno Bauer's 'Sabbath-Jew' but rather against contemporary Jewry.

> And so we find the real nature of today's Jew not only in the Pentateuch and in the Talmud but in contemporary society as well—not as a theoretical but as a highly empirical fact, and not only as the narrowness of the Jew but as the Jewish narrowness of society.[29]

The 'Jewish limitations' of society were for Marx the symbol of the victory of vulgar commercialism in the bourgeois Christian world of America and Europe. Completely distorting the findings of such contemporary European observers of American democracy as Colonel Hamilton, Beaumont and Alexis de Tocqueville, Marx concluded, 'Indeed, the practical dominance of Judaism over the Christian world has reached its unambiguous normal expression in North America'.[30] Although the religious sects in North America were overwhelmingly Protestant, Marx insisted on blaming their reduction of the Christian gospel to 'an article of commerce' on the corrupting influence of Judaism.[31] He drew the same conclusion for European society where 'the Jew has emancipated himself in a Jewish manner' through his financial domination of the market. 'With the Jew and without him, *money* has become a world-power and the practical spirit of the Jews has become the practical spirit of the Christian peoples. The Jews have emancipated themselves to the extent that Christians have become Jews.'[32]

Marx's anti-Semitic myth concerning the so-called universal domination exercised by Jewish money-power was by no means unique in the 1840s. The French socialist Alphonse Toussenel in his *Les Juifs, Rois de L'Époque* (Paris, 1845) repeated much the same thing in more populist language. Marx himself quoted Bruno Bauer with obvious approval on this very theme—namely, the relationship between the Jews and the power of money. 'The Jew, who is, for example, merely tolerated in Vienna, determines by his money-power the fate of the entire German Empire. The Jew, who is without rights in the smallest German state, decides the fate of Europe'.[33]

This quote from Bauer already undermines Marx's claim that his predecessor had viewed Judaism 'as a mere religious criticism of Christianity' or that he had mistaken 'the ideal, abstract nature of the Jew—that is, his religion' for his real essence. In fact Marx had borrowed far more from Bauer's analysis than he was prepared to admit:[34] moreover, where he claimed to be original he was merely repeating the most vulgar anti-Semitic myths in uncritical fashion; and where he touched on the Jewish religion his analysis was inferior to that of Bauer. What was novel in Marx was simply the extreme conclusions which he drew from his own modern, materialistic and pseudo-revolutionary brand of anti-Semitism. 'Thus we recognize in Judaism a universal and *contemporary anti-social* element which has reached its present peak through a historical development in whose harmful aspects the Jews eagerly collaborated, a peak at which it will inevitably disintegrate. The *emancipation of the Jews* means ultimately the emancipation of humanity from *Judaism*.'[35]

It took a baptized, self-hating Jew like Marx to arrive at such a twisted piece of dialectical paradox. Bruno Bauer and the Young Hegelians had demanded that the Jews abandon their religion in order to become worthy of human rights: in other words, they were anti-Semitic, but only to a certain degree, like the French *philosophes* of the eighteenth century.[36] Marx, on the other hand, transformed the issue of Jewish emancipation into its diametrical opposite—the liberation of mankind as a whole from Judaism. He justified this sleight-of-hand by claiming that Bruno Bauer had overlooked the 'real Jew', the 'everyday Jew' whose huckstering was the cold, egoistic heart of the Jewish religion.

> What is the secular basis of Judaism? *Practical* need, selfishness. What is the secular cult of the Jew? *Haggling*. What is his secular god? *Money*. Well, then! Emancipation from *haggling* and *money*, from practical, real Judaism would be the self-emancipation of our time.[37]

What was decisive in Marx's essay was his subjective will to destroy the 'empirical essence' of Judaism, and his tautological equation of the Jews with money-making and the 'egoism' of civil society.[38] The universal domination of money, with its 'materialistic degradation of nature', of the world and of man, is at every point exemplified for Marx by Judaism. 'Money is the jealous God of Israel, beside which no other God may stand. Money degrades all the gods of mankind and turns them into commodities. Money is the universal and self constituted *value* set upon all things.'[39] But money was for the young Marx only a general symbol of the pervasive corruption of Christian society by 'Judaism'. 'The God of the Jews has become secularized and is now a worldly God. The bill of exchange is the true God of the Jew.'[40]

The 'God of the Jews' as interpreted by Marx through the prism of German classical philosophy was simply the ultimate manifestation of human self-alienation. The 'monotheism of the Jew', about which Hegel still had some positive things to say, is reduced by Marx to 'a polytheism of the many needs' and the undisguised worship of the Golden Calf. Judaism is even held responsible for the cultural philistinism of bourgeois society and its degradation of the sexual relationship.

> What is present in abstract form in the Jewish religion—contempt for theory, for art, for history and for man as an end in himself—is an *actual* and *conscious* standpoint, held to be virtuous by the money-man. Even the relations between the sexes, between man and woman etc. become an object of commerce! The woman is auctioned off.[41]

Judaism through its connection with money, the 'alien monster' which dominates man, has brought civil society to its ultimate perfection in the Christian world. Its abolition thereby becomes for Marx a revolutionary necessity—in order to deliver humanity from the clutches of its own total degradation. Hence Marx's closing passages in 'Zur Judenfrage' combine a pseudo-messianic call for human emancipation with the radical, uncomprising demand to *abolish* Judaism.

> As soon as society succeeds in destroying the *empirical* essence of Judaism—buying and selling, and its presuppositions—the Jew will become *impossible*, because his consciousness will no longer have an object. . . . The *social* emancipation of Jewry is the *emancipation of society from Judaism.*[42]

The false universalistic pathos behind this formula was all too clearly an emotional projection of Marx's self-hatred, like his hope that 'if the Jew recognizes the futility of his *practical* existence and strives to put an end to it, he will work away from his previous course of development toward *human emancipation* in general and turn against the *highest practical* expression of human self-alienation.'[43]

In 1844, at the moment when Marx was embarking on his crucial transition to revolutionary socialism, he chose therefore consciously to negate the very possibility of a specifically Jewish existence and identity. Was it pure coincidence that his Judaeophobia appeared in its most pathological form at this time? Was Marx's pre-Marxist anti-Judaism a necessary point of departure for his subsequent critique of capitalist society? Finally, was the 'Marxist' Marx who had already arrived by 1845 at his theory of the class-struggle, of historical materialism and of the revolutionary mission of the proletariat still an anti-Semite?

If we take the *Economic and Philosophical Manuscripts* of 1844 as our criterion, then it would appear that Marx had within a few months purged himself completely of his anti-Semitic phantasmagoria. In these *Paris Manuscripts* which deal with the same general topics of money, species-man, alienation and human essence as one can find in 'Zur Judenfrage', there is no more mention of the Jews. Instead we have a genuinely universalistic perspective as well as a cogent and brilliant statement of Marx's positive humanism.[44] In the *Manuscripts* (not published until 1932) Marx had already outlined the basic programme of his life's work which culminated in his *Critique of Political Economy* (1859) and *Capital* (1867). In these writings there is a certain continuity with the earlier essay on the Jews: the workers now represent the negative side of the universal condition of alienation. They are alienated from their labour and prevented from realizing their human essence, not by the 'Judaism of civil society' but by the capitalist mode of production. The latter (like the money-power of the Jews) is also universal in its drive, which transcends all the frontiers of race, religion and nationality. Robert Misrahi has argued on the basis of the *Paris Manuscripts* that Marx had already overcome the anti-Semitic eruption which briefly surfaced in February 1844.[45] He had sublimated his hostile stereotype of the Jew, transforming him into the *capitalist*, and projected his 'positive image' of suffering on to the worker. The capitalist bourgeoisie were now the motive power of universal self-alienation and the working class, the chosen instrument of ultimate human redemption. Misrahi's argument is that Marx's self-rejection as a Jew made possible his conversion to Marxism, but that once a Marxist, he abandoned anti-Semitism as the aberration of his youth.[46] This theory is made more seductive in so far as Misrahi, unlike other Marxian apologists (such as Isaac Deutscher, Abraham Léon, Maxime Rodinson and István Mészáros) does not gloss over but if anything perhaps overstates the anti-Semitism of 'Zur Judenfrage'.

But this well-intentioned attempt to salvage the 'socialist' Marx from the accusation of Judaeophobia remains unconvincing. For all the available evidence points to the fact that Marx never overcame the self-hatred of his youth as far as Jews were concerned. The most that one can say is that there is no doctrinal *necessity* for anti-Semitism within Marxist theory, simply because Marx was insufficiently interested in the Jewish problem to give it a systematic treatment. As Marx refined and developed his analysis of Western capitalism, of its internal mechanisms and underlying fetishisms, he had no need to fall back on the mythological stereotypes of 'Zur Judenfrage'. But his personal antipathy to Jews as money-men, hucksters and parasites in the pores of feudal society was not in the least modified. To quote only one example from many, in the *Neue Rheinische Zeitung* of 29th April 1849 we discover that 'The Jews of Poland are the dirtiest of all races'. But already *The Holy Family* of 1845 shows us a 'Marxist' Marx, whose view of the Jewish question has not changed in substance from that expressed in the *Deutsch-Französischer Jahrbücher*.[47] An analysis of *The Holy Family* proves that, even after his total break with Bruno Bauer and Young Hegelianism, Karl Marx had not renounced his 'Jewish' anti-Semitism. If this is less conspicuous than in 'Zur Judenfrage' it is largely because he found it tactically convenient to take the side of Jewish critics of Bruno Bauer, against whom his main attack is still directed. 'Judaism' again symbolized the social structure of alienation for Marx, even after he had written the Paris Manuscripts. His critique of Bauer continued to be based on the latter's 'theological' approach to the Jewish problem, not on his intransigent hostility to Judaism.

> Herr Bauer only understands the Jew in so far as he is the direct object of *theology* or the *theologian.* He has no conception, therefore, that real, secular Jews and hence also religious Jews are incessantly produced by existing bourgeois life and receive their final culmination in the money-system.[48]

As in 'Zur Judenfrage', Marx pointed out that Bruno Bauer had 'confused the state with humanity, human rights with man, and political emancipation with human emancipation'. It was only natural, therefore, that Marx supported the 'liberal and rationalist Jews' who had polemicized against Bruno Bauer's idea that atheism was a precondition for Jewish civil equality. Even these 'feeble adversaries' (*tristen Gegner*) were superior to Bauer in their understanding of the doctrine of human rights. Marx also quoted with approval the arguments of Gustav Philippson and S. R. Hirsch showing that Judaism by Bauer's own logic 'must have had some influence on history' and on the formation of modern culture.[49] Marx agreed with these critics of Bauer that the latter's philosophical atheist State, far from solving the Jewish question, would actually lead to State terrorism and the guillotine, since by definition it would have to exclude all Jews and Christians as treasonable elements. Summing up Gabriel Riesser's arguments on this subject, Marx observed, 'As a result, Herr Bauer would have to hang Jews and Christians in his 'critical State'. Marx also quoted Gabriel Riesser (the leading advocate of Jewish emancipation in Germany) with approval, on the meaning of the Jews' demands for civil equality—namely, freedom of trade, freedom of movement, residence and travel.[50]

But this apparent support for the principles of Jewish emancipation was for Marx nothing but a purely formal concession to the internal logic of bourgeois society. It did not imply that he had abandoned his earlier view concerning the anti-social role of the Jews in the contemporary world. On the contrary, Marx continued in *The Holy Family* to emphasize that this omission was the main defect in Bruno Bauer's analysis. The 'theologian' had failed to see the profane, practical meaning of Judaism. Once more Marx repeated his so-called secular, scientific formula as laid down in 'Zur Judenfrage'. 'Let us consider the real worldly Jew, not the *Sabbath* Jew, as Bauer does, but the *everyday* Jew. We will not look for the secret of the Jew in his religion, but we will look for the secret of religion in the real Jew.'[51]

Needless to say, the 'real Jew' as depicted by Marx in *The Holy Family* of 1845 was as much a hostile caricature as his earlier version. Nor had Marx abandoned his anti-Semitic myth about the 'judaized' essence of bourgeois society. If anything, he placed even greater emphasis on the notion that Judaism had survived solely because it was in harmony with the dehumanized commercial and industrial practice of capitalism. It was therefore a revolutionary duty for socialism to abolish the huckstering 'Jewish essence' and free humanity from the 'Judaism of civil society'. Marx regarded Judaism as a synonym for the 'inhumanity of contemporary life-practice'.

> The human emancipation of the Jew or the emancipation of mankind from Judaism is therefore to be understood, not as Herr Bauer believes, as a special task of the Jew, but as the general practical task of the contemporary world, which is Jewish to its innermost core.[52]

Thus although Marx rejected Bauer's 'theological fanaticism' and described states which had failed to emancipate the Jews as politically backward, his basic standpoint had not changed.[53] The novelty in *The Holy Family* was simply the harshness of his polemic against what he saw as Bauer's apologia for the theocratic Prussian State. His rupture with Young Hegelianism had sharpened his opposition to the reactionary implications of Bauer's doctrine of human rights. But support for Jewish emancipation remained for the 'socialist' Marx a purely legalistic concession—necessary only so long as egoism constituted the natural basis of civil society. Once the 'money-system' which incessantly produced 'real, secular Jews' was abolished, then the ultimate problem of human emancipation (and thereby the Jewish question) could be finally solved.

In their articles for the *Neue Rheinische Zeitung* (1848–9) both Marx and Engels continued to identify Jews with petty huckstering, peddling and other unsavoury social activities.[54] In journalistic articles for the *New York Daily Tribune* in the 1850s Marx also vented his spleen against Jewish financiers—notably in a piece entitled 'The Russian Loan'. Here he singled out for attack bankers like Stieglitz, Rothschild and Achille Fould, who aided absolutist rulers such as Tsar Nicholas I, Franz-Joseph of Austria, and Louis Napoleon to maintain their tyrannical sway.

> Thus we find every tyrant backed by a Jew, as is every Pope by a Jesuit. In truth, the cravings of oppressors would be hopeless and the practicability of war out of the question, if there were not an army of Jesuits to smother thought and a handful of Jews to ransack pockets.[55]

Marx deplored the role of Jewish banking-houses and usurers in Europe, who were a 'curse to the people' and whose loan-mongering brought benefit only to 'the houses of the children of Judah'. Ironically enough, much of the information which Marx had acquired about such activities (especially of Amsterdam Jews) came from his Dutch uncle, Lion Philips—himself a banker and a converted Jew. It was of course by no means surprising for socialists to attack the influence of Jewish financiers in nineteenth-century European society. Many anti-Semitic socialists and radicals like Fourier, Toussenel, Proudhon, Bakunin and Pierre Leroux saw in the figure of the Jewish financier a new kind of feudal lord exercising his despotic sway over the rising European industrial civilization. But these socialists were essentially primitive populists, incapable of understanding the economic mechanisms of modern society—the function of credit, exchange, banking and capital accumulation. Hence they tended to personify the complex and anonymous features of modern capitalism, with its restless search for new markets and sources of wealth, in the familiar stereotype of the Jew. This was no longer the case of Marx, who in the *Communist Manifesto* (1848) insisted with great emphasis on the historically necessary and progressive function of the capitalist system. But although Marx ceased after 1845 to make the atavistic error of equating Judaism with capitalism, his personal antipathy to everything 'Jewish' did not diminish in the slightest.

Even more remarkable, it was not balanced by a single expression of concern at the plight of persecuted and oppressed Jews, whether in Russia, Poland, Austria-Hungary or anywhere else in the world. In this context it is worth mentioning an article written by Marx for the *New York Daily Tribune* in April 1854, which has sometimes been wrongly quoted as an example of his alleged compassion for the poor Jews of Jerusalem.[56] In this article, one of a series which Marx wrote on the dispute over the Holy Places at the time of the Crimean War, he mentioned the unequalled misery and sufferings of the Jews in Jerusalem

> inhabiting the most filthy quarter of the town, called *hareth-el-yahoud*, in the quarter of dirt between the Zion and the Moriah where their synagogues are situated—the constant objects of Moslem oppression and intolerance, insulted by the Greeks, persecuted by the Latins, and living upon the scanty alms transmitted by their European brethren. The Jews, however, are not natives, but from different and distant countries, and are only attracted to Jerusalem by the desire of inhabiting the Valley of Jehosaphat; and to die on the very place where the redemption is to be expected.[57]

At first glance, this passage suggests that Marx might have felt some pang of sympathy or even identification with the persecuted Jews of the Eternal City. But such a misleading impression is dispelled once it is realized that this comment was copied almost verbatim out of a contemporary eye-witness report on the Holy Land by the French writer César Famin. The original French text, entitled *Histoire de la Rivalité et du Protectorat des Églises Chrétiennes en Orient* (1853), was considerably more sympathetic in tone than Marx's bowdlerized version:[58] to take one example, the latter substituted the expression "the most filthy quarter" of Jerusalem for Famin's more correct designation of it as the 'Jewish quarter'.[59] Famin actually mentioned several projects to reconstitute the Jews as a nation and re-establish them in Palestine—although he personally regarded the dispersion of the Jews as irreversible. Marx for his part never once considered the 'Zionist' solution to the Jewish problem, although it had been hinted at even by Bruno Bauer in his *Die Judenfrage* (1843), and later in explicit terms by Moses Hess in *Rom und Jerusalem* (1862). Famin also spoke warmly of the Jewish lament for Zion—'*douleur immense dont le spectacle arrache souvent des larmes aux chrétiens eux-mêmes*'—a passage which Marx, not surprisingly, suppressed.[60] Thus the only reference to the existence of 'poor Jews' in the entire work of Marx turns out to have been a diluted plagiarism from a French Catholic author.

Although Marx carefully avoided the slightest hint as to his Jewish antecedents in public, he was not at all averse to attacking other baptized Jews for concealing their origins when it suited him. A classic example of this crude form of projection was his verbal assault on the proprietor of the *Daily Telegraph*, Joseph Moses Levy, a baptized English Jew, whom he lacerated in the most abusive manner in *Herr Vogt* (1860).

> As Eduard Simon wants with all his strength to be among the Romans, thus Levy wants absolutely to be numbered among the Anglo-Saxon race. At least once a month he takes up the cudgels against the un-English politics of Mr Disraeli, for Disraeli (the Asiatic mystery) does not derive, like the *Telegraph* from the Anglo-Saxon race. But what good does it do Levy to attack Mr Disraeli and put a Y for an I, for Mother Nature has written his pedigree in absurd block letters right in the middle of his face?[61]

This was one of Marx's milder references to Levy, who as the proprietor of a leading capitalist newspaper was of course his political enemy. But Marx was in no moral position to criticize Levy's behaviour as a baptized Jew—still less to indulge in such crude racial satire at the expense of the latter's 'Jewish nose'.

The same strictures apply to Marx's repulsive abuse of his fellow revolutionary socialist, Ferdinand Lassalle. The vulgar epithets reserved for Lassalle in the private correspondence of Marx and Engels, ranging from 'Baron Itzig' to 'Jewish nigger', were all the more inexcusable considering that Lassalle generally treated Marx with deference and friendly respect. The way in which Marx reciprocated these attentions reveals to what irrational depths the founder of *scientific* socialism could fall, not excluding the basest racial prejudice. In a letter to Engels of 10th May 1861 Marx managed not only to slander Lassalle, but even to give credence to perhaps the oldest of the many legends invented against the Jews.

> Apropos Lassalle-Lazarus. Lepsius in his great work on Egypt has proved that the exodus of the Jews from Egypt was nothing but the history which Manetho narrates of the expulsion of the 'leprous people' from Egypt. At the head of these lepers was an Egyptian priest, Moses. Lazarus, the leper, is therefore the archetype of the Jew, and Lassalle is the typical Lazarus.[62]

There are a number of points worth noting about this comment, which transcend the cheap sneer at Lassalle's syphilitic condition and the scarcely veiled desire to degrade his rival's importance. Marx was perfectly correct in his assertion that Manetho, a Hellenized Egyptian priest of the third century B.C., was the first authority to report that the ancestors of the Jews had been 'lepers'. This point had equally been made by Richard Lepsius, the nineteenth-century German Orientalist, whose work on ancient Egypt and on the biblical exodus saga was referred to by Marx. What neither Lepsius nor Marx mentioned, however, was that this hoary folk-myth represented the first important attack on the Jews in Greek literature; the legend of the Jews as a 'leprous people' had been circulated by the first-century Alexandrian anti-Semite Apion as part of a systematic defamatory campaign. The legend had been taken up by the Romans, and became a central theme in the pagan, pre-Christian literature of anti-Semitism. It is difficult to believe that Marx, a considerable classical scholar in his own right, did not know this fact, and one can only assume that he shared the Greco-Roman contempt for the social and religious particularism of the Hebrews. But the repetition of this crude anti-Semitic fable also served a more deep-rooted inner compulsion, to utterly repudiate the Jewish people. The descendant of generations of rabbis could find no better method for achieving this dissociation than to reduce the central event of Jewish religious history, the exodus from Egypt, to an expulsion by the Egyptians of Israelite 'lepers'. Moses, the liberator of the Hebrews from Egyptian bondage and the creator of Judaism, thereby becomes identified in Marx's mind with a renegade Egyptian priest at the head of a band of leprous Jews.

Equally absurd were Marx's aspersions on the allegedly 'Negro-Jewish' descent of Lassalle. Marx depicted Lassalle's pushfulness (*Zudringlichkeit*) as a 'nigger' trait, and fancifully attributed his physical appearance to the likelihood that one of his ancestors had 'crossed with a nigger' during the Hebrew exodus from Egypt.[63]

> It is now perfectly clear to me that, as the shape of his head and the growth of his hair indicates, he is descended from the Negroes who joined in Moses's flight from Egypt (unless his mother or grandmother on the father's side were crossed with a nigger). This union of Jew and German on a Negro base was bound to produce an extraordinary hybrid.

Engels was no less vitriolic about Lassalle, whom he liked to describe as 'Baron Itzig', and whom he had characterized to Marx back in March 1856 in the following terms:

> He is a real Jew from the Slav frontier, and he has always been willing to exploit party affairs for private purposes. It is revolting to see how he is always trying to push his way into the aristocratic world. He is a greasy Jew disguised under brilliantine and flashy jewels.[64]

Engels would hardly have written in this fashion to Marx unless he was sure that such a display of Teutonic prejudice would have met with the latter's approval. Similar comments abound in the private correspondence of Marx and Engels, and it serves no useful purpose to catalogue them all.

But is there any evidence to suggest that Marx ever overcame this highly subjective Judaeophobia? Did he begin to revise his hostile attitude to the race from which he descended, in the mellowness of old age?[65] Such reversals of attitude were by no means uncommon among his contemporaries. Heinrich Heine and Moses Hess, fellow-Rhinelanders and radical Jews who in the 1840s had shared some of Marx's Judaeophobia, both returned to their ancestral religion in different ways. Even Friedrich Engels, who as a Gentile was free of this specifically Jewish self-hatred, changed his opinions and after 1878 took an increasingly strong stand against anti-Semitism.[66] In Marx's case the evidence remains purely circumstantial, and his later silence on the Jewish question is open to various interpretations.

One possible reason for this silence is that his own Jewishness was simply of peripheral and secondary concern to Marx—at the most a psychological irritant which he had tried brutally to cast off in the manner described. This might explain why he felt no need to comment on the anti-Semitic agitation which was developing in Germany at the end of the 1870s under the impulse of Adolf Stoecker's Christian-Social party. Nor did he feel moved to react to the Russian pogroms of 1881 which were to lead to a rebirth of Jewish nationalism. The author of *Capital* and the founder of the First International was preoccupied in his last years with more universal issues, and busy perfecting his analysis of the imminent breakdown of the capitalist system under the weight of its own contradictions. He left Engels to deal with Eugen Dühring's racialist aspersions on his ancestry and confined himself to a critique of the latter's economic theories in *Anti-Dühring* (1878).[67] Nor did he comment on Bakunin's grotesque assertions that he was in league with Rothschild[68]—although he had fiercely fought Bakunin's efforts to undermine the International with all the polemical skill and sarcasm of which he was capable. Marx was most probably psychologically incapable of dealing with such anti-Semitic slanders by radical opponents, even assuming that he considered these accusations worth refuting.[69]

However, a more personal reminder of his racial origins could still sting him to the quick, especially where it touched on his marriage to Jenny Marx-Westphalen. His wife had died in 1881, and in an obituary for the French newspaper *La Justice* his son-in-law Charles Longuet (a socialist of the Proudhonian school) suggested that racial prejudice in the Westphalen family had been an obstacle to their marriage. By way of explanation, Longuet was indiscreet enough to mention that 'the famous socialist, as is known, is of Jewish descent'. Marx replied immediately, sending a furious letter to his daughter Jenny Longuet: 'Tout cette histoire is a *simple invention*; there was *no préjugés à vaincre*. I suppose I am not mistaken in crediting Mr Ch. Longuet's inventive genius with literary 'enjolivement'.[70] He added that Longuet would do him a favour if he never mentioned Marx's name again in his writings. What strikes one most about this response is its evident over-reaction to what might have been considered a triviality. Why did Marx feel the need immediately to rebut an assertion which did not on the face of it discredit either him or his deceased wife? Was it the assertion that there had been 'prejudices' in the Westphalen family which so angered him or the public reminder (even in a friendly fashion) that he was a Jew by birth? Whichever of the two assertions provoked Marx's wrath, his own correspondence with Ruge in March 1843 (which we have already quoted) shows that Longuet's account was far from implausible. Marx's over-sensitivity on this point suggests that even at the end of his life the slightest reminder of his Jewishness when it touched him *personally* could awaken a hostile reaction.

Two further pieces of evidence must be considered in examining Marx's attitude to the Jews. In the 1870s we discover him during visits to the Karlsbad spa encountering a whole society of professional Jewish people, scholars, doctors and businessmen, whose company he apparently enjoyed. In particular he established friendly contact with the leading Jewish historian of the nineteenth century, Heinrich Graetz, which led to a brief correspondence in 1877. We find the Jewish historian writing to Marx (1st February 1877) upon the receipt of *Capital*, affably recalling their discussions at Karlsbad, and puzzled as to what gift he might offer Marx in return. His letter implicitly suggests Marx's total lack of interest in Jewish history. Graetz wrote: 'The content of my 12 volume history [on the Jews] lies far, far outside your horizon. Perhaps my work on the 'Preacher Solomon' might be more to your taste'—a reference to Marx's preference for works of earthly realism, rather than the metaphysical consolations of the next world.[71] This allusion in Graetz's letter is indirectly confirmed by the reminiscences of Eleanor Marx, his favourite daughter, who reported to Max Beer 'that her father took no interest in Jewish affairs and had no contact with London Jewry'.[72] Eleanor Marx, on the other hand (although born of a Christian mother, and not strictly speaking a Jewess) displayed a remarkable self-conscious pride in her 'Jewishness'. In this respect she was unique among Marx's three daughters, as well as being the child who physically resembled her father the most. In her private correspondence she sometimes commented ruefully on her Jewish appearance, but it was a source of ironic amusement to her—as she once wrote to Kautsky, 'I, unfortunately, only inherited my father's nose (I used to tell him, I could sue him for damages as his nose had distinctly entailed a loss on me) and not his genius'.[73]

Whether Eleanor Marx's 'Jewish' consciousness owed anything to her father seems highly improbable in view of what has already been said here, but it cannot be completely ruled out. A much more likely explanation for Eleanor's positive attitude was her encounter with the Russian-Jewish immigrant proletariat in the East End of London. As she once exclaimed enthusiastically to Max Beer, 'My happiest moments are when I am in the East End amidst Jewish workpeople'.[74] Like Friedrich Engels, who had originally shared most of Marx's prejudices against the Jews, she found in these working-class immigrants an incarnation of Jewry with which she could identify as a socialist and as a human being. Her spontaneous, passionate reaction to the Dreyfus Affair, just before her tragic suicide in 1898, indicated that this identification was not a superficial affair.[75]

Karl Marx, the assimilated descendant of a distinguished line of rabbis and the greatest theoretician of the world proletariat, did not live to witness this change. He died in 1883, a decade before the emergence of a Jewish labour movement influenced by his ideas, which began to mobilize the impoverished masses in Russia. Nor could he have foreseen the role which the revolutionary Jewish intelligentsia as a whole was to play in the workers' parties of Russia, Central and Western Europe. He did not live long enough to see the birth of political Zionism, which resurrected a Jewish collectivity whose claims he had dismissed in 1844 as those of a 'chimerical nationality of merchants and money-men'.[76] It was left to his disciples to adapt themselves as best they could to Marx's harsh utterances on the Jewish question and apply his legacy to changing circumstances and new challenges.[77]

CHAPTER 2

Ferdinand Lassalle, the Gladiator

'There are two classes of men I cannot bear: journalists and Jews—and unfortunately I belong to both.'

Ferdinand Lassalle

'Slavery demoralizes but it also purifies the soul of the strong and creates idealists and rebels. Thus we find that their humiliating situation has cultivated in stronger and nobler natures among the Jews a sense of freedom and justice and bred a revolutionary spirit.'

Wilhelm Liebknecht

Ferdinand Lassalle, the first President of the General German Workers' Association, the ADAV (Allgemeiner Deutscher Arbeiterverein) and founder of German social democracy, was born on 13th April 1825 in Breslau. His father, who had Germanized his family name to Heyman Lassal, was a prosperous silk-dealer who had raised himself by his own efforts out of abject poverty: originally he had intended to become a rabbi, but difficult economic circumstances obliged him to earn his living as a merchant. Heyman Lassal, the son of a *Maskil* (enlightener) and admirer of Moses Mendelsohn, was himself a liberal in religious matters, and transmitted the values of the German enlightenment to his precocious and self-assertive son. Lassalle's mother, Rosalie (*née* Friedlander), was on the other hand strictly Orthodox, and observed the dietary laws long after Ferdinand had severed his attachment to the traditional observances.

The Silesian city in which Ferdinand grew up was situated on the Slav frontier of Germany. In the late 1830s it was the scene of a fierce conflict between the Orthodox and Reform camps in German Judaism.[1] In 1838 Abraham Geiger, a leader of the Reform movement, was chosen as assistant rabbi by the Breslau community, but could not take up his position due to the strong opposition of Solomon Tiktin, the incumbent Orthodox rabbi. The struggle became a *cause célèbre* in Jewish circles, with Tiktin also enjoying the support of the Prussian bureaucracy and conservative Gentiles until his death in 1843. Geiger, on the other hand, wished to make Judaism an integral part of German and European culture, to eliminate from it any marks of national uniqueness and to abolish those traditional institutions which did not conform to modern ideas.

Both Heyman Lassal and his son sided with Geiger's views in this dispute.[2] From the young Ferdinand's diary we know that he listened to Geiger's sermons and that he took an interest in the disputes which were then animating the Breslau 'Kehilla'. In a diary entry of 2nd February 1840 he wrote, 'I think that I am one of the best Jews in existence, although I disregard the ritual laws'.[3]

The young Lassalle was profoundly shocked by the news of the Damascus blood libel accusations in 1840. The Jews in the city (at that time ruled by Muhammad Ali of Egypt) were accused of having murdered a Capuchin friar and his Muslim servant, in order to use their blood for ritual purposes. The resultant disturbances and the atrocity propaganda greatly troubled Western Jews and enlightened opinion throughout the world. The 14-year-old Lassalle was inspired to comment in his diary:

> I could . . . risk my life to deliver the Jews from their present crushing condition. I would not even shrink from the scaffold could I but once more make of them a respected people. Oh, when I indulge in my childish dreams, so it is ever my favourite idea [*Lieblingsidee*] to

stand armed at the head of the Jews and make them independent.[4]

The passivity of the Syrian Jews drove the young Lassalle, imbued with his Maccabean pride and spirit of revolt, to a frenzy of anger and despair. How could they endure such cruelty and humiliation? 'A people who bears this is hideous; let them suffer or avenge this treatment',[5] he wrote in his diary on 21st May 1840.

> Even the Christians marvel at our sluggish blood, that we do not rise, that we do not rather perish on the battlefield than by torture. . . . Is there a revolution anywhere which could be more just than if the Jews were to rebel, set fire to every quarter of Damascus, blow up the powder magazine and meet death with their persecutors? Cowardly people, you deserve no better fate![6]

With extraordinary vehemence, bordering on the melodramatic, Lassalle continued, 'You do not know how to die, or how to destroy, you know nothing of a just revenge, or how to go down to the same grave as your enemies, tearing their flesh from their bones in the last death-struggle. You were born to be slaves!'[7]

Already in these early entries in his diary the psychological mechanism behind Lassalle's growing estrangement from Judaism is more or less apparent. His passion for liberty and the defiant streak of fanaticism in his character were outraged both by the treatment of his people and by their apparent suffering of insults in silence. There was an imperious quality in the young Lassalle, a manifest desire for self-realization in action which could find no outlet in the parochial disputes of Breslau Jewry. His soul was fired by generous, universal ideals, by his reading of German-Jewish radicals like Heine and Boerne who stood in the forefront of the struggle for human rights. He was no less impatient with the Germans than with the Jews. 'I am reading Boerne's letters, which I find very interesting', he confessed on 23rd July 1840. 'One sees just what a vast prison Germany is, where human rights are stamped under foot and thirty million people are tormented by thirty tyrants. One could weep at the stupidity of these people who do not break their chains although they could if they but had the will.'[8] Inflamed by his own rhetoric, he announced, 'I will proclaim Freedom to the Peoples even if it costs me my life'.[9] His nature cast him for the role of leadership: 'Had I been born a prince, I would have been an aristocrat, body and soul; but circumstances—'as it is, I am a plain son of the middle-classes'—obliged him to be a democrat.[10] Sent by his parents to a Commercial Institute in Leipzig, the young Lassalle was soon straining at the leash, convinced that commerce was no fitting occupation for his special talents. His letters from this period show a curious dissonance, but also an understandable homesickness for his family, to whom he felt closely attached:[11]

> Today was the Passover . . . . Memories of happy past days came back to me. I saw us all sitting at the long festive table, my dear father at the head, with his fine sonorous voice, and next to him my dear pious mother, looking anxiously round to see that all the ritual was being observed as strictly as it had been in her childhood.[12]

Lassalle had not yet lost his interest in the Reform movement within German Judaism, as his remarkable letter, addressed in 1843 to Theodor Creizenach (one of its leaders) reveals.[13] In this letter the 18-year-old partisan of Geiger, boldly set out his objections to an outmoded orthodoxy and the need to permeate Judaism with the spirit of modern philosophy.[14] There could be no question of renovating the Jewish religion through a restoration of Biblical Mosaism. Nor would a return to Talmudism or even a modernized version of 'Jewish' Protestantism represent anything but 'a complete retreat' in the context of 1843. Judaism, like Christianity, had to confront the critical fire of enlightened rationalism if its reform were to keep pace with the achievements of German science and scholarship.[15] There could be only one possible result of this encounter for the young Lassalle—an exodus from the Mosaic desert into the Promised Land of Hegelian philosophy.

In the next two years Lassalle, like his great contemporary Karl Marx, drank deeply at the well of Young Hegelianism. In both cases their definitive break with Judaism was expressed in its tortuous metaphysical language, but the impact of German idealism on the impressionable Lassalle seems to have been more total. In a letter to his father of 13th May 1844 young Ferdinand compared his discovery of Hegel to a spiritual rebirth. 'The philosophy [of Hegel] has got hold of me, and I have been reborn, and [endowed] with a new spirit. That rebirth has given me everything: clarity, self-awareness . . . in brief, it has made me into Reason conscious of itself.'[16]

Lassalle's encounter with Hegel did not inspire him to undertake an immanent critique of the Hegelian system from within or to arrive at an all-embracing total view of the historical process like Marx. It remained a personal discovery, which led Lassalle in later years, under the influence of Fichte, to assert that the goal of philosophy was the realization of subjective freedom. It was Lassalle even more than Marx who sought to transmit the classical heritage of German idealist philosophy to the working classes, without standing it on its head in the form of dialectical materialism. For Lassalle it was simply inconceivable to claim that matter determined spirit, or that social relations of production determined consciousness.

One of the first consequences of Lassalle's infatuation with Hegel was the final complete severance of his residual attachment to

Judaism. In a letter to his 'pious' mother of 30th July 1844, in the course of explaining his social isolation in Berlin, the 19-year-old Ferdinand inexplicably dragged in a long discourse on the obsolescence of Judaism. Taken straight out of the *Philosophy of History* of the deceased Prussian philosopher, and perhaps reflecting his own feelings of self-alienation, Lassalle depicted the Hebrew spirit as 'the world of the wretched personality, [*die Welt der erbärmlichen Persönlichkeit*].[17] What followed might charitably be put down to youthful love of dialectical paradox were it not, like Marx, taken to the pathological extreme which seems to characterize German-Jewish self-hatred.

> One can with every justification say that the world of the Hebrew people represents, if you like, the most perfect ugliness, the most extreme submission of man before God, the most inward fragmentation and lack of principle: in short the most complete self-alienation of the spirit.[18]

In inimitable Hegelian language, Lassalle went on to evoke this Hebrew spirit twisting and turning 'like a worm in the dust before the abstract Godhead'. The Jewish religion was based on hard servitude, and hence the cruel destiny of the Jewish people, its 'indescribable suffering' and oppression, merely reflected the essence of its abstract spirit. But the young philosopher of history hastened to assure his poor mother that this suffering was part of the grand journey of the world-spirit towards self-consciousness—'the spiritual stage which the world must transcend in the Jewish people is the stage of discord, servitude and misfortune'. There was even a certain nobility in the aesthetic 'ugliness' (*Hässlichkeit*) of Judaism, in its very remoteness from nature.[19]

This pseudo-philosophizing would be of little interest were it not so obviously a prelude to Lassalle's casting off the Jewishness in himself, as part of that burden of unhappiness and misfortune which seemed to guide the destiny of Israel.[20] The Young Hegelian intellectual baggage which served as a convenient rationalization for this choice was soon put to a more positive use during Lassalle's stay in Paris during 1845–6. His encounter with the great German poet and essayist Heinrich Heine, whom he had long admired, is of considerable interest—reflecting the differences between two generations of pre-1848 radicals. Heine, unlike Lassalle, was an apostate (he had converted to Lutheranism in 1825) though later he bitterly regretted his opportunism in so doing. He had settled in Paris in 1831 to avoid police harassment, and become the leader in exile of the Young Germany movement. Though severely critical of the Judaism of his day, he began after the Damascus Affair to re-read the Bible and works on Jewish history, coming to a more sympathetic assessment of the ancestral religion. When he first met the young Lassalle in the winter of 1845 (Heine was then forty-eight years old) he was engaged in a dispiriting struggle to regain certain pension rights which his family were withholding.

Lassalle threw himself with alacrity into Heine's cause, impressing the older man with his enthusiasm and energy. The long-suffering poet then wrote a letter of introduction for Lassalle to Varnhagen von Ense which gives one a revealing (though perhaps unduly flattering) portrait of his would-be saviour. 'My friend Herr Lassalle is a young man with remarkable intellectual gifts, with the greatest devotion to study, the widest knowledge and the keenest judgment I have so far met.'[21] Heine went on to observe that Lassalle displayed enormous talent in action, free from any hint of the caution and renunciation which had plagued his own generation.

> This new generation is determined to enjoy and to attain concrete success; we in our time bowed humbly before the invisible, we snatched at shadowy kisses and the thin perfume of flowers; we renounced and smiled a bitter smile. And yet, perhaps our lot was happier than that of these hard young gladiators who march so proudly towards their death-struggle.[22]

The 'hard young gladiator' whom Heine described belonged to the first generation of Jews in Germany who could feel free to act out their self-appointed roles in society without bringing upon themselves an immediate backlash of anti-Semitic prejudice. When he returned to Germany in 1846 Lassalle, having appropriately gallicized his name to that of a French revolutionary general, was a young man in search of a cause. His opportunity came through the Hatzfeldt affair, which brought him widespread publicity, fame and a permanent annual income which ensured his financial independence. In 1846 he had first met the Countess Sophie von Hatzfeldt, who had been unable to secure a divorce from her husband under the existing law, though he had mistreated her, taken mistresses and been given custody of her children. Abandoned by her family, her own caste and without the possibility of a financial settlement in sight, this beautiful, aristocratic woman was regarded by Lassalle as a victim of social injustice. In a letter in 1860 to Sonia Sontsev, he recalled: 'And I, a powerless young Jew, rose up against the world, against the power of rank and the whole aristocracy, against the power of unlimited wealth, against the Government and its officials—the natural allies of rank and wealth—against all possible prejudices'.[23] Though without previous legal experience, Lassalle battled away for eight years on behalf of the Countess, indulging his natural penchant for opposition, flamboyant theatricality and chivalrous gestures.[24]

Lassalle's fame was further promoted by his active role in the 1848

Revolution in Germany, which led to two terms of imprisonment, one connected with stealing documents related to the Hatzfeldt case. Lassalle's defence against his arrest for inciting to violence was printed as a pamphlet under the title *Meine Assisen-Rede* (1849) and became a classic of its kind. Its influence extended far beyond the frontiers of Germany, and made a considerable impression, not least on other Jewish revolutionaries who were brought to socialism by Lassalle's eloquence. Paul Axelrod, one of the founders of Russian social democracy and himself from a poor Jewish background, recalled in his memoirs that Lassalle's speeches had been a major factor in impelling him to work for the emancipation of the poor and the oppressed of Russia. 'Grandiose perspectives' had been sparked off in his mind when he read about Lassalle's fiery conduct at his trials, his attacks on his judges in the name of the Fourth Estate (working classes). 'The proud language and the authoritative tone of the statements of a "subject", a Jew at that, to the ruling power . . . made upon me an immeasurable impression and gave me a profound delight and satisfaction.'[25] At the same time the new horizons opened by Lassallean eloquence led the young Russian revolutionary away from his earlier concern with the plight of the Jewish masses in Russia.

Though Lassalle was eventually imprisoned for six months as a result of his revolutionary activities, this period in jail paradoxically saved him from expulsion and the life of a political émigré. After 1849 he remained the 'last of the Mohicans', fighting on in splendid isolation for the ideas of the democratic revolution in Germany. This brought him closer in the 1850s to Marx, with whom he was in regular correspondence, and whom he sought to help financially and with the publication of his writings in Germany. Though the two men cooperated at first, there were too many sources of friction to make their association a fruitful one. While Marx lived a nightmarish existence of grinding poverty in the first decade of his London exile, Lassalle had been handsomely rewarded by the Countess von Hatzfeldt, and his new-found wealth enabled him to play the role of a high-society dandy and stock-exchange speculator. At the same time his standing as a scholar, poet and jurist had grown with the publication of his work on the Greek philosopher Heraclitus (1857) and his dramatic epic *Franz von Sickingen* (1858). Though these works provoked the criticism (sometimes justified, but more often malicious) of Marx and Engels, they made Lassalle an instant celebrity in the Berlin salons.[26] It was this prestige which he enjoyed as a philosopher, barrister and man of the world which enabled Lassalle to find such response in the working classes when he began his great political campaigns in the 1860s. Though Engels might see in him nothing but 'a greasy Jew' trying to push his way into the aristocratic world, Lassalle was more aware of the fact that nothing could be accomplished in politics without a sense of style. But the differences between Marx and Lassalle transcended personalities and temperaments, they reflected a fundamental divergence of political and philosophical outlook.[27]

Marx was a materialist who regarded the class-struggle as the inexorable unfolding of the laws of economic development; Lassalle saw class conflict as a stage on the road to lifting the human consciousness of the workers to a new level. Marx looked to the ultimate dissolution of the State in a classless society; Lassalle perceived it as the repository of a high ethical mission—as an instrument to fulfil the workers' demands. Marx was the prophet and theorist of an international labour movement; Lassalle became a predominantly German leader. Marx had a long-term strategy based on his historical analysis of capitalism, Lassalle by comparison was an eclectic *Realpolitiker*. In contrast to Marx, Lassalle believed in an alliance with the Prussian State against the liberal middle classes, and to this end he was prepared to accept the idea of a 'Social Monarchy' (*Sozial Volkskönigtum*).[28] Not surprisingly, Lassalle's political philosophy, which sought the integration of the workers into a powerful, united Germany, was considerably more congenial to a conservative Prussian statesman like Bismarck than was that of Marx. Whereas the latter had vilified his fellow-socialist in private correspondence with Engels, Bismarck told the Reichstag on 16th September 1878 that Lassalle was 'one of the most intellectual and gifted men with whom I have ever had intercourse, a man who was ambitious on a grand scale, but by no means a Republican: he had very decided national and monarchical sympathies; the idea which he strove to realize was the German Empire, and in that, we had a point of contact'.[29] One need not necessarily subscribe to this interpretation of Lassalle's politics to recognize that his was indeed an ambition on the grand scale. It was not for nothing that he promised his fiancée that one day he would enter Berlin as President of the German Republic in a chariot drawn by six white horses.

This evident personal ambition and the authoritarian style of leadership which he imposed on the young German labour movement was a further reason for Marx and Engels to distrust him. The General German Workers' Association which he founded on 23rd May 1863 was to be an instrument of dictatorship in the hands of its President. As he told the workers in Ronsdorf, 'We must forge our wills into a single hammer and place this hammer in the hands of a man in whose intelligence, character, and goodwill we have the necessary confidence, so that he can use this hammer to strike with!'[30] The new organization of the German workers was controlled by an absolute monarch, it was a personal creation of Lassalle's will-to-power, bearing the mark of his forceful individuality. This Caesarian tendency in Lassalle's mode of leadership did not make him any the less popular among the German working classes. On the contrary, his political activity between 1860 and

1863 which skilfully exploited the constitutional crisis in Prussia, aroused an unprecedented enthusiasm in the workers. Lassalle came to them as a prestigious personality from the bourgeois world, with a radical message. The workers were to be 'the rock on which the Church of the present age will be built', but first they would have to form their own political party and free themselves from the tutelage of the liberals. Universal suffrage was the indispensable weapon through which they would achieve their emancipation, by overthrowing the grossly inequitable Three-class Electoral System in Prussia. Together with his plan to secure State credit for producers' co-operatives, this was the linchpin of Lassalle's agitational programme in the early 1860s. His tireless propaganda roused the backward, uneducated mass of German workers out of their political stupor. Ceaselessly Lassalle imbued them with the idea that a weak, impotent German bourgeoisie would betray their interests. His defiant spirit, his charismatic self-assurance, his passionate revolt against servitude, his calculated sense of theatrical pomp communicated itself to the workers. In June 1864, during his last political campaign, Lassalle was received by the Rhinelanders like a demigod. There were triumphal marches, hymns of welcome, garlands strewn in his path, lines of carriages which followed the chariot of the 'President'.[31] The 'man of science' who had brought the accomplishments of German philosophy to the workers, the virtual dictator of the labour movement, was already a living legend. Why then has Lassalle's star been on the decline in the twentieth century, as against that of Marx?

In the first place, Lassalle's strengths, his shrewd eye for questions of power, his sense of rhetorical effect, his capacities as an agitator and organizer were by their nature more ephemeral. Lassalle's speeches and writings, while full of freshness and clarity, seem limited in their scope compared to Marx. He thought in terms of Prussia, German nationalism and the practical issues of the time, where Marx wrote in terms of continents, centuries and mankind as a whole. Lassalle was a *grand oseur et grand poseur*, a torchbearer who lacked the scientific power of Marx to translate his concepts into a coherent system; the Marxian prophecies endure not only as an indictment of nineteenth-century industrial civilization but as a philosophy of history and a method of analysis applicable to different periods, places and patterns of civilization. But who knows what would have happened if Marx had been prematurely cut off, like Lassalle, at the age of thirty-nine, before he had completed his *Critique of Political Economy* and *Das Kapital*!

Lassalle's life was shortened by his private weaknesses, by his complete incapacity to compromise in affairs of the heart and his confused judgment of other people—especially of the fair sex. This has given rise to a fair amount of speculation about his character, and offers excellent material for romantic fictional biographies. It is of interest here chiefly because of the light it throws on his attitude to Jews, Judaism and his personal identity. Unlike many other socialists, Lassalle wrote nothing *publicly* concerning the Jewish question—partly because it ceased to concern him after 1844, but also because in his lifetime (he died in 1864) it was not a political issue, even in Germany. Thus we have no evidence to suggest he would have adopted the Marxist class analysis of Judaism, though in view of his known distaste for 'materialism' one may consider it unlikely. Nor was he interested in the Jewish community, though on a visit to Constantinople in 1854 he was momentarily reminded of the religious fervour he had witnessed in Breslau during his youth.[32] On the other hand, he did appear to recognize that the Jews of Western Europe were a religious community of ethnic origin, whereas Russian Jewry constituted a 'nationality'. This much we know from his extraordinary love-letter written in 1860 (in French) to Sophie Sontsev, the 19-year-old Russian girl whom he courted at a spa in Aachen and mistook for a blue-blooded daughter of the Russian aristocracy. In his whirlwind seduction of Miss Sontsev Lassalle appeared to be in two minds concerning the question of marriage. Having vaunted his virtues in the course of his forty-page epistle, Lassalle then went on to enunciate the obstacles to the love-match, including somewhat unexpectedly his Jewish origin.

> But will you be able, Sophie, to withstand the second blow? I am a Jew! My father and mother are Jews, and if I am also as little inwardly Jewish as you are, and perhaps even less, if that is possible, nevertheless I have not yet forsworn this religion since I also do not want to adopt any other. I can well testify that I am no more a Jew but not without lying become a Christian.[33]

Having made this startling confession, Lassalle goes on to explain that it is the reaction of Sophie's Russian countrymen that he has in mind, for there, unlike Germany, Judaism is regarded as a 'nationality', as something alien, and not merely as a religion.

> Your compatriots, Sophie, will despise you for marrying a Jew! You, the descendant of princes, marrying a man, who—truly, if descent has a claim on honours—can be prouder than you all, coming as I do from an older race than all your princes and nobles of a few centuries, from the stock of the first great civilized people in history, from the old Syrian kings.[34]

This declaration seems rather puzzling at first sight, with its curious oscillation between exhibitionist pride and shamefaced apologetics. But there is a sting in the tail—the cult of past grandeur is ultimately a snobbish device to justify Lassalle's Jewish self-hatred:

> I do not like Jews at all. I even detest them in general. I see in them nothing but the degenerate sons of a great, but long past epoch. As a result of centuries of servitude, these people have taken on the characteristics of slaves, and for this reason I am so hostile to them.[35]

In order to drive home his point, Lassalle added that he had no Jewish friends among the society which surrounded him in Berlin (this was not completely true), and that from the social standpoint there was nothing to prevent him converting to Christianity. The problem was political because 'I am a politician, and what is more, the head of a party. And my party must obey the principles of never submitting to prejudice.'[36]

Leaving aside the *sacro egoismo* of Lassalle for a moment (the party to which he referred did not come into existence until two years later), one is struck by the illogicality of all these arguments which culminate in his willingness to undergo conversion at the behest of Sophie's parents, but not otherwise. Three years later, during his ill-fated courtship of Helene von Dönniges he again offered baptism as a last resort to win her hand, wrongly assuming that she was a Catholic.[37] Indeed, he even appealed to his friend, the Catholic bishop von Ketteler, to intervene on his behalf, on this mistaken assumption. Helene von Dönniges was no more a Catholic than Sophie Sontsev was a Russian aristocrat. In fact she was the granddaughter (on her mother's side) of a Jewish banker!

Lassalle's self-hatred as a Jew was in my view a malaise created by his parvenu striving for social status, by his restless opportunism, and desire to be accepted in high society. It had nothing to do with a socialist standpoint or perspective, nor with any analysis of the Jewish question. To some extent Engels was right, therefore, in his assessment of Lassalle's character, though his Teutonic prejudices against East European Jews tended to distort his judgment.[38] Engels really hit the nail on the head in his letter to Marx of 4th September 1864, following the news of Lassalle's death in a senseless duel in Geneva, arising out of his affair with Helene von Dönniges.

> And what an extraordinary way to die. This would-be Don Juan really falls in love with the daughter of a Bavarian ambassador and wants to marry her. Then comes up against a rejected suitor of the lady—who incidentally is a swindler from Rumania—and gets himself shot dead by his rival. That could only happen to Lassalle, with his unique character, part Jew, part cavalier, part clown, part sentimentalist. How can a politician of his calibre let himself be shot dead by a Rumanian adventurer?[39]

In the wake of Lassalle's sudden, dramatic death both Marx and Engels were able temporarily to forget past animosities and resentments. Marx in a letter to the Countess von Hatzfeldt (whom he admired at a distance), gallantly stated that Lassalle had died young 'in triumph, like Achilles'. In another letter to Engels he called his former rival 'one of the old stock and the enemy of our enemies'.[40] Engels agreed with this verdict, adding his own pertinent comment. 'What rejoicings there will be in the ranks of the factory owners and those dirty dogs of the Progressive Party. Lassalle was the only fellow in Germany they really feared.'[41]

Within a few years, however, the founders of scientific socialism, faced with the Lassalle legend in the German labour movement, felt obliged to sharpen their blades. Marx accused his fallen comrade of shameless plagiarism and a nonsensical belief in the readiness of the Prussian State to subsidize class-struggle.[42] In a letter in 1868 to Johann Baptist von Schweitzer, the new leader of the ADAV, Marx further criticized Lassalle's tactical concessions to the Prussian monarchy. There was undoubtedly some truth in this reproach. The Lassalleans had inherited a fanatic illiberalism from their deceased leader, who in his detestation of the German bourgeoisie was prepared to support a Prussian, dynastic solution to German unity. The authoritarianism of the Lassalleans went hand in hand with an anti-Jewish nuance which Lassalle himself had introduced in the early 1860s, in his attacks on 'Manchesterism'—i.e., free-trade liberalism. One of his favourite targets was Aron Bernstein, liberal editor of the *Berliner Volkszeitung*: 'A man who cannot even write German but is slowly but surely corrupting our nation's language and its character with the peculiar gibberish with which he feeds his readers—that so-called Jewish-German—not one sentence without grammatical mistakes!'[43] How far Lassalle (who once confessed that he hated journalists and Jews above all else) might have gone with this demagogy is hard to assess. But there can be little doubt that his supporters were influenced by his rhetorical assaults against Jewish literati and bourgeois intellectuals. Nor is it an accident that his most important successors, von Schweitzer and Hasselmann, admired Bismarck's *Realpolitik*, his power-philosophy and contempt for the middle classes.

The Marxist 'Eisenacher' wing of the party led by Bebel and Liebknecht was on the other hand passionately opposed to Prussian militarism and Bismarck's policy of annexations. They found Leopold Sonnemann, the South German democrat and Jewish proprietor of the liberal *Frankfurter Zeitung*, their most useful ally. This temporary alliance was seized upon by the Lassalleans as evidence that the workers' interests were being sacrificed to those of big capital. Anti-Semitism as initiated by the neo-Lassalleans began to appear in the inner-party polemics of the 1870s.[44]

Wilhelm Hasselmann, editor of the *Neuer Sozial-Demokrat*, was the mainspring of this trend, even branding the Marxists on occasion as 'servants of the Jews' (*Judenknechte*). He asserted that Jewish capitalists sought to protect their fortunes from attack by winning influence in the SPD. He also accused Jewish intellectuals in the party of being agents of *embourgeoisement*, favouring compromise with the middle classes rather than direct action by the workers. Lassalle's bitter opposition to 'Manchesterism' and liberal capitalism had evidently contributed to fomenting this mood among his followers in the SPD.[45]

Lassalle's ambivalence was, however, largely a consequence of his times and of the contradictions in his fiery, romantic temperament. His Jewish background made him an outsider driven to rebel against bourgeois society, but pushed two ways at once: towards the aristocratic élite from which Jewish intellectuals were traditionally excluded and also towards the forgotten working class—the rock on which the 'new Church' would be built. Hence the anomalies in his conduct, the unstable co-existence in the same personality of seemingly incompatible social roles; the scholar and the demagogue, the perfumed dandy and the workers' leader, the speculator and the socialist. Lassalle was simultaneously a conformist, ingratiating himself with the establishment and a revolutionary preaching the overthrow of bourgeois society.

As a Jew in politics, Lassalle stands in significance, ambition and achievement somewhere between Disraeli and Marx.[46] In his aristocratic tastes, his social climbing and flamboyant dandyism, he resembled the English Tory leader. In his passionate revolutionary idealism and messianic faith in the German working classes, he was closer to Marx. Ferdinand Lassalle combined in unique measure the German 'Führer' cult with the Jewish prophetic instinct, even if this inflammable mixture was constantly threatened by an unstable romantic exhibitionism. A poem composed in his honour shortly after his death epitomizes what this Jewish revolutionary meant to the German proletariat.

In Breslau ein Friedhof
Ein Toter im Grab;
Dort schlummert der Eine
Der Schwerte uns gab.[47]

CHAPTER 3

Eduard Bernstein, the Non-conformist

'Jewish emancipation ensued at a time when the bourgeoisie believed in itself, only a new society can complete it.'
Eduard Bernstein

'In the journal we shall be publishing Bernstein will write against the assimilationists; he is on the road to Zionism. . . .'
Chaim Weizmann

Eduard Bernstein, the father of 'revisionism', must rank after Marx and Lassalle as the outstanding Jewish intellectual in the history of the German labour movement. Unlike the founders of German social democracy, he belonged to the post-emancipation generation, for whom assimilation was more or less an accomplished fact. He never had to wrestle with the psychological implications of baptism at an early age as did Marx, or to follow the stormy path of Lassalle to recognition of his merits as a political leader and activist. Bernstein's temperament in any case lacked the revolutionary ardour and pathos of his two predecessors. But his importance was no less great, in formulating the basis of a democratic socialism adapted to the changing conditions of capitalist society. Bernstein was the first German socialist to challenge the fundamental economic assumptions on which the Marxist model of revolution was based; he was the first to question the utopian concentration on the final goal of socialism at the expense of the means and the method by which it was to be achieved.[1]

Eduard Bernstein was born in 1850, into a lower-middle-class family, resident in North Berlin. His paternal ancestors hailed originally from Danzig, where they had in the past supplied the Jewish community with a number of scholars and rabbis.[2] His father Jakob had originally been a plumber's apprentice in Danzig, but after moving to Berlin became an engine-driver, serving in this profession for thirty years, until his retirement in 1874. Bernstein's mother (*née* Johanna Rosenberg) was a hard-working woman who had a lifelong struggle to make ends meet for her fifteen children—five of whom died at an early age.

Jakob Bernstein no longer observed the dietary laws, but he remained a member of the Jewish reform community in Berlin.[3] The family celebrated Christmas 'in the German manner' and brought up their children in an atmosphere free 'from any kind of denominational narrow-mindedness'.[4] The Bernsteins retained a favourable opinion of liberal Christianity, even though they preferred reform Judaism for its greater 'freedom from dogma', and considered themselves patriotic Germans. Eduard recalled in his memoirs that his parents 'were far removed from regarding Judaism as something which separated them nationally from the Germans'.[5]

The fusion of reform Judaism and political liberalism in the family was best personified by its most illustrious figure—Aron Bernstein, the brother of Jakob—who had been educated at a rabbinical seminary. In the 1840s Aron had come under the influence of the 'Young Germany' movement and the radical ideas of Boerne and Heine, as well as forming a close friendship with Leopold Zunz, the famous scholar and pioneer of the Wissenschaft des Judentums ('Science of Judaism') movement. Aron Bernstein threw himself wholeheartedly into the struggle for Jewish equality in Prussia, and also contributed to founding the Jewish reform community. He even wrote stories about Jewish life in the *Shtetl*, such as 'Voegele der Maggid', which became popular in Eastern Europe as well as Germany.[6]

Aron Bernstein was, however, best known as a militant liberal reformer, as the editor of the influential *Berliner Volkszeitung* and as a historian of the 1848 Revolution. He was a partisan of the ideas of Schulze-Delitsch, which earned him the enmity of Ferdinand Lassalle and his followers, and he remained one of the most articulate representatives of the radical bourgeoisie in Germany. Eduard shared a number of his uncle's characteristics—notably his journalistic talent, his liberalism and interest in Jewish affairs; but politically their paths diverged once Eduard became active in German socialism during the 1870s.

Eduard Bernstein joined the Marxist 'Eisenacher' wing of the labour movement in 1872, at a time when he was still a modest employee of the S. & L. Rothschild bank in Berlin. One of the factors which impelled him towards social democracy was the disastrous experiences of the *Gründerzeit*—the speculative fever and resulting depression of German capitalism in the early 1870s.[7] A further influence was the deep impression made on him by the speeches of Johann Jacoby, Bebel and Liebknecht, the German radical and socialist leaders, in the wake of the Franco-Prussian war. Bebel and Liebknecht had consistently defended a pacifist and internationalist position during the war, which led to their trial for high treason in 1871–2.

Bernstein had been disillusioned by the narrow-minded chauvinism which swept Germany following the Prussian victories, and disapproved of Bismarck's policy of annexation. Within a few months Bernstein joined the Eisenachers, whose liberal-democratic, anti-Prussian and internationalist position he found more congenial than the narrow, authoritarian and latently anti-Semitic Lassallean wing of the Socialist Party. In his memoirs Bernstein recalled that the neo-Lassallean tirades of Wilhelm Hasselmann against the 'Jews' in the Marxist wing of the labour movement turned him into a 'passionate enemy of the Lassalleans'.[8]

But Bernstein's reaction to the literary anti-Semitism of the 1870s remained somewhat ambivalent. For example, in the middle of the decade he became an enthusiastic disciple of Eugen Dühring, the blind lecturer in politics, economics and philosophy at the University of Berlin.[9] Dühring was to become after 1880 the leading ideologist of racial anti-Semitism in Germany but in the mid-1870s he still enjoyed great popularity among socialists in Berlin. Bernstein regularly attended his lectures and communicated his admiration for Dühring's *Cursus der National- und- Sozialökonomie* to Johann Most and August Bebel, who hailed it as the most important work on economics since Marx's *Das Kapital*. Bernstein was not particularly concerned by Dühring's Judaeophobia, and was initially convinced that the blind lecturer's theories supplemented Marx with a more 'liberal' outlook![10]

Dühring had attacked, for example, the validity of Hegelian dialectics and of historical-materialist doctrines—criticisms which later recurred in Bernstein's own revision of Marx. He excused his teacher's racial prejudices somewhat speciously, 'since at that time, certain strata of the Jewish population in Germany were pushing themselves into the foreground in a way which deeply shocked many Jews, including myself'.[11]

Bernstein only broke with Dühring in 1879, when the latter began systematically to attack the 'Jewish' press and the 'Judaized' social democracy for corrupting the working class and the German nation as a whole. Once Dühring had joined forces with the organized political anti-Semitism spread by Wilhelm Marr and Adolf Stoecker, no socialist could support him and still remain in the SPD. Reviewing his attitude to Dühring nearly four decades later, Bernstein rather apologetically wrote

> Not until anti-Semitism developed from an accusatory to a persecuting movement did I change my attitude towards it. But in combating it, I always took care to treat the question as one of democratic equality of rights. It never entered my mind to conceive the Jewish question as a question of special national rights or interests of the Jews.[12]

In 1878, following the passing of Bismarck's anti-socialist laws, Bernstein felt obliged to emigrate to Switzerland, where he became the private secretary of Karl Höchberg. This was the beginning of a long period of exile from Germany, which lasted until 1901. The first eleven years were spent in Switzerland, and the next twelve in London.

His new patron was the son of a Jewish banker from Frankfurt, a wealthy socialist who had given his fortune to the German party. Bernstein was strongly impressed by Höchberg's generosity, idealistic principles and noble character, and co-edited with him three issues of the *Jahrbuch für Sozialwissenschaft und Sozialpolitik*, under the pseudonym of Dr Ludwig Richter.[13]

In 1881 Bernstein became editor of the *Sozialdemokrat*, the new official organ of the exiled Social Democratic Party (SPD), published in Zürich and smuggled into Germany. For the next eight years he played a central role in boosting the morale of the labour movement, in its struggle for survival under the anti-socialist laws.

One of the themes which received considerable attention in the *Sozialdemokrat* during the 1880s was the resistance of the German working class to Stoecker's crusading Christian-Social movement. The paper published regular reports from Germany, illustrating the firmness with which the workers repudiated Stoecker, Pinkert,

Henrici and other anti-Semitic agitators: it emphasized that the working class, although repressed under the anti-socialist laws, had no intention of surrendering to the Bismarckian regime and its caricature of 'State socialism'.

At the same time, the *Sozialdemokrat* condemned the passive indifference of the liberals and of German Jewry to the persecution of socialists. While workers had shown themselves ready to risk expulsion and loss of livelihood to defend Jewish equality, liberal German Jews had short-sightedly supported Bismarck's repressive policies. They thereby ignored the common roots of the anti-Semitic and the anti-socialist witch-hunt in Bismarckian Germany.[14]

On 6th February 1881 the *Sozialdemokrat*, in one of its first issues under Bernstein's editorship, noted that it was 'shameful for the ruling classes, that it is we, the persecuted and the despised, who demand and uphold the rights of man for those who helped and still help to outlaw and persecute us'.[15]

Like other Jewish intellectuals who had identified themselves with the labour movement under the anti-socialist laws, Bernstein was sharply critical of the position adopted by the German-Jewish community. There was, however, nothing surprising in Jewish liberal attitudes, considering that the community was a predominantly middle-class, upward-moving, social group who had taken a prominent part in the capitalistic expansion of Germany.[16]

Until the 1890s, when it began to look on the SPD as a possible line of defence against anti-Semitism, the Jewish community had little reason to support an outlawed movement which proclaimed itself revolutionary, threatened the status quo and the free market, and was hostile to liberal and religious values.[17]

Although Bernstein criticized the attitudes of official Jewish representatives in Germany towards the labour movement, he was singularly free of any self-hatred. His personal correspondence with Friedrich Engels during the early 1880s reveals, moreover, that he was very sensitive to the growth of the anti-Semitic movement. As editor of the *Sozialdemokrat* in Zürich, he was in a good position to obtain material on its activities inside Germany, which he began to communicate in July 1881 to Engels, who was resident in London.

The correspondence between the two men on this subject reflects the relative closeness of their relationship. Engels had great confidence in Bernstein's abilities, and fully supported the general line taken by the *Sozialdemokrat*, including its strong condemnation of the anti-Semitic agitation. Although Engels was clearly the master in theoretical matters, their correspondence shows that Bernstein discussed problems on a footing of equality with his veteran adviser in London. In July 1881 he warned Engels that

> One should not underestimate this movement [i.e., anti-Semitism],

> at least not in the practical struggle. . . . In Berlin alone, apart from the conservative and Catholic press, there are no less than seven of these newspapers and their number increases every day in the provinces. . . . The entire civil service, including the judiciary and the higher teaching profession, the petty bourgeoisie and farmers sympathize with anti-Semitism, the former in bad faith, the latter *bona fide*.[18]

Bernstein was sufficiently confident of his ground to disagree with the assessment of Engels, based on Karl Hirsch's reports, that the 'Jew-baitings' (*Judenhetzen*) were an ephemeral phenomenon. Hirsch, a German socialist émigré, and friend of Marx and Engels, had recently visited Berlin and reported that the resentment of the masses against the Jews was much weaker than that against the Government. Engels conveyed Hirsch's opinion to Bernstein, adding his own assessment that the Jew-baitings were orchestrated by the Junkers, and would disappear after the Reichstag elections.[19] Bernstein was unconvinced by this judgment, and on 9th September 1881, he wrote to Engels:

> The reports which I have been receiving from Berlin, etc.—and moreover from pure Germans—sound quite different, and during their most recent visits both Liebknecht and Bebel had an altogether different impression. It is true that the Jew-baiting has been and will continue to be promoted from above, but it falls on a very receptive terrain as far as peasantry, the artisans, officials and teachers etc. are concerned; therefore, I think it would be a great mistake if we were to treat the antisemitic movement simply as a political-religious phenomenon. In Dresden, this has, at any rate, scarcely proved to be tenable.[20]

Bernstein made it clear, moreover, that social democracy could gain by recognizing the *popular* discontent which underlay the anti-Semitic movement: 'If the movement should collapse after the elections, then we will reap its legacy—everything in it which is not official must come over to us'.[21] Thus we find Bernstein already in 1881 hinting at what was to become the official SPD doctrine on anti-Semitism a decade later—namely, that the populist campaign was a herald of socialism, which the masses would eventually realize was 'the only way out of the conflicts in contemporary society'.[22]

Bernstein's correspondence with Engels also shows his concern with an anti-Semitic undercurrent in the SPD during the 1880s. In one letter he complained that some German socialists still regarded the Jews as 'the leading representatives of capitalism' and responsible for commercial malpractices. These socialists were prepared, he suggested, to adopt a racially tinged phraseology, for tactical purposes.[23]

On 10th November 1883 Bernstein wrote to Engels:

> You ought to know for example that like *the majority of the 'intellectuals'* in our party, the gentlemen in Stuttgart are also *anti-Semites* on the quiet. It goes naturally with their petty-bourgeois prejudices. For these gentlemen, Marx is already an outmoded standpoint.[24]

Bernstein may well have been responding to Engels's constant warnings against philistine 'intellectuals' in the German party, whom the latter suspected of opportunism, utopianism and of undermining its proletarian character. Bernstein's revelations about their anti-Semitic tendencies would have tended to reinforce Engels's fear of a further dilution of principles within the SPD.

Both Bernstein and Engels put their faith in the class instincts of the German workers during the heroic period of 'illegality' which the SPD endured in the 1880s. In September 1882 Bernstein singled out this factor, when alluding to the fight of the Berlin workers against Stoecker's clerical anti-Semitism: 'If our workers had not been immunized by their class instinct, their democratic sentiments . . . and their hatred of religion, we would have noticed a much, much stronger defection to Stoecker and Körner'.[25]

The intellectuals in the party (including those of Jewish origin) seemed by contrast to be much less resolute in their attitudes. Bernstein pointed out, for example, in a letter to Engels that Paul Singer, a Jewish merchant who had been put up as a candidate by the SPD in the Berlin municipal elections of 1883, did not want the socialists to enter into an alliance with the radical bourgeoisie to defeat Stoecker. This was all the more astonishing since Singer's candidacy had been a deliberate act by the SPD to defy the 'Berlin movement' and its clerical-conservative crusade. Bernstein interpreted Singer's neutrality as a defensive reaction to the anti-Semitism he had encountered among 'our intellectuals': 'out of an exaggerated conscientiousness, he believes that he himself must play the anti-Semite'.[26] Elsewhere in his correspondence with Engels, Bernstein stigmatized this attitude as 'a heroic form of self-castration', adopted by many Jews in the SPD, including Max Kayser and Karl Höchberg, as well as Paul Singer.[27] It has indeed been a common reaction of assimilated, revolutionary Jews to their own oppressed collectivity, from the time of Marx and Lassalle to the present.

Although Bernstein was not a practising Jew, and although he was as committed as his colleagues in the SPD to the ideal of integration, he remained free of this particular neurosis. His immediate circle of friends were mainly Gentiles, but despite this high degree of personal assimilation, Bernstein never lost his feeling of solidarity with Jews as a persecuted group.

In 1888 Eduard Bernstein was expelled from Switzerland and took refuge in London with his family. He had in the meantime married Regina Zadek ('a sharp little Jewess', according to Engels), who already had two children by a previous marriage. The couple settled in Kentish Town, where Bernstein continued to edit the *Sozialdemokrat* until its closure in September 1890. In its last number Engels in a parting message declared that 'It has been by far the best newspaper the party has ever had'.[28] This was no idle tribute from the co-founder of Marxism. In a letter to Laura Lafargue, Engels remarked, on 25th September 1890, 'Today, the last No. of the *Sozialdemokrat* is published. I shall miss that paper almost as much as the N(eue) Rh(einische) Zeitung'.[29]

The end of the *Sozialdemokrat*, which coincided with the abrogation of the anti-Socialist laws, marked the termination of the first phase of Bernstein's career as a socialist. The next decade, which he spent in the English capital, was to profoundly change his general outlook, and also to mark his attitude to the Jewish question. The more tolerant atmosphere of Victorian England reinforced his liberal sentiments, his horror of brutality and his distaste for revolutionary violence.[30] His consistent Anglophilia (a feature which Bernstein shared with many Continental Jews of his time) derived from a strong attraction to English liberties, common sense, scepticism, respect for facts and toleration of dissent.

Above all, his own revision of Marxism was profoundly shaped by the model of liberal Fabian socialism in England. His wife Regina even translated the Webbs' *History of British Trade-Unionism* into German in 1895, with an epilogue written by Eduard, in which he hinted that the socialist revolution was no longer imminent.

During his London exile in the 1890s Bernstein continued to follow closely events in his native Germany, and to contribute regular articles to the SPD newspaper *Vorwärts* and the *Neue Zeit*. The revival of political anti-Semitism in Germany after 1890, reaching its peak with the election of sixteen anti-Semitic deputies to the Reichstag in 1893, obliged the SPD to redefine its attitude to the new movement. One trend in the German Socialist Party advocated adopting a position of benevolent neutrality towards the *völkisch* agitation, whose anti-capitalist rhetoric seemed likely to benefit the labour movement. Following the lead of well-known publicists like Franz Mehring and Richard Calwer, these socialists concentrated their attack on philo- rather than anti-Semitism. They rather demagogically equated 'philo-Semitism' with 'sycophancy before capitalistic monied Jewry, support for Jewish chauvinism, whitewashing of Jewish injustices'.[31]

Bernstein, in an article for the leading German Marxist review *Neue Zeit* in 1894, protested against this socialist rhetoric, which he regarded as clumsy, ineffective and reminiscent of racialist propaganda. He also noted with regret that Jewish colleagues in the party 'out of otherwise honourable motives, most often declare themselves against "philo-Semitism".'[32] He observed that these comrades 'just because they are themselves of Jewish origin, consider it their special duty to protect the party from all suspicion of favouring Jewish interests'.[33] He sympathized with the dilemma of Jews in the German and Austrian labour movements who feared that their parties might be branded as a 'Jewish protective guard' (*Judenschutztruppe*) if they did not oppose 'philo-Semitism'; but he was convinced that the policy of 'heroic self-castration' which he had already derided in a letter to Engels ten years earlier was self-defeating and morally unacceptable.

Bernstein's own position, as he expressed it in 1894, was still impeccable, from a German Marxist viewpoint. He argued, like Engels, Bebel and Liebknecht, that anti-Semitism was essentially a symptom of *Mittelstand* discontent. He suggested that it would find followers 'only among those who have not yet been enlightened by social democracy and where, as in the case of small farmers, artisans and small businessmen—a falsely conceived self-interest blurs their view'.[34] It was a temporary expression of false consciousness, directed at Jews by the rural and urban *Mittelstand*. The lower middle class, like other disorientated groups in capitalist society, regarded Jewish middlemen as representatives of the hated money-economy. In order to protect themselves from unwelcome competition, they adopted a political ideology whose strength lay in 'the confusion, uncertainty and self-deception over the nature of these evils', encouraged by capitalist society. In common with other German socialists, Bernstein optimistically viewed the *völkisch* agitation as a preliminary stage in the coming victory of socialism.[35]

In 1894 Bernstein also subscribed to the prevailing Marxist standpoint that assimilation was a cultural and historical necessity, entailing the complete renunciation of all inter-group solidarity among Jews:

> with the formal emancipation of the Jews, every excuse for isolation, for a special Jewish solidarity against non-Jews, for a tribal or racial morality in intercourse with non-Jews has been eliminated and where anything of the kind exists, it must be fought against as energetically as possible.[36]

This was certainly an unequivocal statement of the classic assimilationist position; all the more remarkable since only a year earlier the first German-Jewish self-defence organization, the Centralverein deutscher Staatsbürger jüdisches Glaubens—Central Union of German Citizens of the Jewish Faith—had been founded to combat the growing virulence of racial anti-Semitism.[37] Bernstein at this time clearly believed that demonstrations of Jewish solidarity would merely inflame prejudice and call in question the principles of assimilation. By the late 1890s, however, he had revised his earlier standpoint, that anti-Semitism was only a symptom of the general crisis of liberal-bourgeois society.

What caused this change? What underlay Bernstein's growing affirmation of his ethnic identity and led him during the First World War to redefine his attitude to the Jewish community?

In the first place, Bernstein, unlike Marx, Kautsky and many other socialists, had never associated Jews with the worst features of capitalism. He never dwelt on the negative aspects of the medieval ghetto, on the huckstering 'Jewish spirit', or on the isolation of Jews from the rest of humanity. Nor did he assume a posture of cultivated superiority when writing about the East European Jewish masses; Bernstein never argued that Jewish 'peculiarities' (*Eigenthümlichkeiten*) were anti-social traits, which would vanish with the end of capitalism.

Admittedly, like other German Marxists, he was critical of modern nationalism, and before 1914 he was convinced that Jews were destined to lose their group identity. But Bernstein had never accepted the revolutionary Marxist perspective that socialist society necessitated the end of the Jewish community and of Judaism. Hence he was more able and prepared to revise his opinion in the light of changing circumstances: on the Jewish question, he proved in some respects to be closer to the idealism of Gustav Landauer and Martin Buber than to that of Marx and Kautsky.[38]

Bernstein's change of heart, in view of its timing, was clearly related to the broader theoretical challenge he offered to classical Marxism. After the death of Engels in 1895, Bernstein in a series of articles for the *Neue Zeit* entitled 'Problems of Socialism' began to question the revolutionary dogma which had become official doctrine in the SPD.[39] He rejected the theory of an imminent collapse of capitalist society extrapolated from Marx's prognoses concerning the growing misery of the proletariat, the concentration of capital and the sharpening of class antagonisms.[40] Bernstein argued on empirical grounds that the middle class was not declining, that the peasants were not sinking, that crises were not growing larger and mass misery was not increasing.

One of the incidental consequences of this 'revision' of Marx was to undermine the basis of the official theory of anti-Semitism advocated by the SPD in the 1890s. If the German *Mittelstand*, despite all predictions, was not disappearing, or even sinking into the proletariat, then the socialists were unlikely to benefit from the *völkisch* agitation: nor was there a socialist society immanent in the womb of collapsing capitalism which could be counted on to eliminate the Jewish question in the near future.

Equally important, Bernstein questioned the premises of historical materialism, its fatalistic determinism and emphasis on impersonal economic development. In place of Hegelian dialectics, he favoured a combination of piecemeal empiricism and ethical idealism. Bernstein's method, which turned away from the *final* goal of socialism to concentrate on practical social reforms, was more likely to be tolerant of Jewish identity than was the totalistic vision of orthodox Marxism. His evolutionary socialism excluded the dialectical theory of the vanishing of Judaism, based on its inevitable self-dissolution in a post-capitalist society. Bernstein's revisionism, through its endeavour to eliminate the 'utopian' elements in Marxist ideology, implicitly entailed abandonment of the revolutionary perspective on the Jewish question.

Theoretical considerations alone do not explain, however, Bernstein's growing sense of solidarity with Jews in the late 1890s. It was of course the decade which witnessed the election of Karl Lueger in Vienna (1897), the Dreyfus Affair in France, pogroms in Russia, Algeria and Rumania, a noisy anti-Semitic agitation in Germany and anti-alien propaganda in Britain. These events formed the background to the emergence of the Zionist movement: in 1896 Theodor Herzl, the Austrian journalist and founder of political Zionism, wrote in his *Judenstaat*: 'Anti-Semitism increases day by day and hour by hour among the nations; indeed, it is bound to increase because the causes of its growth continue to exist and are ineradicable'.[41]

In this hostile atmosphere Bernstein felt obliged, as he pointed out in 1898 to his English socialist critic, E. Belfort Bax, to defend the Jews: 'Anyone who knows me well, knows that I am not at all sensitive on this point, but under present circumstances, it is a categorical imperative for me to be a 'philo-semite' in the face of all anti-Semitism'.[42]

In an obituary written in the same year for Eleanor Marx, Bernstein significantly stressed her *philo-Semitism*. He must have frequently accompanied the fiery daughter of Karl Marx on her visits to London's East End, with its heavy concentration of Jewish immigrants from Tsarist Russia and Poland. Bernstein affectionately noted 'her strong sympathy for the Jews', especially for 'the Jewish proletarians of the East End'.[43] He found it remarkable that

> At every opportunity she would affirm her descent with a certain defiance; how often I heard her assert with pride from the platform to the crowd below: 'I am a Jewess'—though she was not religious and had no contact with the official representatives of Jewry.[44]

Bernstein also recalled her indignation at the neutrality of the French Marxists during the Dreyfus Affair, her impatience with their rigid conception of class justice. He observed with seeming approval that: 'she did not allow herself to be led astray by her deep-rooted proletarian class feeling whenever the Jew was oppressed as a Jew, but declared herself for the oppressed, irrespective of class-affiliation'.[45]

This summed up in a nutshell one of the central departures of Bernstein and other 'revisionists' from orthodox Marxist attitudes to the Jewish problem.

Whereas classical Marxism insisted that class-interest was the sole decisive criterion, Bernstein's more liberal position was that Jews should be defended *as Jews*, wherever they were persecuted. For him this was an ethical, humanitarian 'categorical imperative' not to be subordinated to the strategy of revolutionary class-struggle.

Bernstein's attitude towards Zionism as a national movement was, however, critical, rather than sympathetic before 1914, despite his disagreements with the Marxist centre of the SPD. After his return to Germany in 1901 and his election as deputy for Breslau West the following year, Bernstein was approached by a number of Zionist sympathizers seeking his support for the new movement. The 27-year-old Chaim Weizmann, future leader of world Zionism, was actually convinced in August 1902 that he had won over the distinguished German socialist to the Zionist cause. In a letter to Vera Khatzman, Weizmann wrote:

> I had a long talk with Bernstein (the famous one) and his daughter in Berlin. I took him to task for taking up the cause of the Armenians, and not taking up the Jewish cause. He declared: 'If I had any Jewish feeling, I should be a Zionist. Perhaps it will come.'[46]

Weizmann added that in the Zionist journal which he hoped to publish in Berlin, Bernstein would 'write against the assimilationists'; he assured his wife-to-be that Bernstein and his step-daughter were 'on the road to Zionism', and that his assistant Kasteliansky was 'working on them adroitly'.

Bernstein's private correspondence at this time shows that he was indeed approached by Kasteliansky, by Alfred Nossig, director of the Verein für jüdische Statistik, and by Theodor Zlocisti with regard to questions connected with Zionism and agricultural colonization in Palestine.[47] Moreover, Bernstein was a regular contributor to the revisionist *Sozialistische Monatshefte*, whose editor Joseph Bloch was a militant Zionist and a close personal friend.

The *Sozialistische Monatshefte* was openly sceptical of the assimilationist solution to the Jewish problem in Eastern Europe advocated by Karl Kautsky's Marxist review, the *Neue Zeit*. This may have been one reason why Kautsky wrote to Julius Motteler in January 1903:

> Nothing would be nicer than if Bernstein were to turn to Zionism, and if I could help bring this about, I should like to do so. The Zionists need a prophet, Bernstein needs believers in his prophecies and we do not need him.[48]

Kautsky, who saw himself as the defender of Marxist orthodoxy against Bernstein's revisionist 'heresy', would doubtless have welcomed an opportunity to rid the SPD of a troublesome dissenter. Kautsky's ironic remarks about Bernstein as a future 'prophet' of Zionism were to be unexpectedly realized over twenty-five years later, when the two men crossed swords after the Palestine riots of 1929.

After 1900 Bernstein did not become a Jewish nationalist, but he did feel a growing concern for the fate of his persecuted co-religionists. Already in his maiden foreign policy speech as a Reichstag deputy, he had passionately denounced the discrimination practised by the Rumanian Government against its Jewish subjects.[49] He called on the German Government to guarantee Jewish civil equality in Rumania, as it was obliged to do by the terms of the Congress of Berlin (1878).

Bernstein also followed the pogroms in Russia in 1903 and 1905 with anguished concern. A number of book reviews which he wrote at this time in the *Dokumente des Sozialismus* indicate that he recognized the special plight of Russian Jewry.[50] Unlike Karl Kautsky, whose article on the Kishinev pogrom (1903) advocated the most rapid dissolution of the compact Jewish community, Bernstein regarded the immediate prospect of de-nationalizing Russian Jewry as remote. He was frankly critical of those socialists who tried to apply Marx's propositions in 'Zur Judenfrage' to the situation in Russia. Eduard Bernstein even suggested that Marx had been guilty of the 'shallowest rationalism' in parts of this essay, a criticism which he subsequently repeated.[51]

Although he rejected Marx's theory on this particular issue, Bernstein showed little sympathy for 'autonomism', a Yiddish-oriented variant of Jewish nationalism, popular in Russia and Austria-Hungary at the beginning of the twentieth century. He did not accept the premise of autonomists like Nathan Birnbaum that the Jews in Eastern Europe constituted an independent nation with their own unique language, history and culture.[52] In arguing against separatist trends in the Jewish labour movement of Russia and Eastern Europe, Bernstein, like other German Marxists, appealed primarily to the common tactical needs of the international proletariat. He was not disposed to concede any validity to the demands for cultural-national autonomy of the Jewish proletariat outside Russia.[53]

On the eve of the First World War, Bernstein's dislike of Jewish nationalism found its harshest expression in a long article for the *Neue Zeit* on the Zionist campaign against the Hilfsverein in Palestine.[54]

The Hilfsverein der deutschen Juden was a philanthropic German organization which had set up a network of schools and technical institutes in Palestine, and contributed considerably to raising cultural and material standards in what was then a backward Turkish province. The director of the Hilfsverein, Paul Nathan, a friend of Bernstein, had run into conflict with Palestinian Jews who accused him of sponsoring German cultural 'imperialism' at the expense of Hebrew education in the Holy Land. Bernstein deplored the 'fanatic chauvinism' of the agitation against Paul Nathan and the lack of political realism among the Zionists. He suggested that the geographic, climatic and economic conditions in Palestine, as well as the 8–1 ratio in favour of the Moslems, made the prospects for large-scale colonization remote. Bernstein concluded his essay on a highly critical note:

> Zionism is a kind of intoxication which acts like an epidemic. It may, and presumably will, also pass away like one. But not overnight. For, in the last resort, it is only part of the great wave of nationalistic reaction which has overflowed the bourgeois world and seeks to invade the socialist world as well.[55]

He proposed that social democracy should subject this nationalistic reaction to a 'fundamental critique'; but the intervention of the First World War greatly modified his viewpoint. It even led him to support the concept of national autonomy for Jews in individual European countries, and to consider Jewish nationalism as reconcilable with modern democratic ideas of self-determination.[56]

This change of perspective was not surprising when taken in the broader context of Bernstein's revisionist outlook. He had approached the Jewish problem since 1900 more as a liberal than as a Marxist; his attitude during the First World War was, moreover, typical of a general intensification of self-consciousness among German Jews. This led him to write in 1917 a remarkable pamphlet entitled *Von den Aufgaben der Juden im Weltkriege*, which perfectly illustrated his changed outlook. This pamphlet was in part a polemic against the ultra-assimilationist patriotism of his co-religionists during the 1914–18 war, whose zeal for the Fatherland made them more papist than the Pope.[57] Bernstein's pacifist sentiments were outraged by the sight of German Jews like Ernst Lissauer (who composed the 'song of hate' against England) leading the chorus of nationalist hysteria against the Allies. Bernstein accused certain Jewish newspaper editors, proprietors and journalists of joining in the inflammatory rhetoric of chauvinist hate-mongering and racial mythology. Both as a socialist and as a Jew, Bernstein felt deeply offended by this *Übernationalismus*.[58]

As a socialist, he had been no less shattered to see the disintegration of the international worker's movement at the outset of the war. His colleagues in the SPD had voted almost unanimously for the war-credits, and many of his revisionist friends in the party favoured an openly imperialist, annexationist policy. Bernstein himself argued passionately against this trend, and after 1915 became a leading spokesman for the neutralist line. This brought about his rupture with previous allies like Joseph Bloch and Eduard David, and a rapprochement with Centrists like Kautsky, who joined him in the USPD, or Independent Social Democratic Party of Germany, an independent splinter group opposed to the Majority Socialist war-policy.[59]

Disillusioned with socialist failure to prevent and oppose the war, Bernstein belatedly discovered the true cosmopolitan 'mission' of the dispersed Jewish people. *Von den Aufgaben* was the disenchanted product of a pacifist imagination, the noble but somewhat utopian statement of enlightened liberal cosmopolitanism amid the chaos of a collapsing civilization. Bernstein upheld the view that Jews had a special historical mission as 'born mediators between the nations'. They were chosen instruments of international reconciliation, '*ein verbindendes Element für die Völker der Kulturwelt*':[60] their heritage was profoundly cosmopolitan and opposed to every form of chauvinist incitement and racial hatred. Hence Bernstein's disgust with those of his over-zealous co-religionists who had rallied to the cause of Pan-German imperialism.

According to Bernstein, the Jews belonged to a race which had renounced its separate national destiny in favour of a higher ideal which he called '*Weltbürgerlicher Patriotismus*'. He argued that this ideal should have a superior claim for Jews over and above their tribal sentiments (*Stammesbewusstsein*) and their patriotic feelings for the adopted fatherland (*Landespatriotismus*). Bernstein appealed to world Jewry, as citizens of all the belligerent nations, to work for this universalist mission of world peace.[61]

Bernstein's pamphlet had virtually nothing to do with Marxism and relatively little to say about Zionism, though it was written shortly before the Russian Revolution and the Balfour Declaration of November 1917. These two momentous events, which confronted world Jewry with the choice between a class and a national orientation in world politics, made Bernstein's liberal ideal of cosmopolitanism seem redundant. While revolutionary and socialist Jews rallied to the messianic internationalism of the October Revolution, those who dreamed of a national renaissance now looked to England and to Zion.

It was significant that Bernstein's previous opposition to Zionism seemed to be wavering, and by 1917 he was even ready to concede to it a qualified support. He acknowledged that the Zionist movement had given a creative *élan* to the impoverished Jewish masses throughout the world, although he remained critical of chauvinist tendencies among Jews. In his 1917 pamphlet he had reaffirmed, 'I am no Zionist. I feel myself too much a German to be able to be one'.[62] In an article for Martin Buber's Zionist publication *Der Jude*, he summed up his new attitude as one of spontaneous solidarity rather than formal adhesion to any Jewish cause. He wrote:

> I am of course conscious of my descent from Jews and feel no need to keep it dark; on the contrary, I have a sense of solidarity with Jews wherever they are treated with contempt, because of their descent; but I cannot bring myself to join any specifically Jewish association, and would consider myself a stranger in relation to such groups, of whatever kind they might be, purely social or political, General Zionist or socialist Zionist.[63]

Bernstein persisted all his life in this refusal to join any specifically Jewish organization. But Salman Rubaschow (Zalman Shazar, later President of Israel), who was the Poale-Zion representative in Berlin during the First World War, recalled that Bernstein warmly welcomed the entry of Poale-Zion into the Socialist International in 1919.[64] Rubaschow insisted that in his meetings with Bernstein he always felt 'a recognition and the decisive weight of generations' on Jewish issues, lacking in his contacts with other European socialists.[65]

In the 1920s Bernstein did belatedly become more sympathetic to Zionist colonization in Palestine.[66] In 1921 his niece Lily Zadek, a German Jewess from Berlin, even emigrated to Palestine, where she died in 1969. In one of her letters she refers to the enormous esteem in which her uncle was held by the Zionist labour movement in Palestine. Like a number of other European social democrats, including the Belgians Emil Vandervelde and Camille Huysmans, the Frenchmen Jean Longuet and Léon Blum, the English socialists George Lansbury and Arthur Henderson, Bernstein also joined the Socialist Committee for a Workers' Palestine in 1928. A year later, after the pogroms in Hebron, the ageing veteran of German socialism broke a lance for the Zionists against his old friend and past rival, Karl Kautsky. The latter had condemned Zionism in an article for *Vorwärts*, the central organ of the SPD, written on 4th October 1929. Not for the first time, he characterized it as a romantic and reactionary utopia, a 'world-ghetto' for the Jewish people which would turn into a death-trap once Anglo-French hegemony in the Middle East vanished.[67]

Bernstein was shocked by Kautsky's denunciations, and stressed the positive achievements of 'co-operative Jewish labour' in Palestine, 'under the most difficult conditions'. He argued that the rise of National Socialism and the difficulties of emigration to other lands made a Jewish national home in Palestine a pressing necessity of the hour. Although as opposed as ever to any chauvinist tendencies, Bernstein defended the idealistic pioneering zeal of the Jewish colonists in Palestine.[68] In June 1930, when the British Government threatened to suspend Jewish immigration to Palestine, the Zionist-socialist leader David Ben-Gurion, through the medium of Marc Jarblum, requested Bernstein's intervention.[69] The Minister in charge at the Colonial Office, with overall responsibility for Palestine at that time, was Lord

Passfield (Sidney Webb), an old friend of Bernstein from the years of his exile in London. We do not know whether Bernstein intervened or not, but that he was asked to do so confirms the regard in which he was held by the Zionists.

Bernstein's last years were overshadowed by the growing menace of Hitlerism and the decline of the Weimar Republic. He was alarmed by the rampant nationalism and xenophobic anti-Semitism of the 1920s, constantly inflamed by Nazi and right-wing *völkisch* propaganda. He now recognized that socialists of his generation had tended to underestimate the strength and tenacity of Judaeophobia: the post-1918 reaction to the immigration of Eastern Jews into Germany illustrated that old prejudices were stronger than ever.[70] Even the German Left found it difficult to resist the new wave of racism, although in 1921 Bernstein had confidently written that in his party 'an outspoken anti-Semite is an impossibility'.[71] Bernstein courageously sought to defend the immigrants from the East against the systematic campaign mounted on the Right.[72]

The world depression of 1929 and the National Socialist breakthrough in the Reichstag elections a year later deeply saddened the octogenarian veteran of the German socialist movement. One of his last letters, addressed to his 'very dear, old comrade', Karl Kautsky, then resident in Vienna, lamented the tragic condition of Germany in these 'miserable times'.[73]

His death on 18th December 1932 spared him by six weeks the accession of Hitler to the Chancellorship of Germany.

CHAPTER 4

Rosa Luxemburg, the Internationalist

'The 'lofty silence of the eternal' in which so many cries have echoed away unheard resounds so strongly within me that I cannot find a special corner in my heart for the ghetto. I feel at home in the entire world wherever there are clouds and birds and human tears.'

Rosa Luxemburg

'Rosa Luxemburg is a unique blend of the German, Polish and Russian characters and of the Jewish temperament.'

Isaac Deutscher

Rosa Luxemburg, perhaps the purest exponent of socialist internationalism among twentieth-century Marxists, was born in 1871, in Zamość, a town in the south-eastern part of Russian Poland. Her father, Eduard (Eliasz) Luxemburg, managed the family timber concern and travelled frequently to Warsaw and Germany on business.[1] He spoke fluent Polish and belonged to the assimilated Jewish middle-class intelligentsia who took a strong interest in Polish affairs. Rosa's mother, *née* Lina Löwenstein, was also a cultivated woman with a passion for the Bible, as well as for classical German and Polish literature.[2] On her mother's side, Rosa Luxemburg descended from a tradition of rabbinical scholarship as impressive as that of Karl Marx.[3] Her maternal grandfather, Rabbi Isaac Löwenstein, from Poznan, was the son of Rabbi Nathan Löwenstein, who died in Lublin in 1834. The outstanding personality on the maternal side of the family was the eighteenth-century *Maskil*, Rabbi Jacob Joshua Falk, himself the descendant of generations of rabbis.[4] This charismatic ancestor had been distinguished by his opposition to the 'tyrannical' sway of the rich and the notables in the Jewish communities of Germany and Poland. His commentaries on the Bible and Talmud showed a keen sense for social injustice and a dialectical skill in argument, nourished by the ancient Jewish tradition of learning.[5] Long before the eighteenth century, the ancestors of Rosa Luxemburg had been rabbis in Hanover, Altona, Tarnov, Brody and Prague. The family tree has even been traced back to include a noted twelfth-century Provençal rabbi and interpreter of the Talmud.

Rosa Luxemburg, like Karl Marx, showed no awareness of the rich cultural tradition of Judaism to which she was heir, but it would be mistaken to assume that it played no role in shaping her personality and outlook. Her intellectual brilliance, her compassionate optimism and passion for justice, found their 'scientific' expression in the dialectics of Marxism: but the ethical content was unconsciously moulded by generations of rabbinical learning and the spirit of biblical humanism. Moreover, one must not forget that Rosa Luxemburg always enjoyed close relations with her family, with her brothers and sisters as with well as her parents. Although none of them showed any specific interest in Jewish affairs, her mother, Lina, was the sister as well as the daughter of a rabbi, and we know that she was fond of quoting the Bible to her daughter.[6] Rosa's birthplace, Zamość, was a city with a markedly Jewish character, more open to the influence of Western culture than the typical Polish-Jewish townlet.[7] The Luxemburgs lived an insulated existence there, largely separated from the more primitive neighbouring Polish population.

When Rosa was three the family moved to Warsaw, which at that time had a higher proportion of Jews than any other large city in Europe. In 1884 she entered an exclusive *gymnasium* for the children of Russian officers and officials, to which few Poles, let alone Jews, were admitted.

In her late teens, probably as a protest against the policy of forced Russification, she became involved in the Polish socialist movement *Proletariat*. To forestall possible arrest by the Tsarist police, she decided, at the age of eighteen, to leave Poland and continue her studies in the West. There is an amusing story told by Rosa, of how her crossing of the Polish border was engineered by a friend who convinced the local priest that his frail, dark-eyed Jewish companion wished to marry her Christian lover, in defiance of parental authority. Eager to assist such a romantic cause, the priest had the rebellious young woman smuggled across the frontier in a peasant's cart.[8]

Rosa Luxemburg not surprisingly chose Switzerland as her haven of refuge, and soon came into contact with Russian and Polish émigré revolutionaries. It was in Zürich that she met Leo Jogiches, a Russified Jewish intellectual and the son of wealthy parents from Vilna, who became the dominant personal and political influence in her life. In 1893 they founded *Sprawa Robotnicza* (The Workers' Cause) in Paris, together with Adolf Warszawski (Warski) and Julian Marchlewski.[9] This newspaper was the nucleus of a new party, the SDKP (The Social Democracy of the Kingdom of Poland), which in December 1899 became the SDKPiL, with the addition of the Lithuanian Social Democracy. Rosa Luxemburg's party was in fact an élite peer-group founded in exile as a breakaway from the PPS (Polish Socialist Party), whose nationalism it bitterly opposed.

The PPS sought to reorganize Polish socialism in the three areas of Poland occupied by Russia, Prussia and Austria. The main plan in its programme was national self-determination, leading to the restoration of historic Poland as an independent nation-state. Rosa Luxemburg opposed this programme with complete intransigence throughout her political career. For her national self-determination was a hollow, reactionary phrase which meant the subordination of the workers' movement to bourgeois ideology.[10] Her vision of revolutionary socialism from the outset precluded any form of nationalism, and the PPS programme would, in her opinion, only retard the class-struggle. Her doctoral thesis at the University of Zürich on the *Industrial Development of Poland* (published in 1898) buttressed her political attitude with arguments from economic history.[11] She set out to prove that the Polish economy was dependent on the Russian market, and that the Polish bourgeoisie desired the rapid integration of Poland into the Russian Empire.

Rosa Luxemburg's attitude to the Polish question was a mirror of her general theoretical approach to Marxism, internationalism and class-struggle. Since nationalism was for her nothing but a 'petty-bourgeois mystification', she was unsympathetic to the claims of the awakening nationalities in the multi-national Russian, Austro-Hungarian and Turkish Empires.[12] She thought that the independent future of third-rank nations like the Poles, the Czechs, the Yugoslavs, the Lithuanians, the Latvians, the Caucasus peoples and the Jews was definitely bleak.[13] In her long article of 1908 on 'The National Question and Autonomy', she applied a rigidly schematic Marxist analysis to the national problem, relying mainly on economic arguments and the predominance of class-struggle over national antagonisms.[14] Ignoring the fact that Marx and Engels had supported Polish and Irish independence on other than economic grounds, she insisted that a national state in Poland would impede economic development and the struggle for socialism. The Polish working class did not need to set up a bourgeois nation-state, the historical instrument of oppression and conquest: such a step would be totally retrograde, since only socialism could in the long run remedy national oppression. In any case, Rosa Luxemburg did not believe in the capacity of small nations to resist large, powerful states. Her vision of the socialist future was based on a deterministic premise derived from Marx—that socialism must dialectically evolve out of large, centralized capitalist states.

Indeed, on the national question she was more centralist than Lenin, although she had criticized him in 1904 for ultra-centralism on organizational matters. Rosa Luxemburg did not recognize that any national sentiments existed independent of material class interests.[15] At the same time, she idealized the working class, believing that its national policy could always be based on an identity of interests with workers of other nationalities. She ignored the national aspirations of the Polish (and Jewish) workers, because she feared this would deflect them from socialism.

Rosa Luxemburg greatly underestimated the revolutionary potential of national liberation movements and the capacity of small nations to defend their culture against outside oppression. Similarly, her theory ignored the coercion of nationalities implicit in multi-national centralized states like the Tsarist Empire. This blinded her to the legitimate national aspirations represented by the PPS and the Jewish Bund on behalf of Polish and Jewish workers in the Russian Empire. Even though she argued for union of the Russian and Polish proletariat, she refused to fuse her own party, the SDKPiL, with the RSDWP (the Russian Social Democratic Workers' Party), or to accept its centralized control. Yet she had supported Lenin's struggle to reduce the Bund to the subordinate status she opposed for her own group.

Rosa Luxemburg's attitude to the General Jewish Workers' Union (the Bund) and Jewish nationalism derived from her general position on national self-determination and her conflict with the PPS. On the theoretical level, she had consistently argued that the development of the world economy and the expansion of monopoly capitalism was eliminating all national, cultural and linguistic differences.[16] Imperialism and world politics in her view made any independent national programme redundant. In this sense, although she had turned Marx on his head over the Polish question, Rosa Luxemburg was his most faithful disciple.[17] She believed, like him, that the national question was secondary to the class-struggle, and could only condemn socialism to impotence, especially in the context of Central and Eastern Europe.

She feared that the Bund, through its increasing emphasis on 'Jewishness' (*Yiddishkeit*) and its cultural-national separatism, would undermine the common class-struggle to overthrow Tsarist absolutism. But, unlike the PPS, she did not demand that the Jewish workers in Russian Poland and Lithuania assimilate to the Polish language and culture, merely to further the Polish *national* cause. Nor did she seriously envisage the integration of the Bund into her own Polish party; the PPS, with its claim to the exclusive right of organizing the working class on 'Polish' territory, was far more dogmatic in this respect.[18]

Rosa Luxemburg's critical attitude to the Bund derived primarily from her internationalist belief in a united class-struggle of all the nationalities in the Russian Empire. Her close associate Adolf Warszawski, the leading organizer of the SDKPiL, summed it up in a letter of 20th May 1903 to Kautsky: 'the Bund ever more nationalistically tinged, increasingly demonstrates a tendency to separate party organization'.[19] At the same time, although rejecting its claim to defend the separate national interests of Jewish workers, Warszawski, like Rosa, thought highly of its achievements in propaganda and organization. He specifically praised the 'revolutionary enthusiasm' and mass support it enjoyed among the Jewish proletariat in Russian Poland, thanks to its use of Yiddish.[20] Rosa Luxemburg had expressed a similar standpoint in her review of a Bund pamphlet against the PPS in April 1903. She regarded an organization like the Bund as necessary, mainly because it alone was able to reach the mass of Yiddish-speaking workers in Russia and Poland, and win them to social democracy.[21]

But Rosa Luxemburg's perspective on Jewish emancipation in Tsarist Russia was consistently internationalist, and therefore opposed to that of the Bund. She argued that it was in the general interest of Russian and Polish revolutionaries to abolish the Pale of Settlement (see p. 172), eradicate the pogroms and guarantee Jewish civic equality along with other political freedoms in a democratic Russian Republic. A specific struggle for these goals, as waged by the Bund, within a separate Jewish labour movement was in her view unnecessary.[22] Only the all-Russian struggle of the revolutionary proletariat could solve the national problem in the Tsarist Empire.

In the SDKPiL organ *Czerwony Sztandar* (Red Flag) she wrote in April 1905:

> It was visible to everyone that here, for the first time, the whole gigantic proletarian mass of the Russian Empire emerged as *one* working-class in the political arena—without difference of nationality and religion—Russians, Poles, Lithuanians, Armenians, Latvians and Jews, striving for a common, political goal through common action.[23]

The Russian Revolution of 1905 confirmed for her the bankruptcy of 'social-patriotism' and PPS attempts to sever the historic 'Kingdom of Poland' from Russia. In the conflict between the PPS and the Bund she tended to sympathize with the Jewish labour movement, without subscribing to its general principles.[24] She readily agreed that the PPS had inflamed anti-Semitism among Polish workers with its attacks on the Bund as an 'agent' of Russification and a tool of the Jewish bourgeoisie. She accepted that the PPS had exhibited an aggressive chauvinism and exclusivist intolerance with regard to the Bund, rooted in its general 'contempt for other nationalities and national aspirations'.[25] Unlike the Bund, however, Rosa Luxemburg regarded PPS policy on the Jewish question as an inevitable corollary of 'social patriotism'. Every form of nationalism, whether bourgeois or socialist, was by its nature 'exclusive' and incapable of recognizing the self-determination of its adversaries. The PPS was itself 'separatist' in Prussian Poland, yet adamantly opposed to a 'separatist' Jewish labour movement in Russian Poland or Austrian Galicia.[26]

Rosa Luxemburg's position was more consistent than that of many Marxists, since it arose out of her rigorous internationalism, directed equally against Russian, Polish, Austrian and German, as well as Jewish, contemporaries. This was one of the reasons why the leaders of the Bund placed more confidence in her than in the PPS, whose national-revolutionary traditions were alien to them. Close personal ties had, moreover, existed in the 1890s between Leo Jogiches and the future leaders of the Bund in Vilna and Switzerland. Jogiches and Luxemburg used the Vilna social democrats as a channel for smuggling revolutionary literature to the masses in Russia; moreover, they both frequently saw John Mill, later one of the most influential figures in the Jewish labour movement, on his visits to Zürich.[27] Although Mill failed to win them for any specifically Jewish causes, their relations were friendly for a number of years, and in his memoirs he left a sympathetic picture of Rosa Luxemburg.[28]

After the foundation of the Bund in 1897 Rosa's attitude to the Jewish labour movement cooled somewhat.[29] But she must have been aware that the Bund leaders, though not sharing her radical negation of Polish independence, felt closer to her all-Russian orientation than to the nationalist PPS.[30] The ethnic background of Rosa Luxemburg, Leo Jogiches and Adolf Warszawski spared them the sharp distrust which the Bund leaders felt for the main wing of Polish socialism.

The differences between Luxemburg's SDKPiL and the Bund were typical of the rift between the Jewish Marxist intelligentsia in Eastern Europe and the Jewish masses who had retained many of their national characteristics. Rosa Luxemburg, divorced as she was from the Jewish working class, knowing no Hebrew and little Yiddish, could not see any prospect for a viable Jewish culture in Poland. In 1910 she outlined her own Marxist justification for 'assimilation' in a polemic which was also directed at the Bundist theoretician, Bronislaw Grosser.

> Obviously, all the efforts undertaken by a handful of publicists and translators of Yiddish, are out of the question. The only manifestation of a truly modern culture on a Jewish foundation is the Social Democratic movement of the Jewish proletariat. By its very nature, this movement can least of all replace the historical lack of a bourgeois-national Jewish culture since it is itself the manifestation of a culture that is international and proletarian.[31]

Rosa Luxemburg's main argument against the Bundist advocates of extra-territorial Jewish autonomy in Russian Poland was that the Jews had no *national* culture. The 'peculiarity' of the Jewish nationality in Poland was rooted, in her opinion, in East European small-town life. The material basis of economic existence in the *Shtetl* was, however, too narrow to perpetuate a separate nationality. According to Rosa, the Jews were a historically backward nationality, whose characteristics were based 'on socially backward, petty-bourgeois production, petty-commerce, small-town life'.[32] Like most cosmopolitan Marxists, she probably expected the Jewish nationality' to disappear with the growth of capitalist centralization in Eastern Europe.

It is hardly surprising, therefore, that she opposed Zionism, though this was much more marginal to her concerns than Bundism. Already in January 1894 *Sprawa Robotnicza*, under Rosa's editorship, contained an article by Leo Jogiches which praised Russian-Jewish workers for their opposition to 'Zionism'.[33] The article, which obviously reflected the SDKP view of the problem, reviewed the May Day Speeches of Jewish workers in Vilna (1892), regarded by some historians as a turning point in the Jewish labour movement in Russia.[34] This article is interesting for two reasons: it shows that Jogiches and Luxemburg regarded 'Zionism' (represented at that time by the Hovevei-ẓion circles) as a 'social-patriotic' deviation, and secondly that they welcomed the Jewish proletarians as 'new comrades' in the joint struggle of the Russian and Polish working class.[35] The 'Palestinian' solution to the Jewish question, by pursuing the illusion of an independent state (*niezależne pânstwo*) would divide Jewish workers from their Polish and Russian class 'brothers'. It would lead 'to a hatred of other nationalities', and in no way destroy capitalism, even if a Jewish State were one day established. The goal of Zionism—'a utopian Jewish State'—could not change by one iota the situation of the working-people, and Jogiches applauded the Vilna speakers for recognizing this fact.[36] Rosa Luxemburg undoubtedly agreed with this negative assessment of Zionism; moreover, the latter seemed far too remote from her perspective of world-revolution to merit further attention.

Her attitude to anti-Semitism was rather more complex, for this involved personal, emotional factors as well as general ideological principles. On one occasion she quoted Marx's 'Zur Judenfrage' in a polemic against 'leftist' Polish anti-Semites, who had claimed inspiration for their racial doctrines from the founders of socialism. According to Rosa Luxemburg, however, Marx had

> for the first time removed the Jewish question from the religious and racial sphere and given it a *social* foundation, proving that what is usually described and persecuted as "Judaism", is nothing *but the spirit of huckstering and swindle*, which appears in *every* society, where *exploitation* reigns.[37]

Like most socialists, she felt obliged to 'edit' Marx, inferring that he had proved 'that Jewish emancipation is above all an emancipation of society from *this* "Judaism"—i.e., the *abolition of exploitation*'.[38]

In reply to her Polish anti-Semitic adversaries, Rosa Luxemburg declared, with rather more justification, that Marxism rejected any attempt to mystify concepts such as 'nation' and 'race'.[39] International social democracy, she pointed out, divided the world into 'two nations'—the exploiters and the exploited—and two religions, those of capital and labour. The anti-Semites, by contrast, argued that the nation was a homogeneous racial entity which existed above and beyond the class-struggle.

Rosa Luxemburg emphasized that Marxism regarded anti-Semitism as a specific pathology of *bourgeois* society, rather than as an independent issue.

> For the followers of Marx, as for the working class, the *Jewish question as such does not exist*, just as the "Negro question" or the "Yellow Peril" does not exist. From the standpoint of the working class, the

> Jewish question . . . is a question of *racial hatred as a symptom* of social *reaction*, which, to a certain extent, is an indivisible part of all societies based on class antagonism.[40]

The logic of this analysis was that 'only a fundamental transformation of the capitalist system can eliminate the radical attacks on "Jewry" '.[41]

Rosa Luxemburg conceded that there was also another dimension to the problem in Russia—namely, the 'civil equality of the Jews'. But, in her view, this was simply '*one of a thousand social tasks*, whose only common solution one must seek elsewhere'.[42]

From her Marxist standpoint, the Jewish question was a social problem, no different in kind from other issues such as education, the nationalities question, regional autonomy, etc. All these problems were produced by the 'political system', and they could only be resolved by a proletarian revolution, carried out by all nationalities in the Russian Empire.

Rosa Luxemburg argued that to place the 'Jewish question' in the centre of political discussion was a classic manoeuvre of the Counter-Revolution.[43] Its sole purpose was to divert attention from genuine class and political antagonisms, thereby damming up the mass movement of the proletariat and mobilizing the counter-revolutionary 'scum of society'. Rosa Luxemburg, herself unmistakably Jewish in appearance, sharply polemical and constantly vulnerable to the anti-Semitic eruptions in Polish and Russian society, could speak here from personal experience. For a part of the Polish 'free-thinking' intelligentsia, her cosmopolitan SDKPiL was inevitably a symbol of anti-patriotism, and the alleged 'anti-goyism' of the Jews.

Andrej Niemojewski, one of her most virulent detractors in Poland, wrote in his *Mysl Niepodległa* (Independent Thoughts) in 1910, 'As all Jews hate non-Jews, so Luxemburg's Social Democrats have a passionate hatred for Poland'.[44]

The PPS papers *Naprzód* (Forward) and *Przedświt* (Dawn) were not slow in seizing their cue from Niemojewski, and asserting that the SDKPiL served the 'Jewish', not the proletarian, interest. Julian Unszlicht (Sedecki) and Emil Haecker led a scurrilous campaign in the PPS press against Rosa Luxemburg and her party, whom they accused of seeking to 'russify' Poland.[45] Sedecki blamed her party, as well as the Bund, for 'Social-Litvakism'—a pejorative reference to the overrunning of Poland by Litvak Jews, with their 'alien' customs.[46]

Rosa Luxemburg, in a series of stinging articles for the SDKPiL organ *Młot* (The Hammer) in November 1910 hit back at these anti-Semitic slurs, concentrating her fire against the Polish 'progressive' press. She lashed out at the 'mongrel' and 'half-wit' Niemojewski, who symbolized to her the moral decay of the Polish bourgeoisie in the aftermath of the 1905 Revolution. She concluded that the political purpose of such slanders was twofold: to make the Jews a scapegoat for the growing influence of socialism, and to settle accounts with the Polish workers for the wave of strikes in 1905. She characterized the anti-Jewish campaign in the Warsaw press as a literary pogrom, morally even more despicable than the primitive violence of Purishkevitch and his Russian Black Hundred gangs.[47] It was unforgivable that the cream of the Polish intelligentsia in Warsaw had given 'free rein to their zoological instincts'; like the Black Hundreds, the Polish 'progressives' claimed only to be against the 'Jewish revolutionaries'. But, as Rosa Luxemburg pointed out, it was 'in any case impossible to maintain strict order among the pogromist bands'.[48]

The 'progressive' campaign aimed to unite the whole of bourgeois society in one camp, by preaching that Jews were the enemies of the Polish nation: 'Anti-Semitism has become the common platform of the Endek realists, the "christian", clerical Reaction and the "progressive" free-thinkers—the common banner of political backwardness and cultural barbarism'.[49] The social and material foundation of this intellectual alliance was a common hatred of the proletarian class-enemy: the 'hooligan' elements of Polish progressivism had taken the lead in spreading the 'bestial cretinism' of Black Hundred anti-Semitic propaganda to mask their surrender to clerical and nationalist reaction in Poland.

The virulence of Rosa Luxemburg's language in answering the 'zoological anti-Semitism' of Niemojewski and his followers was quite exceptional. On the whole, she seems, like most Jewish revolutionaries, to have made a conscious effort *not* to make a special case out of anti-Semitism.[50] In contrast to her denunciation of the literary 'pogrom' in Warsaw, she had very little to say about the Russian pogroms and their effect on the Jewish population. The SDKPiL admittedly deplored the Kishinev pogrom of 1903 as well as the smaller-scale violence on Polish soil. Rosa Luxemburg and Adolf Warszawski immediately appealed to Polish workers to rally to their Jewish comrades; but at the same time they stepped up their criticism of the Bund's 'separatism'. Both were delighted when Karl Kautsky responded to their request for an article on the Kishinev massacres for the SDKPiL review *Przegląd Socjaldemokratyczny* (Social Democratic Review). The article, which depicted the Russian revolutionary movement as the sole salvation for the Jews and criticized Zionism for maintaining Jewish 'isolation', proved a useful weapon in their polemics with the Bund.[51]

Not once, however, did Rosa Luxemburg, for all her socialist humanism and defence of oppressed minorities like the Armenians and Poles in Germany, ever express a word of sympathy for the victims of the pogroms.[52] This fact became all the more striking when one contrasts it with the genuine outrage provoked in (Gentile) socialists like Lenin, Bebel and Kautsky or in Russian intellectuals like Tolstoy, Chekhov and Gorky by these events. Since Rosa Luxemburg regarded the Tsarist regime with no less passionate a hatred, one can only assume that she had deliberately suppressed any feelings of emotional identification with the Jewish people. Her casual reference to the Black Hundred massacres in a pamphlet entitled *Co Dalej?* (What next?) in 1906 would be difficult to surpass in its analytical detachment.

> The Jewish pogroms, the most important method of attack by absolutism in the first phase of the Revolution, have already become a worn-out and useless weapon. Their only consistent result was to compromise Tsarism abroad. In Russia itself, and in Poland, the triggering-off of pogroms was already impossible wherever there existed enlightened and revolutionary workers. Jew-baiting was already an impossibility in Poland, Petersburg, Moscow, Riga, in all the important centres of the Revolution. It is only still possible in small, remote villages in Southern Russia and Bessarabia—namely, where the revolutionary movement is weak or non-existent. In short, pogroms are only possible where they are not needed, and impossible there where they should serve as a tool against the Revolution.[53]

This comment exemplifies Rosa's evident determination not to single out 'Jewish' victims as deserving any special attention: like so many Jewish Marxists, she exhibited an unresolved guilt-complex when it came to the pogroms and the need to resist brutal anti-Semitism in practice. Her sharp reply from prison to Mathilde Wurm in February 1917 illustrates her impatience with Jewish concerns. 'Why do you come with your special Jewish sorrows? I feel just as sorry for the wretched Indian victims in Putamayo, the negroes in Africa . . . I cannot find a special corner in my heart for the ghetto.'[54]

Her most authoritative biographer, Peter Nettl, accepts this at its face value, as proof of her genuine internationalism.[55] But what kind of universalism is it which expresses abstract concern at a distance for all of suffering humanity but ignores the immediate, concrete misery of the ghetto? What kind of selective humanism is it which abhors the oppression of Indians and Negroes but neglects or represses the consciousness of pogroms? Rosa Luxemburg herself wrote in one of her classic letters from prison, 'To be human is the main thing, and that means to be strong and clear, and of good cheer, in spite and because of everything, for tears are the preoccupation of weakness'.[56] In this positive life-giving optimism which affirmed the world and life, 'in spite of everything', there was perhaps something of Rosa Luxemburg's proud rabbinical heritage: in her disregard for 'special

Jewish sorrows' there was only the confusion and vulnerability of the self-denying internationalist.

Rosa Luxemburg was especially evasive with regard to anti-Semitism in Western Europe. She had followed events in France during the Dreyfus Affair with careful attention, publishing a series of short, unsigned articles in the *Sächsische Arbeiterzeitung* (Dresden) in the summer of 1898.[57] These reports, based on material supplied to her by Leo Jogiches and Boris Krichevskii, were unconditionally pro-Dreyfusard and supported the campaign of the French socialist leader Jean Jaurès for the rehabilitation of Dreyfus. Rosa Luxemburg praised his 'energetic campaign against the clerico-military oligarchy' and his vehement denunciations of the 'nationalist virus' of Rochefort and Drumont.[58] But this was virtually the only allusion which she made to the virulent anti-Jewish campaign in France waged by the anti-Dreyfusard forces. This is the more surprising since anti-Semitism was not only a central issue in France during the Dreyfus Affair but was also a cause of dissension on the French Left.

Nevertheless, in her subsequent articles on the events in France, written for the *Neue Zeit*, she scarcely mentioned the organized campaign against the Jews.[59] Only in reply to an international questionnaire sponsored by Jaurès's paper *La Petite République* in 1899 did she list anti-Semitism as one of 'four social factors' which gave the Dreyfus Affair 'the mark of a question involving the class-struggle'.[60] Nevertheless, she saw no reason to deviate from her general policy of submerging it under other social issues. Rosa Luxemburg considered it a socialist duty to intervene in the Dreyfus Affair, not because Dreyfus was a Jew, or even the victim of a miscarriage of justice, but solely because the working class would gain.

By waging a general campaign against 'militarism, clericalism, nationalism and anti-Semitism', the socialists would strengthen proletarian class-consciousness. It was precisely on these grounds that she later opposed Jaurès's tactics of class-collaboration with the radical bourgeoisie, which flowed logically from his involvement in the Affair. Once she had reversed her attitude to Jaurès, the Dreyfus Affair only interested her as a stick with which to beat the 'revisionists' of Marxism in France and Germany.

It is therefore decidedly misleading to imply that 'she felt particularly concerned by the struggle against anti-Semitism' as a Jewess.[61] The evidence suggests precisely the opposite. Nor was her extreme reticence on anti-Semitism due to lack of provocation in Germany, for Rosa Luxemburg was well aware 'of the peculiar reception' which she and 'other non-Germans' had to put up with in the SPD.

She had arrived in Berlin on 12th May 1898, and after having obtained German citizenship by a sham marriage, her main involvement was henceforth to be in German party affairs. The SPD was the leading socialist party of the Second International, and it was from its left wing that she sought to influence international socialism. Although the SPD had an enviable record in combating anti-Semitism, the reaction to Rosa Luxemburg in many circles of the party was one of scarcely disguised hostility. Some of this criticism was anti-Semitically tinged, although this was by no means the only prejudice to which she was subject. As a woman, an ultra-revolutionary and an 'Easterner', the odds were already stacked against her: her passionate temperament, intellectual superiority and biting sarcasm did not help matters.

It would be mistaken to imagine that the response she provoked was a matter of indifference to someone as sensitive as Rosa Luxemburg:[62] it clearly influenced her anti-Establishment position within the party, and the acidity with which she answered her political opponents. In a letter to Leo Jogiches, nearly a year after her arrival in Berlin, she gave vent to her frustration at the way she was treated by the party executive. Quoting a Polish anti-Semitic proverb, she remarked, '*Jak bieda to do żyda, po biedzie precz zydie*' ('to the Jews for help—and when it is over, away with you, Jews.')[63]

It is unlikely that this bitter comment reflected a consciously Jewish identification in Rosa Luxemburg: according to Peter Nettl, she always stressed her Polish rather than her Jewish identity in Germany, to differentiate herself from the Prussians she so disliked.[64] The remark therefore probably testified to her feeling of being an outsider even in the SPD, which could only have been reinforced by allusions to her origin, made by her opponents in the party. By throwing herself into the 'revisionist' controversy, and becoming the spearhead of the radical Left in the defence of revolutionary Marxism, she had in any event assured herself many enemies on the right wing of the German party.

At the Party Congresses of 1898–9 she unmercifully flayed Wolfgang Heine as a scapegoat for the absent Bernstein, and lectured the trade-unions on their 'Sisyphus-work' in the class-struggle.[65] Her insistence on the final aims of socialism and on militant strike-agitation inevitably alienated the reformist Bavarian wing of the party: they particularly resented the intellectual self-confidence and tactlessness of this 'foreigner', and her sharp, lecturing tone. The trade-union bureaucracy equally detested the impulsive, ultra-leftist young woman from the East who ignored their organizational achievements and chided them with quotations from Marx.

Resentment against Frau Dr Luxemburg and her fellow Russian Jewish émigré Alexander Israel Helphand (Parvus) increased as the revisionist controversy stirred up passions in the party. Shortly before the Lübeck Congress of 1901 the German socialist leader Bebel wrote to Kautsky, 'You cannot imagine the animosity against Parvus and also La Rosa in the Party, and even if I am not of the opinion that we should be guided by such prejudices, we cannot at the same time afford to ignore them completely'.[66]

The barrage of criticism directed at Rosa Luxemburg and Parvus during the Lübeck Congress confirmed this judgment. The 'new arrivals from the East' were angrily caricatured by Richard Fischer, business manager of *Vorwärts*, as a pair of 'literary ruffians', intolerant of any criticism.[67] Wolfgang Heine, a leading supporter of Bernstein's revisionism, declared that the 'Russian and Polish Jews' by their tactless statements had abused German hospitality.[68] He suggested that their behaviour had 'made the struggle against anti-Semitism more difficult', and had strained the internationalism of the SPD to its limits. He compared the behaviour of Parvus and Rosa Luxemburg to that of guests who 'come to us and spit in our parlour'. The mood of other delegates also reflected a Russophobic, anti-Semitic undercurrent in the German party. Only Clara Zetkin rose to defend the absent Rosa and Parvus as 'party comrades' who 'stand with us for the same programme and share our struggles'.[69]

Rosa Luxemburg, who was not present when these attacks were made, was undoubtedly indignant at such personal slurs. In a letter to Kautsky—who had refused to publish her reply to Richard Fischer in the *Neue Zeit*—she upbraided him for cowardice and gave vent to her wounded feelings.

> Well, I am sickened at the thought of having to insist upon rights if these are only to be granted amid sighs and gnashing of teeth, when people not only grab me by the arm and thus expect me to 'defend' myself, but try in addition to beat me to a pulp, in the hope that I may thus be persuaded to renounce my rights.[70]

It is difficult to say which aspect of the personal abuse directed at her activities grated on her most.[71]

At the conscious level, Rosa did seem 'impervious' to the many slights on her womanhood and foreignness which she had to endure in the SPD and outside it. She regarded them as proof that, politically, her opponents had a weak case. Nevertheless, it is astonishing that she made no allusion in her voluminous German writings or in her private correspondence to the widespread anti-Semitism in Imperial Germany.[72]

In 1905, when she sought to draw lessons from the Russian Revolution for the benefit of the German working class, the campaign against 'bloody Rosa' in the bourgeois press took an openly anti-Semitic colouring. Caricatures appeared of her and other Jewish members of the SPD, including Paul Singer and Arthur Stadthagen, under captions insinuating a conspiracy of 'The Great Sanhedrin'.[73]

Her physical ugliness was accentuated, and long-nosed 'Rosa with the snout' was depicted as the centre of this 'Semitic' plot, in the rabid style later adopted by *Der Stürmer*.[74]

The right-wing press called for the expulsion from Germany of the subversive Polish Jewess and 'vagrant' revolutionary. Even in the SPD, her emphasis on mass strikes earned her some notoriety, and in revisionist circles she was regarded as a 'Russian patriot' for her enthusiastic articles on the Russian revolution.[75] Gustav Noske, the SPD expert on military and naval affairs, felt a particular antipathy towards this *déclassé* Easterner, who had stepped forward, as he put it, to 'instruct the German proletariat'. In his memoirs, published in 1947, Noske insisted that it had 'nothing to do with anti-Semitism' when he observed that East European Jewish Marxists in the SPD had a special gift for 'transforming socialism into a dogma and platitudes into articles of faith'.[76] Noske asserted that the East European Jews had evolved a 'secret science' of Marxism, which 'remained incomprehensible to the German workers'.[77] Like some other right-wing socialists in the SPD, he resented the presence of these cosmopolitan Jewish revolutionaries in the German party, who appeared to have won the confidence of the leadership. Their moral pathos, their vibrant internationalism, their rootlessness and sincere idealism seemed 'alien' to the average party functionary.

In 1919 Noske was people's commissar for military affairs in the Socialist Government, when Rosa Luxemburg was brutally murdered by *Freikorps* officers, called in by him to quell the Spartacist revolt. Whether he actually ordered her execution is not certain, but he did nothing to stop his henchmen carrying it out. It was to be one of the tragic ironies of Rosa Luxemburg's political life that she laid down her life for a society to which she never felt attached, and which regarded her in turn with profound suspicion.

Even in the German labour movement this perpetual gadfly and trenchant critic of bureaucratic immobilism remained somewhat isolated. The SPD was for her primarily a springboard to propagate her international ideal of the proletarian 'fatherland': the abandonment by the SPD in August 1914 of the fundamental premises of international socialism deprived her of a viable political base. It was her world as much as that of civilized, bourgeois Europe which came to an end at Sarajevo.

The ease with which a cosmopolitan intellectual like Rosa Luxemburg could straddle three cultures—the German, the Polish and the Russian—her very freedom from national prejudices, proved in the end a disadvantage in terms of practical politics. Isaac Deutscher in his essay on the 'non-Jewish Jew' idealized this feature of Rosa Luxemburg's outlook by arguing somewhat nebulously that hers was 'the ultimate victory' over her assassins.[78] For Deutscher Rosa Luxemburg's 'rootlessness' was a disadvantage only when 'religious intolerance or nationalist emotion was on the ascendant'.[79] This comment completely ignores the historical experience of European Jewry, whose fate was determined by the *failure* of socialist and democratic forces to counter nationalist anti-Semitism. It was precisely Rosa Luxemburg's inability to comprehend the strength of nationalist sentiment in Germany, Russia and Poland which was the reason for the collapse of her internationalist policy. There was perhaps nothing specifically 'Jewish' in her negation of nationalism, but it was surely not a coincidence that other Jewish revolutionaries like Trotsky, Radek, Warszawski and Leo Jogiches resembled her most on this point.

All these revolutionaries who by class, culture and Jewish background belonged to bourgeois society paid the ultimate price for their efforts to overthrow it. Rosa Luxemburg's battered body was thrown into the Landwehr Canal by her *Freikorps* assassins. Leo Jogiches was shot in the back 'while trying to escape'; Radek and Warszawski were victims of Stalin's purges, and Trotsky was assassinated by a Stalinist agent in Mexico. In Rosa Luxemburg's case, posterity has somewhat romanticized this small, frail and slightly deformed woman who aroused so much controversy in her time. For the Social Democrats she remains a theorist of the front-rank, memorable chiefly for her defence of democratic freedoms and her critique of the Bolshevik Revolution. For the Communists her importance was assured by her martyrdom during the abortive German Revolution of 1918–19 and her status as co-founder of the KPD. This final epilogue to her political life has also made her the spiritual godmother of East German Communism. Similarly, in Poland she remains the outstanding revolutionary personality produced by the Polish labour movement—though after the 'anti-Zionist' campaigns of 1967–8 her Jewish origin must be something of an embarrassment. The neo-anti-Semitism of Polish Communists would surely have made her turn in her grave.

On another level, the New Left also has a claim to Rosa Luxemburg, as an inveterate critic of socialist bureaucracy and a most compelling spokeswoman for the creative 'spontaneity' of the masses. All these rival claims for her revolutionary inheritance have their justification and legitimacy. None of them in any way needs to invalidate the existence of an elusive Jewish component in her personality which I have tried to elucidate. The ardent idealism, temperamental impatience and passion for abstract logic allied to her belief in the *final* goal of socialism—all coalesced into a militant universalism whose most eloquent apostles have often been Jewish revolutionaries.

Her last article in *Rote Fahne* (January 1919), sarcastically entitled 'Order reigns in Berlin', acknowledged the 'temporary' defeat of Spartacus and the German Revolution. But a message of defiant millennial hope lit up the debacle as if echoing across the centuries some strange Yahwic incantation. 'Order rules in Berlin!' You stupid lackeys! Your 'order' is built on sand. Tomorrow the revolution will rear its head once more and announce to your horror amid the brass of trumpets: 'I was, I am, I shall always be![80]

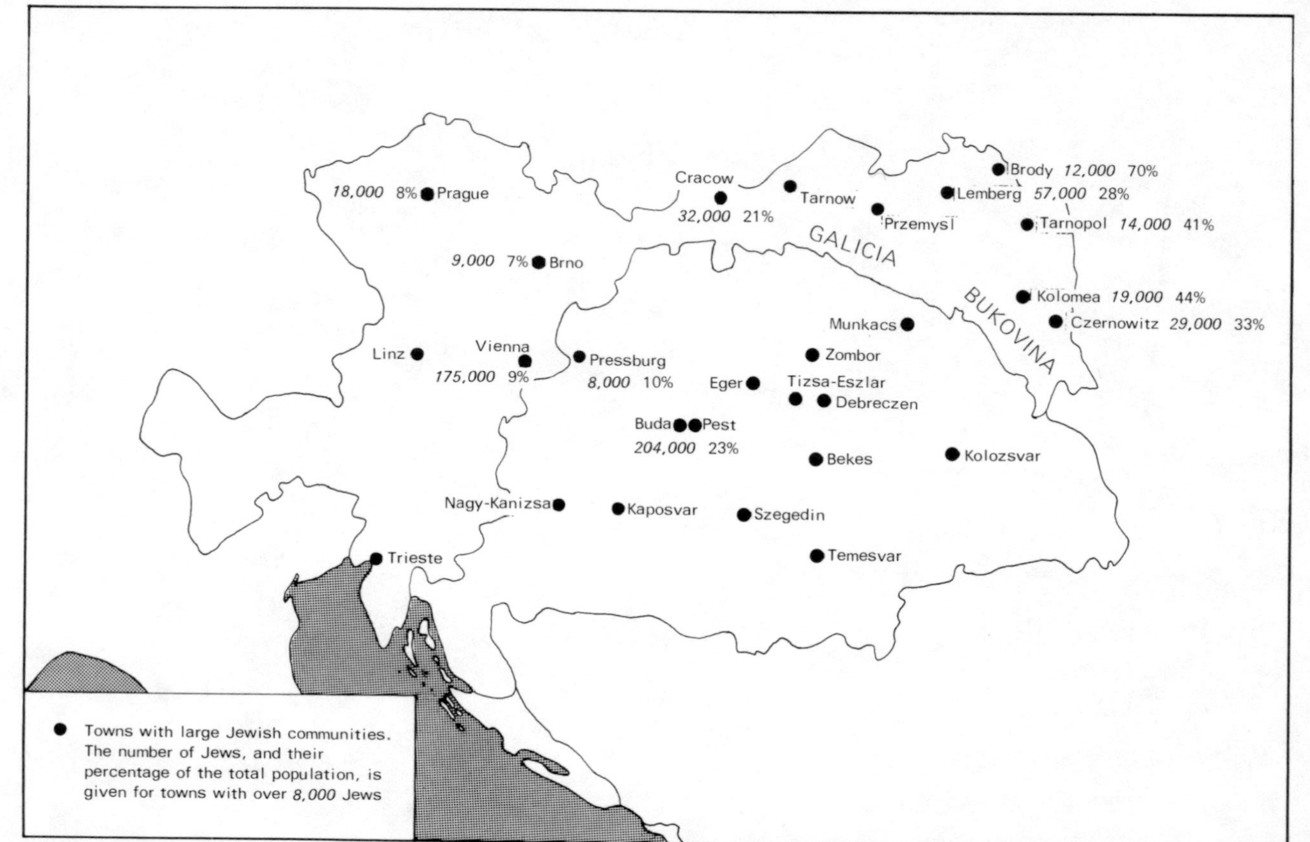

Austria-Hungary, 1910

Austria-Hungary

Victor Adler and Otto Bauer

'Who created the liberal movement in Austria? The Jews. . . . Who betrayed and deserted the Jews? The liberals. Who created the German national movement in Austria? The Jews. And who deserted them, who spat on them like dogs? . . . Exactly the same will happen with Socialism and Communism. Once the soup has been served, you'll be chased from the dinner table. It was always like this, and it always will be'.

Arthur Schnitzler

In perhaps no other region did the Jews play so striking a role in the labour movement as in the multi-national Austro-Hungarian Empire. This was especially evident at the turn of the century, a time when Jewish genius flourished everywhere in the musical, theatrical, literary, scientific and economic life of the Habsburg monarchy. The central axis of this dramatic explosion of creativity lay in the large and powerful Jewish communities of Vienna and Budapest, but Jews were also in the forefront of cultural life in Prague, Cracow, Lemberg (Lvov), Czernowitz and other towns. Austria-Hungary was at the same time the cradle of modern political anti-Semitism, which was endemic to almost all the nationalities in the Habsburg State. It was in pre-1914 Vienna that Adolf Hitler discovered the potential of anti-Semitism as the basis of a mass movement, from his German-Austrian teachers, Karl Lueger, leader of the Christian-Social Party, and Georg von Schoenerer, the founder of racist Pan-Germanism.

In the next two chapters we shall examine the personalities and outlook of two outstanding Jewish intellectuals in the Austrian labour movement, Victor Adler and Otto Bauer. Adler, a physician, educator, humanist and father-figure of the socialist movement in Austria-Hungary, enjoyed a rare prestige among the labour leaders of the Second International. His disciple Otto Bauer, while also rejecting Judaism as national or religious affiliation, profoundly believed in the socialist humanism of his teacher. But neither of these two socialist leaders could rid themselves of their emotional antipathy to the Jewish community, which reflected the strength of anti-Semitism among large strata of the German-Austrian population.

Austrian Jews, like their German co-religionists, did not enjoy civil rights before 1848 despite the prominence of individual Jews in the modernization and expansion of Austrian industry and commerce. During the Metternich era even such a powerful figure as the Jewish banker Salomon von Rothschild could not accede to citizenship. Various restrictions concerning the freedom of movement and rights to own property continued to affect Austrian Jewry until 1860 (except for the brief interlude of the 1848 Revolution). The new Constitution of Austria-Hungary, promulgated on 21st December 1867, first abolished discrimination on the basis of religion. The Viennese Jewish community now began to show signs of rapid growth, attracting an influx of immigrants from all parts of the Monarchy. By 1910 there were 175 318 Jews in Vienna (8·7 per cent of the total population), making it the largest Jewish city in Europe after Warsaw and Budapest. In the same year it was estimated that there were 1 313 698 Jews in the Austrian Empire, as well as approximately 750 000 Jews in Hungary. The Jews constituted 4·6 per cent of the total population of the Dual Monarchy. They were more numerous than the Slovenes, Serbo-Croats, Italians and Rumanians—who, were formally recognized by Habsburg officialdom, unlike the Jews, as 'nationalities'.

Two-thirds of Austrian Jewry were concentrated in the Polish province of Galicia, where they lived in compact masses, speaking Yiddish and remaining distinct in religion, customs and culture from the surrounding population. Throughout the Empire the Jews found themselves caught in the crossfire of nationality conflicts between Germans and Czechs (Bohemia), Poles and Ukrainians (Galicia), Magyars and Slovaks (Hungary). This fact, together with the prevalence of anti-Semitism in all these regions, explains why Zionism and Jewish nationalism found a considerable echo among the non-assimilated Jewish masses of the Austro-Hungarian lands.

The anti-Semitic movement which developed in the 1880s was especially important in German Austria, though its importance in Galicia, Hungary (the Tisza-Eszlar blood-libel case, 1882) and in Bohemia (the Hilsner ritual-murder trial, 1899) should not be underestimated. The Pan-German movement under Schoenerer attacked Jewish capitalism and sought to halt the influx of 'foreign' Jews from other parts of the Monarchy into German Austria. By 1885 it systematically excluded all Jews from membership in German-national organizations on racial grounds, although many Jews had been fervent supporters of the Pan-German cause. The Christian-Social Party under Lueger (who became Mayor of Vienna in 1897) was fiercely anti-capitalist in its early phase, when its main target was the prominence of Jews in banking, the press and Austro-liberalism. After Lueger took office, however, his anti-Semitism became largely verbal, though life was made difficult for immigrant Jewish pedlars.

The political orientation of Austrian Jewry, as in Germany, had traditionally been liberal. The socio-economic interests of assimilated German-speaking Jewry in Austria-Hungary did not encourage support for the working-class movement. Nevertheless, with the weakening of Austro-liberalism at the turn of the century, and the virtual exclusion of Jews from the clerical and nationalist parties, the available options narrowed. The radical Jewish intelligentsia increasingly emerged in the forefront of the Austrian Socialist Party, whose unification was the achievement of Victor Adler. Although the labour movement was in these years far from adopting a 'philo-Semitic' posture, let alone intent on vigorously combating anti-Jewish propaganda, social democracy remained the best long-term hope for the Jewish intelligentsia. Apart from Victor Adler and Otto Bauer, a whole galaxy of able personalities such as Friedrich and Max Adler, Wilhelm Ellenbogen, Friedrich Austerlitz, Julius Deutsch, Robert Danneberg, Oskar Pollack, Thérèse Schlesinger and Helen Bauer (wife of Otto Bauer) took their place in the socialist leadership.

This fact inevitably encouraged anti-Semitic invectives, especially after 1918, when Austria had been reduced to a rump state. Clerical and nationalist propaganda, stimulated by difficult economic conditions and the rise of Austro-fascism, further reinforced anti-Jewish feeling, especially in rural regions. In 1918 there were 300 000 Jews in the Austrian Republic, two-thirds concentrated in Vienna, a socialist stronghold. The spectre of 'Red Vienna' dominated by Jews and communists became an effective rallying-cry of the right-wing parties. The suppression of the Social Democrats in 1934 led to a decline in the Jewish situation, though the clerical regimes of Dollfuss and Schuschnigg were less hostile to Jews than broad strata of the population. The liquidation of Austrian Jewry was brought about by the *Anschluss* (annexation to Germany) on 13th March 1938, which resulted in a wave of racial laws, pogroms and systematic terror on a scale more radical than anything practised in the German Reich at that time.

CHAPTER 5

Victor Adler, the Father-figure

'The last anti-Semite will disappear with the last Jew.'

Victor Adler

'One day Victor Adler described this phenomenon. I asked him what he thinks of anti-Semitism, and with his usual humour this Prague Jew replies: "My dear comrade, one must have Jews, only not too many"'.

Camille Huysmans

Victor Adler, the founder and father-figure of Austrian socialism, was born in Prague in 1852. His parents originally came from Lipnik (Moravia) near the Galician frontier, and moved to Prague only a year before Victor's birth. His father, Salomon Marcus Adler, the son of an orthodox Jew, had been educated in the local Talmud School and then sent to Prague to study the Bible and Hebrew. He subsequently became a merchant and married Johanna, daughter of Wolf Herzl of Nicolsburg in Moravia. Salomon Adler moved to Vienna with the family when Victor was four years old, and at first they lived in the Leopoldstadt ghetto. However, in the liberal climate of the 1860s, as new business opportunities opened up for Austrian Jewry, Salomon Marcus was able to acquire a comfortable residence in a fashionable part of Vienna. His business acumen on the stock-exchange and in real estate had turned him into a wealthy man; but towards the end of his life he ceased to be a conscious Jew and was eventually converted to Catholicism.

Victor Adler was not brought up in a religious atmosphere, though his teacher in religion had been none other than Moritz Güdemann, later the Chief Rabbi of Vienna. Victor appears to have had little taste for Judaism, and at a very early age to have enthusiastically embraced the credo of assimilation to German culture.[1]

He was sent by his parents to the famous Schottengymnasium, the best grammar school in Vienna. At this predominantly Catholic school Adler confronted the Jewish problem at the age of thirteen in an incident which to some extent foreshadowed his future attitude to his own heritage.[2] When his classmate and lifelong friend, Engelbert Pernerstorfer (later Adler's right-hand man in the Austrian Socialist Party), proposed to adopt a Roman constitution in the classroom, with tribunes separately elected by Jewish and Christian pupils, Adler strongly protested. He reproached his friend for failing to regard his classmates 'simply as colleagues, not as Jews and Christians'. Pernerstorfer's approach was 'seemingly tolerant', but Adler did not want tolerance, only equality. 'Where is the equality of all colleagues? If that is done you might as well erect a Jewish ghetto in our school again, and separate the Jews from the Christians by a brick wall.'[3] Adler had adopted the position which he was to defend through thick and thin in all his future political battles—that of 'a Jew who demands justice, not privileges'.[4] Neither at school, university or later in politics did Victor Adler succeed, however, in ridding himself of the Jewish predicament, which in the words of his biographer 'weighed on him even in manhood like a millstone'.[5]

Despite his genuine efforts to repress Jewish traits in his own personality, Adler could not avoid feeling slighted by the anti-Semitism of close friends.[6] Already in adolescence he developed that predilection for self-deprecating irony which was a characteristic quality of many Central European Jews. In a letter to his friend Pernerstorfer, the nineteen-year-old Adler wrote of his encounter with an attractive, cultivated Christian girl 'Imagine: me, a poor, stammering ugly Jew, boorish and clumsy, and she, beautiful, brilliant, cultured—how do I manage it?'[7]

It was as a medical student at the University of Vienna that Victor Adler, like his eminent Jewish contemporaries, Sigmund Freud (against whom he once fought a duel) and Arthur Schnitzler, first encountered the endemic anti-Semitism of the Austrian *Burschenschaften* (fraternities).[8] The distinguished Viennese surgeon Theodor Billroth had echoed widespread sentiments when he expressed alarm at the inundation of the medical faculties by hordes of poor Jewish students from Galicia and Hungary. Billroth, who ironically enough later became a supporter of the Verein zur Abwehr des Antisemitismus (Association for combating Anti-Semitism) acknowledged Jewish talent and energy: but he insisted that the racial chasm between Germans and Jews was as wide as that which had existed between ancient Teutons and the Phoenicians.[9] Adler was stung to reply in his first public appearance before the *Leseverein* of Viennese students. He did not take issue with Billroth's assertion, that Jews were flooding the university faculties, but he did challenge the theory of an unalterable Jewish 'tribal character', which had found such a fertile terrain in Austria. The young medical student maintained that '. . . Jewish blood has flowed in German battles', and although 'this does not entitle the Jews to the gratitude of the German nation', nevertheless it created 'a bond which would tie the next generation of Jews more firmly to the German people'. It was up to the Austro-Germans to choose 'whether they prefer the thorn in their flesh, or whether they will assimilate these remnants of a tribe'.[10] Somewhat apologetically, Adler added: 'I do not know whether my personal attitude to this question is not obscured by the fact that I am myself a Jew.'[11]

Two years later, in 1878, Adler resolved his doubts by adopting Protestantism, the minority religion in Catholic Austria. Both his parents subsequently followed suit—his father Salomon became a Catholic in 1884 and made a pilgrimage to Rome shortly before his death. Victor Adler's mother, who came originally from an orthodox Jewish household, was strangely enough the only member of the family to be converted out of genuine religious conviction. Years afterwards, in his Testament of 1913, Victor Adler justified his personal decision by arguing that his children would thus be spared from becoming pariahs. 'I have only become a Protestant to make complete severance from Judaism easier for my children, and to save them the stupid troubles connected in Austria with agnosticism [*Konfessionslosigkeit*].'[12] Victor Adler doubtless believed that such a step had made things easier for his children, but ironically enough, his son Friedrich, who had been baptized at the age of seven, ended up marrying a Lithuanian Jewess from an Orthodox family.

Friedrich's wife, Katharina Jacobovna Germaniskaya, insisted that they be married in a religious ceremony. When the worried Friedrich asked for his father's opinion Victor replied, 'A Jewish heart after all is also a heart, and this is more important than our cultural and aesthetic requirements'.[13] This comment reflects how far Victor Adler (and his son) had absorbed the patronizing feelings of cultivated superiority to non-assimilated Jews typical of their milieu and epoch.

Victor Adler's own conversion in 1878, the year of his marriage to a Jewess, Emma Braun (who did not undergo baptism), exemplified the commonplace desire of many Jews in Catholic Austria to throw off an awkward inheritance. Such famous contemporaries as Karl Kraus, Otto Weininger or Gustav Mahler, not to speak of Adler's brother-in-law and fellow-socialist Heinrich Braun, similarly decided to cut the Gordian knot which bound them to a despised minority. None of these individuals thereby eliminated their subjective Jewish problem; if anything it was intensified in an era where anti-Semitism had become racial as well as religious.[14] The logic of baptism did, however, push Adler towards a militant, cultural form of Pan-Germanism in the late 1870s, which was accompanied by the almost obligatory enthusiasm for Richard Wagner's music.[15] With his friend Pernerstorfer, Victor Adler became an ardent Wagnerian and member of the Deutschnationale Verein. His Pan-Germanism expressed the strong desire of many assimilationist Jews in Austria to identify with the dominant German culture, without sacrificing their liberal and radical yearnings.[16]

Pan-Germanism in the late 1870s was still anti-clerical, republican, democratic and opposed to the status quo in Austria. It therefore appeared to offer a radical alternative to the stagnation of Habsburg politics. Not only Adler but such Jewish student contemporaries as Freud and Theodor Herzl responded to its appeal until the rise of racialist anti-Semitism in the early 1880s definitely excluded all non-Aryans from the German-national camp.[17] In 1881 Adler could still contribute an article to Pernerstorfer's ultra-nationalist periodical *Deutsche Worte*, attacking the cosmopolitan liberalism of the *Neue Freie Presse*—the leading newspaper of the Monarchy, which remained a favourite target throughout his career.[18] It is difficult to assess the long-term impact of Adler's Pan-German sympathies on his socialist outlook, though there can be little doubt that they have been underestimated. In the cultural life of Austria at the time when Victor Adler was growing up, it is clear that Pan-Germanism was the dominant trend. Adler was probably a socialist at heart as early as 1870, but he saw nothing incompatible with radical German nationalism in its teachings—especially since Lassalle rather than Marx was its standard-bearer in Austria. If socialism offered the only solution to the 'social question', German nationalism stood for the revival of an Austria in danger of losing its German character.

Adler's home in the 1870s had been the meeting-place for a circle of like-minded spirits, including Pernerstorfer, Friedjung, Max Grüber, Heinrich Braun and Siegfried Lipiner, who all felt a deep sympathy for the newly founded German Empire created by Prussian force of arms. This enthusiasm was to shock the young socialist Karl Kautsky, who first came into contact with Adler's Pan-German milieu of artists and intellectuals a few years later. The ideals of these Pan-German radicals were at first somewhat vague and nebulous—born out of their alienation and discontent with nineteenth-century liberalism. They read Schopenhauer (Adler's favourite author in his younger days), Wagner and Nietzsche and dreamt of a new and vital German culture which would combine intellectual and emotional elements into a creative whole. The idealization of the German *Volk* was the strongest political element in the anti-liberal ideology of these student radicals. The regeneration of German culture through art and music remained its common intellectual starting-point. The involvement of Victor Adler in the student reading societies and then in the *deutschnational* movement was therefore perfectly understandable in the context of his time. Anti-Semitism was as yet not an article of faith in the movement, and the irrationalist implications of its aesthetic, symbolic style of politics by no means evident. The high-point of Adler's Pan-German involvement came in 1882, when he collaborated with Georg Ritter von Schoenerer, the leader of the German nationalist movement in Habsburg Austria, on the Linz Programme.[19] Schoenerer and the nationalist historian Heinrich Friedjung (an assimilated Jew) were preoccupied primarily with the encirclement of the Austro-Germans by the more numerous and culturally more backward Slavs. At the same time, Schoenerer also had a feeling for social issues, and it was this part of his political programme which Victor Adler helped to formulate. Radical Pan-Germanism proved, however, no more than a stepping-stone for Victor Adler on his road to creating a new kind of Marxist politics in Austria.

Adler's conversion to socialism grew out of a number of circumstances, only some of them connected with his ethnic background. The *Armeleut-Doktor* after completing his medical studies had opened a practice at 19 Berggasse, Alsergrund. Increasingly he realized the appalling conditions under which the industrial proletariat laboured. In the 1880s Viennese workers faced a seventy-hour week, for which many factories still employed child and female labour, while the housing crisis and high cost of living caused further ravages in the health of the workers. Victor Adler was increasingly aware that the social question was of decisive importance, and could not be solved by the feudal or bourgeois parties, blinded as they were by their egoistic class interests.

His 1883 encounters with Engels in England and Bebel in Germany first made Adler conscious of the Marxist solution to the problems of an emerging industrial society. But without the racialism of the Schoenerer movement, which in 1885 had introduced a specifically anti-Jewish paragraph into the Linz Programme, it is doubtful whether Adler would have turned to socialism.[20] By then it had already become impossible, even for a converted Jew, to be active within the Deutschnationale Verein.

The exclusion of Pan-German Jews like Adler from *völkisch* clubs, societies and associations revealed the rapid progress which fanatical nationalism was making in Austria. This heightened the attraction that socialist ideology began to exert on those Germanized Jews like Adler and Heinrich Braun who had never abandoned their youthful radicalism, and found themselves thrust into a marginal position within the majority culture. Since they were already alienated from Jewish tradition, and excluded by the clerical and nationalist parties from any active political role, the labour movement appeared to offer them a perfect escape from their marginality, and the ultimate revenge on bourgeois society. For these Jewish intellectuals, Marxism became more than just a new political home, it was the universalist, *charismatic* idea of the future which had replaced the faith of their fathers.[21]

Significantly, Victor Adler waited until 1886, the year of his father's death, before finally commiting himself to the Austrian labour movement. In a letter to Karl Kautsky he wrote, 'Now that my father is dead, I have become my own master'.[22] His correspondence with Kautsky from this period indicates that he had by no means abandoned the *Deutschnationalismus* of his Wagnerite student years. He remained as opposed as his former comrade Schoenerer to the 'Slavization' of Austria, and in 1886 told Kautsky that to be genuinely 'communist' one had first to be 'national'.[23]

It was self-evident to Adler, that social-democratic internationalism in Austria presupposed German cultural hegemony. 'As Germans, we may not care very much whether the Czechs learn German, but as social democrats, we must positively desire it.'[24] Not only German nationalism but also something of the liberal heritage was transmitted by Victor Adler to the Austrian labour movement of which from 1889 until his death in 1918 he was the father-figure and undisputed leader. Although the Austrian social democrats, like the German nationalists and Christian-Socials, were anti-liberal in their mass appeal, their language and moral values were essentially those of reason, moderation, progress and enlightenment.[25]

The movement which Victor Adler personified before the First World War believed in the theoretical inevitability of revolution, but its methods remained rational, its preoccupations educational, and its tactics conciliatory. Not for nothing was Victor Adler known as the *Hofrat* (councillor) of the revolution, although his party's programme challenged the antiquated Habsburg regime. Adler's supreme virtue as a socialist leader was his tactical acumen and ability to play the honest broker among opposing factions of his own party.[26] It was this essentially practical intelligence and diplomatic skill which enabled him to preserve Austrian socialist unity in the period before 1914. Already in August 1886, in a letter to Kautsky, he ironically alluded to his capacity for negotiation and compromise as a 'Jewish' quality. Mentioning the new socialist newspaper *Gleichheit*, which he had set up, and largely financed out of his own pocket, Adler added:

> I haven't the slightest vocation for quiet academic work, but I believe myself a very serviceable hawker of foreign ideas (we Jews seem to be almost predestined for peddling)—whether as an agitator, or as a journalist—I will try both.[27]

As a 'peddler' of socialism, Adler did indeed prove remarkably successful, for within three years he had healed the split between radicals and moderates, which had bedevilled Austrian socialism throughout the 1880s. After the Hainfeld Party Congress of 1889, which finally put social democracy on the political map of Austria, Adler was undisputed leader of the party. Only a superb politican and masterful tactician could have preserved the unity of the party, under the conditions prevailing in the Habsburg Monarchy. Not surprisingly, Kautsky, Bebel and Engels were full of admiration for the political realism, the tenacity and devotion, of the Austrian leader, so free of fanaticism and utopian illusions about the prospects of the labour movement under Habsburg rule. Friedrich Engels, in a letter of 1890 to an Austrian correspondent condemning anti-Semitism, singled out the sacrifices of 'my friend Victor Adler' as a proof of how much socialism owed to the Jews.[28] Even such a scathing critic of Austro-Marxism as Trotsky could write in 1917 that Adler's great strength as a leader was his understanding of men and his sense of the possible. Trotsky also recalled that 'Adler, a psychiatrist in his old field, medicine, frequently approached political events from a psychopathological viewpoint, "especially in Austria", as he would ironically say'.[29]

For all his passionate belief in socialism, there was an element of profound pessimism in Victor Adler's view of human nature. The attacks to which he was subjected as a Jew as well as a Marxist in Habsburg Vienna doubtless reinforced the ironic scepticism with which he viewed society and politics in his native land.

The 'Jewish question' could not be banished to the periphery of Austrian political life, once it became an ideological linchpin of two rival movements, which competed after 1889 for mass support with the Social Democrats. Karl Lueger's Christian-Social Party and Schoenerer's Pan-Germans exploited the anti-Semitism of the economically declining petty bourgeoisie, the lower clergy, the students, shopkeepers and petty officialdom, with growing success in the 1890s.

The involvement of Jews in Austrian social democracy simply added a new dimension to the backlash against liberalism which kept the 'Jewish question' in the centre of public attention. The fact that some Jews had embraced an ideology which was so obviously subversive of traditional society was grist to the mill of the Austrian anti-Semites.

After 1889 Victor Adler found himself the target of an extraordinarily vulgar campaign directed at the 'Jewish' leadership of the Social Democratic Party. The Luegerites accused him of having been subsidized by 'Semitic' businessmen, though his anti-liberalism was as pronounced as their own; the Schoenerites attacked his incitement of the 'Aryan' workers, though Adler's *Deutschnationalismus* ceded nothing in conviction to that of the Pan-Germans.

Victor Adler's attitude to such aspersions was exceedingly ambivalent, as was his whole position on the Jewish issue. Indeed, no socialist in the German-speaking world since Marx and Lassalle was to go so far in his willingness to compromise with anti-Semitism. In one of his earliest comments on the Jewish question, in 1887, Adler felt compelled to admit, 'Whoever participates in Austrian public life finds the greatest difficulty in not becoming an anti-Semite'.[30] His own paper *Gleichheit* (Equality) consistently warned the Austrian workers not to 'commit themselves to the Jews in their stand against anti-Semitism', but to maintain strict neutrality.[31] Adler opposed Schoenerer's proposed legislation against the immigration of foreign Jews to German Austria, not because it was anti-Semitic, but because he recognized that such agitation might one day be directed against the labour movement.[32] However, Adler still tried to approach the issue from an objective Marxist standpoint: he argued that the Jews had become scapegoats because certain hereditary qualities, nourished by the ghetto, had blossomed in the liberal era and transformed them into dangerous economic competitors. 'During the period when the law of might prevailed, they were nothing, but when the law of exchange predominated, they emerged into the foreground.'[33] They had admittedly heightened some of the worst features of capitalism, but 'if the Jews are "the kings of the epoch", then the epoch is responsible, not the Jews'.[34]

As a Marxist, Adler recognized that Jews had not originated capitalism, nor did they have any monopoly on exploitation, as the anti-Semites pretended. The peasantry and impoverished craftsmen who blamed them for their misery were ignorant and incapable of understanding the mechanisms of the world economy. The solution to anti-Semitism could only come in a 'socialist society which will lead Ahasuerus, the wandering Jew to the grave!' In such a society, Adler emphasized, 'Jewish' qualities would lose their power and influence. As for the working class, it should not be bamboozled 'either by Jews or by anti-Semites into pulling their chestnuts out of the fire'.

Adler was theoretically in favour of neutrality towards anti-

Semitism, but in practice *Gleichheit* directed its fire far more severely against liberal 'philo-Semitism'. Adler never tired of ridiculing liberal apologetics against the new movement, and lampooning its attempts to enlist socialist support against the anti-Semites. 'When the class-conscious workers, who are first and foremost anti-capitalist, and therefore prepared for anything but the defence of capitalist Jewry, take a stand against the ravings of anti-Semitism, then there is a shout of Hallelujah!'[35] Adler insinuated that liberal efforts to secure working-class support against Lueger and Schoenerer only heightened distrust of the middle classes in proletarian ranks. The proletariat was indifferent to the internecine conflict between 'Aryan' and 'Jewish' capital, and would never become a tool of either feudal-clerical or liberal interests. In the philo- and anti-Semitic debate, Adler was primarily concerned with preventing the labour movement from taking sides. In an article in *Gleichheit*, written in January 1889, he declared, 'The workers of Austria want neither "Jewish" nor "Christian" exploitation and will not allow themselves to be used as a battering-ram either for or against the Jews'.[36]

The socialist press sought to follow Adler's example by exposing the hypocrisy of both protagonists, and the essential unity of interests between rich Jews and the anti-Semites. The latter were criticized for ignoring the Christian millionaires, while the Viennese 'Jew-press' was pilloried for ignoring the social question and whitewashing capitalist interests. Where money was involved, *Gleichheit* noted, Jewish bankers and press magnates became 'respectable' and the Don Quixotes of Austrian anti-Semitism fell silent:

> The Jewish proletarian, the poor Jewish woman peddlar is treated with all the brutality of true Aryan race-pride; while the "Jewish question" is being solved by such humane methods, kings are compelled to open their doors to Jewish money-lenders; and anti-Semitism does not rear its head! Poor Jews are hanged, but rich Jews are presented at Court.[37]

Victor Adler's reaction to the emergence of Austrian anti-Semitism was determined not only by the Marxist ideology of the class-struggle, but also by his marked personal antipathy to capitalist Jewry and the powerful liberal press which was partly controlled by Jews.

Liberal papers like the *Neue Freie Presse,* the *Wiener Allgemeine Zeitung* and the *Österreichische Volkszeitung* were especially attacked by socialists when they made overtures to the working class. In Adler's opinion the flattering comments about the 'enlightened' and intelligent workers to be found in the Establishment press were a pathetic admission of weakness. They were motivated solely by Austro-liberal fears at the success of the Christian-Social anti-Semites in the municipal elections. Already in January 1889 Victor Adler had written, 'The fear of the anti-Semites felt by the Jews is only equalled by the fear of the Jews by the anti-Semites'.[38] It was typical of Adler's whole approach to the Jewish problem that he always insisted on equating philo- and anti-Semitism, as if they were somehow comparable phenomena, of equal danger to the labour movement. The Marxist rationale for this strange posture consisted of saying that philo-Semitism was identical with the defence of 'Jewish' capitalism: on these very dubious grounds, Victor Adler emphasized with obvious satisfaction that socialists would never protect the interests of the Jewish community. With some pride, the Viennese *Arbeiter-Zeitung* noted in November 1889 that the socialist press 'gives as little satisfaction to the Jewish exploiters as the anti-Semitic press. This success is sufficient for us and shows that in this matter we are moving in the right direction'.[39]

The social and political conditions which held sway in Vienna at the end of the nineteenth century, to some extent explain this attitude. Jewish influence in the press, the banks, commerce, the arts and sciences was indeed strong—though by no means as omnipresent as anti-Semites maintained. Similarly, the so-called 'Jewish' press did largely mould liberal opinion, which socialists attacked for its failure to extend the suffrage to the workers. The Marxist labour movement fought above all for the democratization of the political system, and this only appeared possible by undermining the liberal status quo. The Austrian proletariat was completely disenfranchized until 1897, and universal suffrage was only introduced in 1907; the socialists looked in the 1890s to the Christian-Social and German nationalist anti-Semites to accomplish this task, and not to a largely defunct Austro-liberalism. It seemed tactically more astute to Victor Adler and his colleagues to allow the anti-Semites to crush Austro-liberalism, thus allowing the socialists to emerge as the main opposition party. In advancing towards its Marxist utopia, the Austrian labour movement was prepared to do business with the 'socialism of fools', even if the Jews were to be the first victims of this detour.

Under Victor Adler's leadership, the Austrian party, unlike the SPD in Germany, adopted the view that the racialism of the Christian masses had to be mollycoddled and cajoled and blame laid at the door of the Jewish community.[40] The prejudices of the mindless mob were tolerantly excused, but any action of Jewish self-defence was either ridiculed or condemned outright. This policy cannot be explained simply by reference to the 'Marxist' neutrality advocated by Victor Adler in his theoretical assessment of anti-Semitism. Instead of mobilizing a movement dedicated to the removal of all inequality and discrimination, against racial fanaticism and anti-Semitic propaganda, Victor Adler seemed more preoccupied with proving that the Austrian socialists were not a 'Jewish protective-guard' (*Judenschutztruppe*).[41] On 25th April, 1890, for example, the *Arbeiter-Zeitung* reminded a Jewish sympathizer:

> For speculators, there has never been any room, neither will the workers let themselves be used as a battering-ram against the anti-Semites; . . . if Dr Elbogen expects them to form a voluntary security guard against anti-Semitism—then we can only pity him.[42]

This was typical of the kind of argument put forward by Victor Adler to justify his non-intervention in the anti-Semitic campaign being waged with great effect by Karl Lueger's Christian-Social Party in the 1890s. The fear of being identified with unpopular Jewish interests clearly played a predominant role in determining this strategy. It also underlay Adler's attitude at the International Socialist Congress in Brussels (1891), where he influenced fellow-socialists against passing a resolution expressing solidarity with the persecuted Russian-Jewish workers.[43] Instead, the Congress produced a resolution which condemned equally 'anti- and philo-Semitic excitations' as diversions from the class struggle. This was precisely the policy which Adler had adopted in the Austrian labour movement, and at the Brussels Congress it was supported by a number of anti-Semitic French socialists.

During the 1890s Victor Adler faithfully followed the line laid down at Brussels, opposing any deviation of the socialist movement 'into philo- or anti-Semitic channels'. Far from expressing concern at the anti-Semitic successes in the Landtag elections, Adler actually welcomed them, declaring in 1896, 'The Social Democrats desired an anti-Semitic victory, so that the latter could show publicly how their promises will appear in practice'.[44] Since the Luegerites were eliminating the last bastions of liberal influence in the municipal council, their progress was not only desirable but historically inevitable in Marxist terms. Indeed, by the mid-1890s Adler and the Austrian socialists even began to adopt anti-Semitic rhetoric themselves, referring publicly to 'Jewish' exploiters lording it over 'Aryan' workers. Adler's favourite reproach against Karl Lueger, the Christian-Social leader who stood poised for election as Mayor of Vienna in 1897, was his friendship with wealthy Jews.[45] It gave him an excellent opportunity to hit back at the mindless propaganda about the 'Jew-ridden' Social Democratic Party. Sarcastically, he observed that 'even though the anti-Semites have recently invited the richest Jews to the annual ball of the City of Vienna, they maintain that the Socialist Party is led by Jews'.[46]

The constant accusations against the 'Jewish leadership' of the Socialist Party were, however, an unending source of embarrassment to Victor Adler. Neither his conversion, his indifference bordering on self-hatred towards his own ancestry, nor his onslaughts against the

'Jew-press' made any difference to his unscrupulous opponents. During the electoral campaign of 1897 a German nationalist speaker, Dr Mayreder, took Adler to task for leading the 'Aryan' working class astray. The Socialist leader retorted somewhat defensively:

> Dr Mayreder takes the position that the socialist workers are splendid fellows but that their leaders are evil men. The gentlemen speak, however, only of the 'Jewish' leaders (there are among the anti-Semites more Jews than among us) but they never speak of the great mass of leading Aryan comrades.[47]

Not only did this kind of reply implicitly accept a quasi-racist terminology, it consciously sought to make the stigma of 'Jewishness' boomerang on the anti-Semites. It became a favoured technique of Adler and his colleagues to brand their Christian-Social opponents as *Judenknechte*, accomplices of 'Jewish' capitalism in the exploitation of 'Aryan' labour.[48] This type of socialist propaganda amply demonstrated that, on the Left as well as the Right, the term 'Jew' was identified with 'capitalist'. At the 1897 Socialist Party Congress a Jewish delegate from Lipnik (Moravia), Jakob Brod, confronted Victor Adler with the dangerous ambiguity of his policy. Brod pointed out:

> Until now, the party has been at pains to avoid the impression of being a Jewish party. It wanted to prove that the Social Democrats were not lackeys to the Jew. But I say to you that even if we live a hundred years, we will never convince the Viennese petty-bourgeois that the terms "Jew" and "capitalist" are not synonymous.[49]

Brod went on to criticize Adler for indifference to the Jewish proletariat in Galicia, Bukovina and the Leopoldstadt ghetto—'the most oppressed, miserable and backward proletariat of all'.[50] He complained that the party under Adler's leadership had departed from the principles of socialist internationalism and pursued a policy which encouraged general distrust of the Jews. The replies of the party executive, led by 'Comrade' Adler, could only have confirmed these suspicions, for the mood of the Congress was unmistakably hostile. Victor Adler himself reminded delegates that 'the capitalist bourgeoisie here in Vienna has a Jewish complexion. That the Jews must suffer this is sad, but we are also tired of always finding Jews in our soup'.[51]

He also maintained that 'the importance of the Jewish question has been greatly exaggerated . . . because of the anti-Semites, rich Jews appear as miserable and oppressed paupers. . . '[52] Adler dismissed anti-Semitism as an empty slogan of the Luegerites who intended to preserve capitalism whether it was 'Jewish' or 'Christian' in character. Adler noted that since Lueger had assumed office as Mayor of

Vienna he no longer spoke about 'liberation from the yoke of Jewish capital'. He drove home his critique of Christian-Social hypocrisy by remarking that Christian capitalism 'is no less Jewish than Jewish capitalism'.[53]

Adler's comment at the 1897 Party Congress underlined his one-sided view of the Jewish question, above all his anxiety to prevent Austrian social democracy from being identified with 'Jewish' interests.[54] This even extended to the point of introducing an unofficial 'Aryan' paragraph in the selection of Socialist candidates for the parliamentary elections of 1897.[55] Although Jewish intellectuals already played a prominent role in the life of the party, only Wilhelm Ellenbogen was actually put forward as a candidate, in a remote Silesian constituency. Jakob Brod in a letter to Kautsky complained bitterly about this discrimination, which he blamed on Adler's 'prejudices' and the latent anti-Semitism among Austrian socialists.[56] Adler himself confessed that he did not want to overload the party with Jewish intellectuals, and he regarded his own origins as a heavy enough cross for Austrian social democracy to bear. Such an acceptance of popular prejudices may seem surprising in a man with the human warmth, generosity, idealism and sceptical rationalism of Victor Adler; but one should not underestimate the galvanizing force which this self-hatred could have in driving socialists who had rejected their background to identify all the more strongly with the working classes.[57]

Adler's frequent juxtaposition of the Christian masses and the 'Jewish' exploiters faithfully reflected his subconscious wish to become a non-Jew by ostentatiously repudiating capitalism. By placing his personal fortune at the disposition of the party, and devoting his energies to serving the proletarian cause, Adler partly accomplished this dream. Only the clerical and populist anti-Semitism directed at the *Judensozi* (the 'Jewish' social democrats) prevented its complete fulfilment. Such rhetoric could also be turned, however, against the Christian-Socials, just as Adler's party had used it against the Austro-liberals in the early 1890s. For example, Karl Lueger, the 'Christian' Mayor of Vienna, was bitterly satirized in the socialist press after 1897 for his friendship with the Jewish business class and newspaper magnates. He was frequently depicted as the 'betrayer' of the impoverished petty-bourgeoisie who had voted him to power, and as the protector of Rothschild and the Jewish capitalist class.[58]

Victor Adler did nothing to discourage this campaign, and at the 1898 Party Congress informed delegates that Lueger had been branded as a *Judenknecht* by some of his more fanatic followers. He aroused widespread mirth by adding that 'the last anti-Semite will disappear with the last Jew'—a somewhat cynical comment which epitomized his general attitude.[59] His friend and chief lieutenant, Engelbert Pernerstorfer, went still further in his speech on anti-Semitism, claiming that Schoenerer's *völkisch* propaganda was based on an indisputable truth—'Namely, that the Jews are Jews'.[60] The pity of it, according to Pernerstorfer, was that Karl Marx had said much the same thing as Schoenerer, with far more wit, in his 'Zur Judenfrage', over fifty years earlier.[61] Austro-Marxists like Adler and Pernerstorfer evidently regarded Marx's essay as the last word on the Jewish problem. It was indeed a convenient ideological rationalization for prejudices with which they had been imbued as German nationalist students.

In 1898, as the Schoenerite agitation found renewed support among the Sudeten Germans, Adler opposed the demands of social-democratic organizations in Bohemia to combat it more vigorously. Once again, as with the Christian-Social movement of the early 1890s, the official socialist position was to support any agitation which undermined the status quo, even when it was openly chauvinist in character.[62]

Adler also reacted with indifference to the two great *causes célèbres* at the turn of the twentieth century, where Jews were victimized for racial and religious reasons.

The Hilsner Affair of 1899 underlined the fact that the medieval blood-libel against the Jews could still mobilize popular feelings in a so-called 'civilized' state. An innocent Jewish shoemaker's assistant, Leopold Hilsner, had been charged with the ritual murder of a young Christian girl at Polna, in Bohemia. The socialist press naturally opposed the clerical and nationalist agitation in Bohemia which built up around the Affair, but carefully avoided taking any stand which could be construed as sympathetic to the Jews.[63] Similarly, it played down the anti-Semitic crusade in France which developed out of the Dreyfus Affair—concentrating its fire against the liberal press in Vienna for adopting a pro-Jewish position.[64] In Victor Adler's opinion, the whole Affair was merely a storm in a teacup, grossly inflated by liberals and anti-Semites for propaganda purposes.

Having already demonstrated his indifference to the hapless Hilsner (who had been sentenced to death—later commuted to life imprisonment) and the unfortunate Dreyfus, it was not surprising that Adler should also resist any intervention on behalf of Menahem Beilis of Kiev.

The Beilis case of 1911–13, like the Hilsner Affair, was based on the grotesque charge of ritual murder, directed this time at an innocent Jewish cobbler. Despite the world-wide outcry against the trial, and protests made by many socialists, Adler refused to associate himself in any way with efforts to secure justice for Beilis. His attitude was rigidly faithful to the line he had laid down for the Austrian labour movement after 1889—namely, that there should be no diversion of the class-struggle into 'philo- or anti-Semitic channels'. In an era when anti-Semitic movements were constantly gaining ground in Europe, when Lueger was master of Vienna, when the Dreyfus Affair shook France, when millions of Jews were fleeing pogroms in Russia, Victor Adler and his Austrian socialist party felt no obligation to revise their position. Indeed, Adler was reported by one source as exclaiming in exasperation at the Beilis case, 'The Jews, always the Jews. As if the whole world revolved around the Jews!'[65]

Adler's strategy in dealing with the Jewish problem was primarily dictated by his embarrassment at any reminder of his own origins. The various Marxist rationalizations of socialist 'neutrality' on this issue were secondary to the psychological factor which distorted his whole perspective. Neither Bebel, Kautsky or Lenin felt any inner compulsion to link 'Jewish exploiters' with the anti-Semites as common enemies of social democracy. Admittedly, Lueger's rule in Vienna proved detrimental only to the poor Jewish peddlers and did not undermine the prosperity of Jewish bankers and industrialists like Rothschild, Guttmann and Taussig; this provided a convenient justification for the attitude of Austrian socialists.

However, the fact is that the Adlerian social democrats before 1914 scarcely bothered with the plight of the Jewish proletariat in Galicia and Bukovina, except to oppose their aspirations for cultural-national autonomy. Had they taken their own doctrine of class-struggle more seriously they would have paid far more attention to the broad mass of impoverished Jews, who were numerous enough even in the Leopoldstadt ghetto of Vienna. Instead, they chose to concentrate almost exclusively on the financial and commercial élite of Austrian Jewry, whose position they were as eager to undermine as their anti-Semitic adversaries.

The Jewish masses in the hinterlands of the Habsburg Monarchy were primarily Yiddish-speaking *Ostjuden*, whose rapidly declining economic conditions remained of peripheral concern to assimilated German-speaking socialists like Victor Adler and his followers.[66] The problem only impinged on their consciousness when Jewish workers in Galicia began to demand the right to separate proletarian organizations able to defend their specific cultural and economic needs.[67] A conflict developed between the so-called Jewish 'separatists' and the narrowly nationalistic Polish Socialist Party of Galicia, which advocated total assimilation of the Jewish masses to the Polish culture and language. Victor Adler and his colleagues, predictably enough, backed the Galician Poles to the hilt in their intransigent hostility to Jewish autonomy, whether it was advanced by the Jewish Social Democrats (ZPSD) or by the Austrian Poale-Zion.

Even modest demands for cultural autonomy based on the Austrian social-democratic programme of 1899, when they were proposed by Jewish working-class autonomists, were categorically repudiated. For assimilated Austro-Marxists like Victor Adler, any manifestation of Jewish nationalism, whether Zionist or anti-Zionist, was futile, irrelevant and unacceptable. The notion of a 'Jewish nationality' could not be taken seriously by a socialist leader, deeply impregnated with *Deutschnationalismus* and preoccupied with preserving the unity of the Pan-Austrian party he had so painstakingly built up in the 1890s. A man of Adler's background and general outlook clearly had no interest either in a separate Jewish labour movement, or in Zionism. In this respect at least his views were identical with those of the majority of liberal, assimilated Jews in Vienna, Budapest, Prague and Western Austria, whose capitalistic role he otherwise so vigorously combated.

The Marxist intelligentsia in Austria, like their liberal opponents, condemned Jewish nationalism as 'reactionary'; it was the demise of capitalism which would finally bring about the extinction of the 'Jewish nation'. Zionism was nothing but a hopeless and ridiculous attempt in their eyes to revive the defunct corpse of a people doomed to irreversible dissolution. Adler's paper, the Viennese *Arbeiter-Zeitung*, in its deprecation of Zionism as an impractical, romantic and ultra-reactionary utopia, showed the same tendency to despise the Jews as in its earlier attacks on the liberal press.[68] The popular stereotypes which had emerged in its long campaign against liberal capitalism were simply transferred to Zionism, as the last attempt by the Jews to escape their 'inevitable' fate—absorption in the majority culture.

Victor Adler's negative attitude to the Jewish question had clearly been conditioned by his own conversion, his early attraction to German nationalism and his assimilationist convictions. Marxism subsequently offered a seemingly rational justification for his deep-rooted desire to throw off a burden that seemed to him no more than an anachronism. The potency of anti-Semitism in Austrian politics ensured, however, that he was never allowed to forget his origins. The result was that, although he showed great tenacity and courage in the defence of his Marxist beliefs, he was evasive and unconvincing when it came to the Jewish issue. His attitude was best summed up by the Belgian socialist Camille Huysmans, who had pressed him for his opinion about anti-Semitism during the First World War. With his inimitable irony, Adler had replied, 'One must have Jews, comrade, but not too many'.[69]

Would Victor Adler have revised his views had he lived to see the emergence of Nazism, the Holocaust and the birth of the State of Israel? One cannot, of course, say with absolute certainty, but the subsequent attitude of his son, Friedrich (1879–1960), who survived the Hitler era and was a leading figure in the Socialist International, suggests a likely answer. In 1949, in an article for the Swiss socialist paper *Volksrecht*, Friedrich Adler wrote:

> I, like my father, always considered the complete assimilation of the Jews not only desirable but also possible, and even the bestialities of

> Hitler have not shaken my view that Jewish nationalism is bound to lead to reactionary tendencies—namely, to the resurrection of a language which has been dead for almost two thousand years and to the rebirth of an antiquated religion.

Not even the advent of Hitlerian fascism had made Friedrich Adler change his mind. Like his father, he rejected Zionism, for trying to impede what he mistakenly considered to be an inevitable process of assimilation.

CHAPTER 6

Otto Bauer, the Fatalist

'Judaism has always reached the summit of its achievement wherever Jewish natural talents and European cultural traditions have met and cross-fertilized each other.'

Otto Bauer

'This is how I imagine the young Marx'.

Karl Kautsky

Otto Bauer, the most brilliant theoretician of Austro-Marxism and leader of the Austrian Social Democratic Party in the inter-war period, was born in Vienna in September 1881. Like many leading Austrian socialists of Jewish origin, his family originated from Bohemia. His father Philip Bauer was a wealthy industrialist who owned textile factories in Nachód (North Bohemia) and Warnsdorf, near the Saxon border.[1] His mother, Kathe, to whom Otto was strongly attached, was a pious, somewhat ascetic woman who seems to have transmitted her sense of order and diligence to her precocious son. Otto Bauer grew up, then, in the liberal-humanist milieu of the Jewish bourgeoisie, which provided so many leaders of the socialist movement in the last decades of the Austro-Hungarian Monarchy. There is no evidence to suggest that he had any interest in or knowledge of Judaism, or that he was acquainted with the Yiddish language—still the lingua franca of the Jewish masses in the Habsburg Empire. Otto Bauer's parents were already thoroughly assimilated to German culture, though they also spoke Czech, which gave a more cosmopolitan flavour to the household. The one characteristic feature of the Jewish heritage which they probably did communicate to their son was a love of learning for its own sake. The multi-faceted interests of Otto Bauer, which later extended to sociology, history, philosophy, literature, anthropology and pyschology as well as Marxist politics, were first developed as a child. Already at the age of ten he had written a play about the fall of Napoleon, which was unusual for its historical knowledge and rich vocabulary.[2]

Otto Bauer had been attracted to socialism in his teens, and after obtaining a law degree from the University of Vienna he became active in the Marx-Study Circle in the imperial capital. Together with the economist Rudolf Hilferding, the philosopher Max Adler and the jurist Karl Renner, Otto Bauer was from 1904 onward a leader of the Neo-Marxian school in Vienna. The most original feature of Bauer's contribution to Marxist thought was his reassessment of the 'national question'. It was in this context that he also came to consider the Jewish problem, though remaining himself personally remote from Jewish concerns. Bauer's preoccupation with the national problem was not surprising at a time when nationality conflicts were threatening to tear the Habsburg monarchy asunder. It was clear that if the Austrian Social Democrats were to make any headway as a political force in the Monarchy they would have to give some consideration to the strength of nationalist feelings. The conflict between Germans and Czechs in particular threatened the federal structure of the Social Democratic Party in Austria, which was the only supra-national political grouping in the Monarchy. The Brünn programme of the Socialist Party (1899) had shown the way forward to a reorientation of Marxist thought on the national problem in Austria-Hungary. The writings of Karl Renner had dealt with the constitutional aspects of the issue, seeking to defuse the political passions generated by national differences. But it was left to Otto Bauer in his classic work *Die Nationalitätenfrage und die Sozialdemokratie* (1907) to make an original and coherent synthesis of the existing literature, and indeed to open entirely new horizons for Marxist research. This was an impressive enough achievement for a 26-year-old theorist, whose intellectual gifts had prompted Karl Kautsky to remark to Friedrich Adler two years earlier that this was how he imagined the young Marx.[3] In the same year (1907) Bauer was appointed secretary to the Parliamentary socialist group in the Austrian Parliament, and became one of the founders and editors of *Der Kampf*, a monthly review which soon emerged as the chief theoretical organ of Austrian social democracy.[4]

Kautsky's comparison of Otto Bauer with the young Marx is particularly interesting if we apply it to their respective analyses of the Jewish question. Both of these 'non-Jewish Jews' were approximately the same age when they came to formulate their views on this problem—and in both cases it was dealt with as an incidental feature of a broader theoretical structure. Judaism in itself was of no concern either to Marx or to the young Otto Bauer. What had interested the former was its relation to political and human emancipation in general; what concerned Otto Bauer was whether the Jews were a nation and its implications for his theory of the national problem. In both cases theory was also related to a practical issue—the struggle for Jewish emancipation in Germany during the 1840s and the demand for Jewish national autonomy in Austria-Hungary at the turn of the twentieth century. Finally, as I intend to show, Otto Bauer no less than Karl Marx showed a clear psychological bias in his treatment of this issue—which was not unrelated to the unconscious suppression of his own origins.[5]

Bauer's approach to the 'Jewish question', considered in the context of his definition of the nation as 'an aggregate of people bound into a community of character by a community of fate', contained an anomaly from the outset. The definition of nationality in terms of 'community of fate' (*Schicksalsgemeinschaft*)—a fruitful and novel concept in Marxist literature—did not specifically link it with one territory or one language, let alone a state. Were not the Jews perhaps the best surviving example of a 'community of fate', having preserved their national character, religion and sense of solidarity for over two millennia, despite their dispersion and their lack of a state? Was it not a 'community of fate' which had marked them off from other peoples and enabled them to transmit their physical and spiritual characteristics intact down through the generations? This was the kind of approach to the problem one might have expected from Otto Bauer, given the definitions and terminology he had employed throughout his study. Moreover, in the early part of his book he had explicitly admitted, 'The Jews have no common language, and nevertheless they are a nation'.

But in his chapter on Jewish autonomy Otto Bauer suddenly discarded the framework of analysis which he had so profitably used to illuminate problems of national psychology, cultural divergences and their relationship to material factors and processes of class differentiation.[6] Instead he returned to the view of the young Marx that Jews had survived in medieval feudal society as a 'nation' only because they were moneylenders, bankers and traders. With the rise of capitalism the Christians were becoming Jews according to the famous formula of Marx. By this Otto Bauer evidently meant that Judaism, like Christianity, was no more than superstructure erected on a capitalist economic basis, which would dissolve once the social conditions which had produced it disappeared.

Bauer, who was writing sixty years after Marx about the Jews of Russia, Poland, and Lithuania, as well as the non-assimilated masses in Galicia and Bukovina, was applying an outmoded and highly questionable analysis to a very different group of people.[7] In order to preserve the theory he had to do violence to the facts. Thus the Jews, a pre-eminently 'historical' people, become in Bauer's definition a non-historical nation, a 'historyless people'.

> In so far as the Jews in Europe are still a nation, they have the character of a historyless nation. For since they do not possess those classes which are above all bearers of cultural development in a class society, their culture is stunted, their language decayed and they have no national literature.[8]

This assertion was manifestly untrue, and could perhaps be explained by Otto Bauer's ignorance of Yiddish literature and of the cultural renaissance of East European Jewry at the very time he was writing. But there are passages in his book where he does show an awareness of the national dimension of Yiddish literature, and of the psychological transformation in the ghetto Jew after the Russian revolution of 1905. The stature of the Jewish labour movement in Russia as a result of the self-defence organized by the Jewish Bund against the pogroms had given a new heroic dimension to the struggle of the Jewish masses for their social and national liberation. Otto Bauer mentioned these facts, but gave them a distorted interpretation which brought them in line with his faulty Marxist premises regarding the Jewish problem. Instead of dealing with the concrete issue of whether or not Jews had the same right to self-determination as other nationalities in the Habsburg Empire—Germans, Poles, Czechs, Slovaks, Slovenes, Ukrainians (Ruthenes), etc.—Bauer shifted his attention to those processes of modern capitalism which were undermining their distinct identity.

Bauer's main argument was that Western and Central European

Jewry was undergoing an irreversible process of de-nationalization.[9] As an extra-territorial people without a common language or culture, the Jews were particularly vulnerable to the assimilatory power of modern capitalism. They were gradually being forced to adopt the culture, habits and customs of the nations in whose midst they lived. Capitalist production, by making Jew and Christian economically interdependent and eliminating the specifically Jewish economic functions, was levelling out the last distinct characteristics of the Jews. This process of assimilation would inevitably penetrate even the economically backward areas of Austria-Hungary like Galicia and Bukovina, thereby dissolving the last untouched reservoir of Jewish nationhood. It would free the Jews of the Polish ghetto from their grinding poverty, grant them social mobility and the possibility of dispersing into diverse branches of modern industrial production.

The essence of Bauer's case was to prove that the Jews had no future as a nation, and that therefore it could not be in the interests of the Jewish workers of Galicia to demand cultural-national autonomy. This was one might have thought, a matter for the Jews themselves rather than for Bauer or any other theoretician to comment on. Marx and Engels had been rash enough in 1848 to assert that the Czechs and the South-Slav peoples were nations without a future, and their predictions, as Otto Bauer well knew, had proved mistaken.[10] Why then did he repeat their mistake, and deviate from his own theory of nationality, in the case of the Jews? Moreover, was there not an element of emotional prejudice, perhaps even anti-Semitism, in Bauer's denial to the Jewish workers of elementary rights which he conceded to other national minorities—including the most backward peasant nations of the Austro-Hungarian Empire?

One can see this feature of Bauer's discussion most clearly in his picture of the Galician ghetto-Jew. He evidently believed that the Yiddish language (spoken by 90 per cent of Galician Jews) reflected the 'social psychology of a dead epoch', and that Yiddish schools exercised a pernicious influence on the schoolchildren. It imbued them 'with a medieval *Weltanschauung* and the life-habits of a Jewish tavern-keeper'.[11] Worse still, it would perpetuate a traditional way of life that was uncivilized, obsolete and completely out of tune with the dominant majority culture.

> Imagine Jewish children being taught in Yiddish in their independent schools! There the children will be taught the culture of a nation without a history, the culture of a people totally isolated from the mainstream of European civilization, a people held together by the heritage of an outmoded system of thought and by the dead weight of observances transmitted from generation to generation.[12]

Otto Bauer's harsh verdict on the traditional culture of orthodox Galician Jews was not untypical of the judgments of assimilated Jewish intellectuals in Vienna on their East European brethren. The unconditional belief in assimilation, and outright condemnation of anything which retarded the process was as widespread in this milieu as the snobbish dislike of the *Ghettomensch*.[13] An anti-Semitic Viennese Jew like Karl Kraus, regarding himself as the guardian of Christian-Germanic values against the semi-Asiatic hybrid Jews who had clung to their traditions, religion and language, summed it up in a nutshell: 'Despite every respect for the equality of all faiths: oriental enclaves in European civilization are a nonsense'.[14] Otto Bauer's position seems to have been based on the same 'enlightened' form of intolerance. Jewish workers in Galicia would have to be re-educated and liberated from their undesirable 'Jewish' national characteristics and throw off their (historyless?) past, so that they could be completely absorbed in the majority culture. As a result 'the Jews of the East, too, will cease to be a separate nation and merge in their environment (*unter den Nationen aufgehen*) as the Jews of the West merged long ago'.[15] The Jewish proletarian would have to adopt 'the culture of the people among whom he finds his employment'. He would abandon his broken 'German' dialect, his strange clothing, his kaftan and ringlets and other distinctive traits which aroused 'feelings of instinctive opposition and aesthetic repulsion' in Christian workers.[16] Having abandoned his traditional culture and religion, the Jewish worker was ripe for socialism. 'Only then will his special Jewish misery disappear and he will be left with nothing but the common proletarian misery which he will fight and prevail over, in the common struggle, shoulder to shoulder with his Aryan colleagues.'[17]

It is apparent from this and similar passages that the young Otto Bauer was no more free from the unconscious inferiority complexes produced by assimilation than were most of his Jewish middle-class contemporaries in Vienna. The traditional Jew with his kaftan and beard, his indifference to modernism and fashion, was an acute embarrassment. The Jewish worker who came from a similar milieu and was imbued with the same ghetto psychology was likely to provoke anti-Semitism among his Christian 'Aryan' class-comrades. It was significant, moreover, that Otto Bauer frequently used this polarization of 'Aryan' and 'Jew', which was itself a typical sign of how deeply racial thought had percolated into the popular consciousness at the turn of the century. In a passage where he is defining anti-Semitism as a 'primitive expression of anti-capitalism' in Central Europe, Bauer observed that the Jews were very prominent in the capitalist class. 'The Jewish manufacturer very often confronts the Aryan worker, the Jewish middleman faces the Aryan craftsman, and the Jewish moneylender, the Aryan peasant.'[18]

This terminology was an intrinsic element in *völkisch* ideology, but comparatively rare in socialist literature, which did not pay much attention to race. Otto Bauer was also an exception among Marxist thinkers in the enormous positive value which he placed on national individuality (except for the Jews) and in his insistence on the general importance of physical and spiritual characteristics in differentiating nations.[19] It is not inconceivable that a certain predilection for the neo-romantic, organicist model of society, which Bauer skilfully infused into his Marxist dialectics, may have contributed towards his ambivalent attitude to anti-Semitism. But this ambivalence was so prevalent among Austrian socialists of his generation that one really does not need to have recourse to such explanations. Otto Bauer himself wrote in 1910, 'Marx's 'Zur Judenfrage' already differentiated us sharply from liberal philo-Semitism. Social democracy has never been a "Jewish protective guard"'.[20] This was the classic approach of Austrian socialists to anti-Semitism, as laid down by Victor Adler—and what we have said of him applies more or less to Otto Bauer, as the ablest of his disciples. Thus Bauer distinguished sharply, for example, between the 'progressive' and reactionary features of Christian 'socialism'. He regarded Christian-Social anti-Semitism as a progressive (!) social phenomenon during the 1880s and early 1890s, when it sought to overthrow a bankrupt Austro-liberalism which had become 'alien to the people'.[21] Hence he praised Karl von Vogelsang, editor of the clerical-conservative *Das Vaterland*, spiritual mentor of Karl Lueger and founder of Christian 'socialism' in Austria, for his attacks on Jewish capitalism. Bauer quoted with approval a passage from Vogelsang which he found to be 'entirely in the spirit of Marx's 'Judenfrage': 'If through some miracle all of our 1 400 000 Jews should, one happy day, be driven out, it would help us little: for the Jewish spirit has infected us all, it is embodied in our institutions, in our whole way of life, trade and commerce is impregnated with it'.[22]

It is psychologically most revealing that Otto Bauer should have been impressed by such a passage. The point is not so much the accuracy of the objective parallel between Marx and Vogelsang, who were both arguing that the 'Christians' had become 'Jews' as a result of economic liberalism, but Bauer's apparent indifference to the anti-Semitic implications of this argument. Vogelsang (and his disciple Lueger) had inculcated the Christian-Social party with a theoretical abhorrence of capitalism, the free market, and the worship of Mammon, which were all falsely equated with 'Jewish' materialism. Since the Jews were particularly prominent in Austrian capitalism, this gave a sharp anti-Semitic edge to 'Christian Socialism', which it exploited in a most unscrupulous fashion. But Marxist socialists like Adler, Bauer, Austerlitz (who were Jews) and Schuhmeier, Pernerstorfer or Daszyński (who were not) accepted this anti-Semitism as long as it was anti-capitalist in orientation. On the other hand, Bauer's attitude to Jewish nationalism derived logically enough from the arguments he had put forward in the chapter on Jewish autonomy we have already mentioned. He had concluded this chapter by arguing that 'in general capitalist society makes it impossible for them [the Jews] to continue as a nation' because 'the Jews have no closed territory of settlement [*geschlossenes Siedlungsgebiet*]'. Because they lacked a territory, the Jews—unlike the Czechs, for instance—could not resist the process of assimilation. But this was in clear contradiction to Bauer's own theory of nationality (which denied that common territory was a necessary characteristic of a nation) and to the Brünn programme of 1899 (whereby the Austrian social democrats accepted the principle of national autonomy for extra-territorial minorities). Lenin in a polemic against Otto Bauer in 1913 did not hesitate for his own purposes to single out Bauer's self-contradiction on this point: 'This proves . . . how inconsistent Otto Bauer is, and how little he believes in his idea for he excludes the *only* extra-territorial nation (the Jews) from his plan for extra-territorial national autonomy'.[23] Stalin in his essay on *Marxism and the National Question* (1913) made much the same point in more laboured language.[24] Neither Lenin nor Stalin was of course arguing for the recognition of a Jewish nationality, but rather *against* the whole concept of cultural-national autonomy. Indeed, Lenin even acknowledged that with regard to the Jewish national problem he had been influenced by Otto Bauer's theory of assimilation.

Assimilation was not only a law of economic development for Otto Bauer, it was a progressive, civilizing factor in human history. He instinctively identified himself with 'names like Spinoza, Disraeli, Marx, Lassalle, Heine and many others', whose contributions to human society and thought represented the highest achievement of Jewry, and were a product of successful cross fertilization with European culture.[25] At the same time, while looking forward to the time when intermarriage (or as he poetically put it, 'the courtship of young men and the affections of young girls') would resolve the 'last of all Jewish questions', Bauer did not regard assimilation as entailing a complete disappearance of Jewish 'genius'. Despite a full fusion with the surrounding European peoples, the 'specific spiritual qualities' of the Jewish nation would somehow be passed on into the common genetic pool.[26] It was, however, one thing for Otto Bauer to point to the great contribution of individual assimilated Jews to humanity, and an altogether different matter to argue that this choice was open to the Jewish masses in Eastern Europe. In the multi-national Habsburg state the Jews found themselves caught in a crossfire of irreconcilable national conflicts between Germans and Czechs in Bohemia, Poles and Ruthenes (Ukrainians) in Galicia, Magyars and Slovaks in Hungary. The anti-Semitic attitudes prevalent among all these nationalities made the emergence of Jewish nationalism in the Dual Monarchy almost inevitable. Bauer, however, played down the anti-

Semitism of Polish workers who went along with an economic boycott of Jewish labour in the factories: instead he lamented the fact that the Jewish masses in Galicia clung to their separate culture, thus making 'the union of the Jewish proletarians with their Slav class-comrades very difficult'.[27]

This was a rather one-sided viewpoint considering the very considerable racial, religious and linguistic differences separating the Jews from their Slav neighbours.[28] It was essentially a political concession to the Polish socialists in Galicia, who demanded the complete assimilation of the Jewish masses to Polish culture in order to strengthen their own national position. Otto Bauer for his part regarded such assimilation as 'natural' because it broke down the barriers between proletarians. A separate Jewish labour movement (which had emerged in Galicia after 1905) would simply fragment the forces of social democracy. What special objectives could the Jewish workers have which were divergent from those of their Polish or Ruthenian comrades?[29] Since capitalism was irresistibly producing a common class-consciousness in the proletariat, Jewish nationalism must be considered 'petty-bourgeois, reactionary and utopian'. In 1912 Bauer wrote, 'Any attempt to artificially hinder assimilation and nurture an ideology hostile to it in Jewry is retrograde and reactionary'.[30] As support for his thesis of assimilation, Bauer had written an interesting sociological essay in *Der Kampf* discussing the historical conditions which determined the general viability of national minorities.[31] He argued that the Jewish bourgeoisie in Austria-Hungary, like the ruling class of other nationalities, had been the first stratum to be absorbed. In the Czech lands they had been 'Germanized', in Hungary they were 'Magyarized' and in Galicia they were becoming 'Polonized'. Assimilation was more difficult for the Jewish petty-bourgeoisie and working class, since capitalism had not yet broken up traditional social relationships in Eastern Europe and created the prerequisites for a common class-struggle.[32] Thus the Jews in Poland would remain unassimilable as long as they existed in the pores of a peasant economy producing primarily for its own needs. He predicted, however, that Polish Jewry would eventually disappear like the German minority between the fourteenth and sixteenth centuries, once the money-economy had fully penetrated Polish society. Emigration overseas and internal migration within Central Europe would disperse the Jews, who would gradually dissolve as a group since they lacked 'a closed territory'.

Bauer curiously ignored the attempts of the Zionist movement to create precisely such a 'closed territory' in Palestine by transplanting Jewry from the ghettoes of Russia and Eastern Europe. Nor would he at any time in the future seriously consider the Zionist solution to the Jewish problem—one of the surprising omissions in his writings.

Nevertheless, Bauer clearly recognized that nationalist persecution and racial intolerance remained a major obstacle to the completion of assimilation. He briefly mentioned that the 1881 pogroms in Russia had greatly reduced the prospects of integration in the Tsarist Empire and produced a Jewish nationalist ideology hostile to this trend. He also admitted that even in advanced capitalist countries, 'racial instincts and racial prejudices outlive assimilation', and that 'mixed marriages between Aryans and assimilated Jews are relatively rare'.[33] But although he conceded that this made 'the complete absorption of the Jewish minority by the Aryan majority more difficult', he apparently retained his faith in the irresistible assimilative power of capitalism, at least until 1914.

In the greatly diminished post-1918 Austrian Republic, which no longer contained the non-assimilated Jewish masses of Galicia and Bukovina, what had been a Habsburg now became a Polish, Hungarian or Rumanian problem. On the other hand, the mass immigration of Galician Jews to Vienna during the First World War exacerbated the indigenous Austrian anti-Semitism which had been lying dormant in the last years of the Habsburg Monarchy. Bauer, who had been imprisoned on the Russian front during the war, returned to Austria to assume leadership of the left wing of Austrian socialism. When Victor Adler died in 1918 he took over as Foreign Minister of the new Republic and fought hard to secure the approval of the Allies for *Anschluss* with Germany.[34] Bauer was convinced that a truncated Austria was not economically viable, and that the Austrian workers' movement could only benefit from union with a 'Red Germany' dominated by its powerful labour movement. In the Marxian perspective, *Anschluss* with Germany was to be the proletarian finale to the abortive bourgeois revolution of 1848;[35] it would rescue the Alpine Republic from its miserable status as a 'dwarf State', doomed to a life of petty provincialism. The 'greater German Reich' offered the prospect of participating in 'the exciting life of a great nation', as opposed to 'a life of smallness and pettiness in which nothing noble can prosper, least of all the noblest thing we know—socialism'.[36]

It was supremely ironic that a Jew and a Marxist intellectual should strive so passionately as Foreign Minister for the *Anschluss* and for keeping the Sudeten Germans inside Austria.[37] His ardent defence of the interests of *Deutschtum* was soon forgotten, however, once the intransigence of French imperialism had blocked the road to union with Germany and provoked his resignation as Foreign Minister in 1919. Nevertheless, even after this dream had evaporated in the nightmare of Hitler's invasion of 1938, Otto Bauer, by that time a refugee in Paris, still clung to his belief that only an all-German revolution could save Austria. In the April 1938 issue of the émigré journal *Der Sozialistische Kampf* Bauer wrote that the restoration of Austrian independence was a reactionary mirage:

> The watchword with which we oppose foreign rule over Austria by satraps from the Reich cannot be the reactionary slogan of the restoration of Austrian independence, but rather only the revolutionary watchword of the all-German revolution, which alone can free the Austrian *Stamm* of the nation from the fascist tyrants along with the other German *Stammen* [tribes].[38]

Otto Bauer was as mistaken on this issue as he had been on the Jewish question: like many Austrian socialists before the second World War, he clung to a cultural form of Pan-Germanism which reflected the insecure national identity of most Austrians in the First Republic. Moreover, as a socialist he had always held an idealized view of Germany and its labour movement which influenced his judgment on a whole range of political issues.

As the leader of Austrian social democracy between 1918 and 1934, Otto Bauer was faced with a difficult political situation from the tactical viewpoint. Although the Social Democrats were the single largest party with a stable vote, ranging from 40 to 45 per cent of the electorate and control of the municipal administration in Vienna, the hostility of the bourgeois parties, the external menace of fascism and a permanent siege mentality reduced the room for manœuvre. The Social Democratic leadership adopted a strategy of *Attentismus* in this situation, not so dissimilar from that practised by the SPD in Imperial Germany and by the Left in the Weimar Republic. A radical Marxist phraseology compensated for the wait-and-see tactics of the party, which was determined at all costs to maintain its impressive array of organizations, even if this meant postponing crucial decisions regarding their attitude to State power. Direct confrontation with the class-enemy was avoided, although the Linz Programme of 1926 had called on the proletariat to set up a defensive proletarian dictatorship, should democracy be threatened by monarchist or fascist forces.[39]

Otto Bauer, who epitomized the Austro-Marxist search for a middle road 'between Reformism and Bolshevism', was perfectly conscious of the ambiguity in his policy towards the bourgeois state. His whole theory of socialism was impregnated with a strong belief in historical inevitability and the irreversible logic of events.[40] In his case it seems to have reinforced a certain Hamletian paralysis of the will at critical moments, which perhaps contributed to the fiasco of the Austrian labour movement in 1934.

It is extremely difficult to assess what role his Jewish origin played in multiplying the obstacles facing him as leader of the Austrian workers' movement under the harsh conditions of the First Republic. The literary critic and left-wing intellectual Ernst Fischer rightly observed that in Austria anti-Semitism was inseparable from anti-intellectualism.[41] We have already seen how under Victor Adler's leadership anti-Semitic feelings were quite prevalent, even in the labour movement, despite its exceptionally high proportion of leading Jewish personalities. Bauer could not have been impervious to this fact, and to the potency of the myth of 'Jewish Bolshevism', which was as effective in Austria as in Germany after 1918. Fischer records in his memoirs that he once asked Otto Bauer why he had never formally left the Jewish community; the latter's reply suggests a suppressed bitterness and also a defiance, not without dignity: 'How could you possibly understand? You've never heard anyone muttering "dirty Yid" behind your back.'[42]

Nevertheless, whatever his private feelings, Bauer's attitude to post-1918 anti-Semitism in Austria followed the same pattern laid down by Victor Adler before the war. He insisted on presenting the Christian-Social Party and the Pan-Germans as pseudo-anti-Semites, who accepted the support of high finance, and would close ranks with their 'Jewish' allies against the labour movement. The anti-Semitism of the Pan-Germans and the Christian-Socialists according to Otto Bauer simply served the interests of the big bourgeoisie, which was 'largely Jewish'. Thus in 1924 he wrote:

> Nevertheless, even today, these parties cannot completely dispense with anti-Semitism. They need popular anti-Semitic catchwords in the struggle against social democracy. . . . The Jewish capitalist readily bears the costs of printing anti-Semitic electoral leaflets to weaken the social democrats.[43]

The anti-Semitism of the 1920s was in his view much more reactionary than the original movement which had begun forty years earlier in 'the liberation of the petty and middle bourgeoisie from the hegemony of the predominantly Jewish big bourgeoisie'.[44] 'Liberation from Jewish domination' (*Befreiung von der Judenherrschaft*) had been transformed from a 'progressive'(!) into a reactionary slogan by Seipel and his Christian-Social followers. Bauer refused to take this phenomenon seriously, completely underestimating the mesmeric influence it exercised on the petty-bourgeois masses and peasantry in Catholic Austria, who hated atheistic 'Red Vienna' and the radical Jewish intelligentsia, whether liberal or Marxian.[45]

Instead of vigorously countering this propaganda, the Austrian socialists under Bauer tried to turn it against their Christian-Social adversaries. Following the first significant electoral breakthrough by the Austrian Nazis, in April 1932, as a result of which National Socialists entered the regional legislatures of Lower Austria, Salzburg, Vienna, Carinthia and Styria, the situation had changed, however. Although the Social Democrats did not lose any votes to the National Socialists, it was evident that the Christian-Socials and the other bourgeois parties (including the fascist Heimatblock) had lost ground. Although anti-Semitism was much more integral to the ideology of the Austrian Nazis than it had been to the followers of Seipel, Bauer viewed it with remarkable equanimity in an article in *Der Kampf* of May 1932.

> The ex Christian-Social petty-bourgeois who voted Nazi the other day has not become a German nationalist. But he frets at his old party, which has become so statesmanlike that it no longer dares to be anti-Semitic. It takes money from Jewish industrialists and gives away the people's wealth to the Jew-banks.[46]

This was the classic Marxian riposte to anti-Semitism, which always asserted the primacy of class interests above race, religion or nationality. The implication was that the labour movement must be equally opposed to both Jewish and 'Aryan' capitalists who manipulated anti-Semitism as a smokescreen to hoodwink the masses.[47] The bankruptcy of this theory was exposed by German Nazism, but even in 1934 Otto Bauer regarded Hitler's anti-Semitism as a 'utopian, petty-bourgeois, anti-capitalist' diversion, intended to mask from his more radical followers the establishment of a new capitalist dictatorship in Germany.

Otto Bauer's general theory of fascism was much more subtle than his simplistic view of the Jewish question, though until 1927 it had been a rather marginal issue in his writings. The rise of the Austrian Heimwehr in the late 1920s, the world economic crisis, and the successes of the German Nazis prompted Bauer to deal more extensively with the fascist phenomenon. At first he tended to regard the Heimwehr merely as the creature of high finance and the bourgeois parties.[48] But after 1932 he became more aware of the immanence of the fascist danger and the strength of its mass base among such socially threatened strata of the population as students and unemployed workers etc.

With Hitler's accession to power in Germany in January 1933, followed two months later by the dissolution of the Austrian Parliament and the Dollfuss coup, Otto Bauer became profoundly pessimistic about the prospects of resistance to Austrian 'clerico-fascism'.[49] He opposed the brave but hopeless uprising of the Austrian workers in February 1934 which obliged him to flee with Julius Deutsch and other party leaders to neighbouring Czechoslovakia.

In exile Otto Bauer had the opportunity to elaborate further his theory of fascism while at the same time maintaining contact with the illegal socialist movement in Austria. Despite the fiasco of 1934 and the growing influence of anti-Semitism (even in the workers' movement) Bauer, though in exile, enjoyed an extraordinary hold over his followers. His personal authority survived the party split and his vision of the 'revolution' as a certain if remote goal, continued to inspire faith in the rank-and-file. In these last sad years of his life, Bauer continued to write prolifically and reflect on events. In 1936 he predicted a new world war because the militarist elements in the ruling-classes of the fascist states had gained the upper hand.[50] Increasingly he began to regard fascism as an imperialistic phenomenon based on State regulation of the economy by a bureaucratic caste and a terroristic dictatorship over all social classes including the bourgeoisie.[51] Though his theoretical model of fascism had come closer to that of the Communists, Bauer emphasized much more than them the disastrous effects of a weakening of democratic traditions. Above all he saw a parallel between fascist and Bolshevik dictatorship, though not quite in the sense of the modern theory of totalitarianism. Thus in 1936 in his book *Zwischen Zwei Weltkriegen* Bauer wrote:

> Fascist dictatorship destroys the results of the political emancipation of the individual, in order to prevent the social emancipation of the masses. The dictatorship of the proletariat abolishes the political emancipation of the individual in order to force the social emancipation of the masses. But however deep and important this contrast, they have it in common that they both destroy what the era of bourgeois revolution conquered in terms of freedom and humanity: thereby they undo what was the most valuable result of four centuries of struggle, the most important consequence of the whole bourgeois epoch of history, and the foundation of all civilization in our time.[52]

The final blow to Otto Bauer's hopes that Austria might be saved from Hitlerian fascism came with the *Anschluss* of 1938, whereby the country was juridically and administratively incorporated into the Nazi power-structure. One of the most immediate and most tragic consequences of these events was the rapidly deteriorating situation of Austrian Jewry. Immediately the new regime introduced decrees and perpetrated acts of violence against the Jewish community of even greater cruelty and scope than those in Nazi Germany itself. These facts were not unknown to Otto Bauer, who had by now taken refuge in Paris. They deeply saddened him, and finally brought him to abandon his earlier views on the inevitability of assimilation. The curtain was going down on a whole era of German-Jewish creativity in Central Europe.

In the last article which he wrote before his premature death in Paris at the age of fifty-six, Bauer appealed to 'the world conscience' to save the 300 000 Jews in Austria from Nazi aggression.[53] He asked the Western democracies to open their doors to the oppressed victims of fascism, the members of a 'national' minority entitled to protection under the Treaty of Saint-Germain. The appeal appeared in the *News*

Chronicle on 5th July 1938—the day after Bauer's death in Paris of exhaustion, and perhaps also from a broken heart. The majority of his Austrian countrymen greeted Hitler with rapturous enthusiasm, and a few of them were to play a significant part in the extermination of European Jewry.[54]

France

Bernard Lazare and Léon Blum

'Emancipation? What will your emancipation give me? It will afford me a social situation which will allow me to refine myself; thanks to this I shall acquire new capacities for feeling, and consequently I shall find it more difficult to suffer; it will develop within me a greater sensibility yet it will not cause the things that wound that sensibility to disappear—on the contrary. Out of a wretch sometimes numbed by his wretchedness, it will make a sensitive being who feel doubly every pinprick. . . . Out of an unconscious pariah it will make a conscious pariah.'

Bernard Lazare (*Jewish Nationalism and Emancipation*)

It was the French Revolution which first emancipated the Jews in the name of the Rights of Man. It was also in France at the end of the nineteenth century that the full political potential of anti-Semitism was revealed at the time of the Dreyfus Affair. It was the French model of civic equality and assimilation which had everywhere inspired Jewish emancipation on the European continent: it was also the explosion of anti-Semitic hysteria in France during the 1890s which prompted Theodor Herzl to write his epoch-making Zionist pamphlet *The Jewish State*, while living as a foreign correspondent in Paris. In the next two chapters we shall describe how two prominent Jews in the French Left came to re-examine the 'Jewish question' in the light of those events which seemed to Herzl to have undermined the ideals of 1789.

At the end of the eighteenth century there were approximately 40 000 Jews living in France, mainly concentrated in Alsace Lorraine, and Yiddish speaking. The Consistorial system was established under Napoleon, whereby the French State officially recognized Judaism as a religion and placed it under centralized government control. Before 1848 the Jewish community had already consolidated its social and economic position, and the Rothschilds, Péreire brothers and Fould were extremely prominent in the Parisian *haute banque*. This early Jewish dominance in French banking was an important factor in the leftist anti-Semitism of leading French socialists of the period, such as Fourier, Proudhon and Toussenel. Although a number of Jews were also active apostles of the 'philo-Semitic' Saint-Simonian school of French socialism, the community as a whole tended to be identified with the prosperous bourgeoisie. Under the Second Empire this impression was strengthened by the spectacular involvement of Jewish financiers in French railway construction and capitalist enterprise. By 1869 there were 80 000 Jews in France,

30 000 of them in Paris—but the loss of Alsace Lorraine to Germany led to a temporary decline in numbers. Nevertheless, many Alsatian Jews (including the unfortunate Dreyfus family) opted for French citizenship. A further influx of Jews from Eastern Europe following the Russian pogroms in 1881 and immigration from Ottoman Europe (the Balkans), brought the French Jewish community back to its earlier level.

The French Jews were among the most assimilated in Western Europe, scattered throughout the social structure, including many middle-class people in business and the liberal professions, and towards the end of the nineteenth century a substantial artisan class. By 1880 two-thirds of the Jewish community was concentrated in Paris. Official French Judaism was overwhelmingly liberal in character, and increasingly adapted itself to French ways and customs. Its secular religion was attachment to the principles of the French Revolution, which in political terms meant espousing a moderate Republicanism. There were no obstacles in France to the entry of Jews into the bureaucracy, army and higher academic positions such as existed in Germany and Austria-Hungary. One result of this civic equality was the relative indifference, even hostility of most French Jews to socialist or anarchist doctrines. Under the Third Republic the prevailing assimilationist ideology encouraged support of the status quo.

Anti-Semitism did not emerge as a significant political trend until the 1880s. The initial impetus derived from the crash of the Catholic bank Union Générale, which was widely attributed to the machinations of the Rothschilds. In Catholic and Royalist circles, opposition to the legacy of the French Revolution, and a desire to restore the declining influence of the Catholic Church, was one factor in encouraging its propagation. On the Left the traditional suspicion of Jewish banking capital also played its part. In 1886 Edouard Drumont, who was to become the driving-force of French anti-Semitism, published his sensational best-seller, *La France Juive*. Drumont enjoyed considerable popular support among the lower clergy, the petty-bourgeoisie, students and officers—especially after the Panama scandal (1893) had implicated a number of German-Jewish financiers in parliamentary corruption. But it was the arrest of Captain Dreyfus, accused in 1894 of selling military secrets to Germany, which unleashed a wave of anti-Semitic feeling in France which eventually threatened the whole edifice of republican institutions. In the great struggle which ensued, only a handful of Jews played any role, led by the Republican politician Joseph Reinach. The majority of the community preserved a discreet silence, even during the widespread and violent anti-Semitic riots of January-February 1898. Bernard Lazare, and to a lesser degree Léon Blum, were among the few Jewish intellectuals who were deeply involved in the events surrounding the Dreyfus Affair. Lazare in particular evolved a theory of

Jewish nationalism which was unique in its revolutionary implications, though it found little echo outside a few Jewish immigrant and working-class circles.

For the majority of the French Jewish community the belief in assimilation and in liberal Republican France remained unshaken, at least until the advent of the Vichy regime in 1940. This was in spite of the fact that anti-Semitism was a significant factor in French public life between the two world wars, as the career of Léon Blum attests. The extreme Right, led by Maurras and Daudet, attacked him unceasingly as the symbol of 'Jewish revolutionary' subversion, though his policies were always moderate and gradualist. Even the leaders of French Jewry were unhappy about his accession to the Premiership in 1936 at a time of mounting social unrest, xenophobia and racism in France. The Jewish immigrants from Eastern Europe, on the other hand, who constituted an ever-growing proportion of French Jewry in the 1930s, welcomed his Popular Front government. The fact that Blum did not conceal his Jewish identity, unlike so many of his assimilated co-religionists, was much admired. As a Yiddish-language paper in Paris observed in May 1936:

> Blum is not only a Jew, but an authentic Jew who has a Jewish heart and mentality, who takes an interest in the establishment of a Jewish national home in Ereẓ Israel and the fact that such a Jew is Prime Minister of one of the greatest countries in Europe . . . is a unique fact in modern history.

Léon Blum was no less a Frenchman, no less of a socialist, for that.

CHAPTER 7

Bernard Lazare, Dreyfusard Prophet

'I believe that for internationalism to take root, it is necessary that human groups should previously have won their autonomy; it is necessary for them to be able to express themselves freely, it is necessary for them to be aware of what they are.'

Bernard Lazare

'He was a Jew of the great race, the prophetic race, the race which says "a just man" where others say "a saint"'.

Léon Blum

There are few intellectual journeys in modern Jewish history more remarkable and illuminating than the path traversed by Bernard Lazare, the forgotten prophet of the Dreyfus Affair. A revolutionary anarchist and a deeply sincere internationalist, he came to embrace a radical form of nationalist particularism which remains altogether distinct both in the history of socialism and in that of Zionism.[1] Nothing in his social or family background predestined him to become the lonely 'Prophet of Israel' whose crusade for Dreyfus redeemed the honour of French Jewry. But his metamorphosis from self-hating Jew to tribune of his people offers the observer a unique vantage-point from which to study the psychology of the authentic Jewish revolutionary.

Lazare Marcus Bernard was born in 1865 in the ancient French city of Nîmes in the Languedoc. Like a number of other provincial towns in the South, Nîmes had a small, cohesive, practising Jewish community which could trace its French roots back over many generations. In the Middle Ages Provençe had been a centre of Hebrew learning, and the Jews had lived peacefully for centuries with their neighbours, under special papal protection. By the time of the third Republic traditional Jewish customs had, however, lost much of their original meaning and significance, though they were still observed. This was the case with Lazare's parents, Jonas Bernard and Douce Noémi Rouget, who celebrated the Passover and other festivals at home without transmitting any specifically Jewish education to their four sons.[2] The children learnt their *bar-mitzvah* recital by rote, without really understanding it. They were already integrated thoroughly into French culture and society; Fernand became a colonel in the French Army, Armand a doctor, Edmond a picture-frame dealer, and the family had great hopes that Lazare might become a lawyer. But the ambitions of the young Lazare were first and foremost literary, and in 1886 he left his home town for the bright lights of Paris.

At first he studied palaeography and history at the Sorbonne, but with the help of his cousin Georges Michel (Ephraïm Mikhaël), he was soon introduced into the bohemian, avant-garde circles of Parisian literary life. Both Mikhaël and Lazare Bernard were strongly attracted by the Symbolist movement whose high-priest was the poet Mallarmé, and their joint literary début, *La Fiancée de Corinthe*, reflected this influence. By the early 1890s Bernard Lazare (this was the pen-name he henceforth adopted) had become a leading literary critic of the Symbolist group, respected for his fearless and sometimes harsh judgment on his contemporaries.[3] His conception of the writer's role already reflected both the passionate, fighting nature of his temperament and his profound conviction that literature had to serve the cause of social justice.[4] This belief, allied to Lazare's involvement with the Symbolists, led him to embrace anarchism as the universal hope of the future.

From 1892, when he became director of the Symbolist organ *Entretiens politiques et littéraires*, Lazare increasingly began to interpret art as a form of social action, whose mission was to oppose all authority and dogma and help prepare the revolution from below. It was also in the *Entretiens* that Bernard Lazare contributed his first two articles on the Jewish question, a subject which he had as yet not studied in any depth. These two articles, which appeared in September-October 1890, manifested a radical Jewish self-hatred which makes Lazare's subsequent Dreyfusard odyssey and conversion to Zionism all the more remarkable.

The 25-year-old Southerner from Nîmes was prompted to comment on the Jewish issue by the noisy anti-Semitic campaign organized by Drumont and the Marquis de Morès in Paris. The Bible of this new political movement—which had unsuccessfully contested the municipal elections in February 1890—was Drumont's *La France Juive*. This turgid and sinister work had enjoyed a sensational vogue since its publication in 1886. Drumont traced the decline of France since the Revolution to *la conquête juive*, to the alleged success of a small but cohesive minority in gaining control of French institutions, politics, economy and culture.[5] Drumont openly called for the expulsion of the Jews from France, under the watchword of *La France aux Français*.

Lazare's two articles offered an altogether unexpected confirmation of Drumont's contentions—indeed, if anything, they outdid the father of modern French anti-Semitism in their rabid intolerance. In so far as Lazare was a Jew, his point of departure was, however, necessarily different from that of Drumont, as were his fundamental motivations: what they had in common was a vehement hatred of the 'Jew' as an alien, as a rich capitalist and a venal agent of corruption. Lazare's anti-Semitism depended, however, on a sharp differentiation between *Juifs* and *Israélites*, whom he depicted as two altogether different species of being. He unreservedly applied all of Drumont's strictures to the former: the foreign 'Jews', whether rich or poor, whom he designated as *Juifs* were utterly depraved creatures, wanderers without a home, a herd of cosmopolitan bedouin who would contaminate everyone and everything with which they came into contact. They were mean, narrow-minded, sly and unscrupulous, owing their allegiance only to the 'Golden Calf'. Their philosophy of life was based on the sectarianism of the Talmud, and had nothing to do with the cultivated French Israelites, who had absorbed the blessings of Latin civilization. The Israelites of France were honest, upright, decent people, indistinguishable from their compatriots. They could be counted upon to support Drumont as long as he confined himself to attacking the *Juifs*.[6]

Lazare's second article, entitled 'La Solidarité juive', pursued this theme, focusing its attack on the Alliance Israélite Universelle which had been set up by Adolphe Crémieux to give succour and aid to oppressed Jews all over the world. This French philanthropic organization had been violently attacked by Drumont in *La France Juive* as a secret conspiracy to achieve Jewish world-domination. Lazare joined in this attack, though from a different standpoint. The Alliance had in his view been guilty of the unpardonable error of trying to protect the persecuted Jews in Algeria, in Russia, Eastern Europe and the Balkans. The doors of France had been opened as a result to a flood of coarse, uncultivated, money-grubbing nomads.[7] They had 'swarmed down on our country like locusts', inevitably breeding the anti-Semitic backlash with which the young Lazare identified himself.[8] 'Thanks to these hordes with whom we are confused, it is forgotten that we have lived in France for nearly two thousand years, like the Franks who invaded this country . . .'[9] With all the arrogance of an assimilated 'Israélite' proud of his roots of two millennia on French soil, Bernard Lazare declared: 'We have nothing in common with those who are constantly being thrown in our face, and we should abandon them'.[10] He advised his fellow-Israelites to 'halt, to dam up if they can, the perpetual immigration of these predatory, vulgar and dirty Tartars who come to feed unduly on a country which is not their own.[11] These impoverished immigrants threatened the previously secure identity of the French Israelites. As rootless *Juifs* from Russia and Central Europe, imbued with the ghetto mentality and incapable of assimilation, their misery and suffering would transform a free country into a pig-sty. With almost sadistic wrath and a haughty indifference, the young Lazare could write:

> Russian usurers, Galician tavern-keepers and money-lenders, secondhand pedlars from Prague, Polish horse-dealers, money-merchants from Frankfurt, what do they mean to me, a French Israelite? In the name of what supposed fraternity should I care about measures taken by the Tsar against subjects who appear to him as harmful?[12]

The man who was later to devote his tragically short life to the cause of Jewish brotherhood and liberty could, in 1890, only recommend his fellow 'Israelites' to kick out the alien 'lepers' in their midst.

At this time Bernard Lazare was already a well-known critic and anarchist committed to the cause of social revolution. His writing on social problems was characterized by unusual vehemence, high-minded sectarianism, a marked capacity for hatred and complete loathing for authority. The milieu in which he moved was thoroughly infiltrated with anti-Semitism, which in nineteenth-century France had long been a feature of the Left. Hatred of the Rothschild 'dynasty' was almost obligatory in socialist and anarchist circles. Even nationalist anti-Semites like Drumont, Rochefort and Maurice

Barrès by using a populist, anti-capitalist phraseology achieved respectability in left-wing circles. Hence there was nothing especially surprising in the fact that a young Jew, ignorant of his tradition and history, should identify with the commonplace anti-Semitic stereotypes of the time.[13] This was true above all when that individual was as preoccupied as Bernard Lazare with the problem of demonstrating his full integration in French society.

What was nevertheless to distinguish Lazare from so many other revolutionary Jews was his restless search for a personal identity and his independence of mind which could not be satisfied by purely political doctrines. In some ways his intellectual evolution was reminiscent of Maurice Barrès, the great French writer and anarchist who also turned later to integral nationalism. Barrès, like Lazare, was intensely suspicious of official socialism, of political parties and of the new era of industrialism through which *fin-de-siècle* France was passing.[14] His anti-Semitism was partly the result of an obsession with the loss of spiritual roots, though in his case it eventually became a demagogic slogan to win popular support for an openly racialist platform. This option was not open to Lazare once anti-Semitism in France began to assume the character of a mass movement and to adopt an exclusivist racial mystique. In the 1890s the campaign unleashed by Drumont rapidly began to outgrow its original left-wing orientation and to attack not only Jewish bankers but also assimilated Jews in all walks of life, including the Army.

This development prompted Bernard Lazare to undertake a remarkable, wide-ranging study entitled *L'Antisémitisme, son histoire et ses causes* (1894). The early sections of this book first appeared as review articles in 1891 and 1892, and they seem to reflect the earlier anti-Jewish bias of the author. To a large extent, Lazare considered that 'the Jews were themselves, in part, at least, the cause of their own ills'.[15] Though they did not determine the particular character of anti-Semitism in any time or place, they were the one constant factor in its development. It was the 'unsocial' character of the Jew, rooted in his religion with its strict and precise ritual and his tenacious patriotism which was ultimately responsible for anti-Semitism.[16] The Jews had everywhere remained part of a long, unbroken chain of tradition, a nationality of the confessional type, refusing to merge with their neighbours.[17] Lazare agreed with Drumont that this had made them a state within the State, and in 1894 he still disapproved strongly of the fact. The Jews, indoctrinated by the Talmud and convinced of their own superiority to other nations, had remained refractory to all attempts at assimilating them.[18] Jew-hatred was primarily a reaction of the Gentile nations to this obdurate survival of an alien minority in their midst: until the seventeenth century, its causes had been primarily religious, but in modern times it had assumed new forms, partly economic and partly nationalist in character.

Lazare parted company with Drumont, however, over his assertion that the Jews could *never* assimilate. The anti-Semites, he argued, were caught in a 'perpetual and fundamental contradiction', once they embraced the pseudo-scientific doctrine of racial exclusivism. Their reliance on false analogies from biology and anthropology had turned anti-Semitism into a self-fulfilling prophecy:

> anti-Semitism was born in modern societies because the Jew did not assimilate, did not cease to be a people, but when anti-Semitism had ascertained that the Jews were not assimilated, it violently reproached them for it, and at the same time whenever possible, it took all necessary steps to prevent their future assimilation.[19]

In his chapter on modern anti-Semitism, Lazare began to abandon the neutral tone of his earlier discussion and to take issue with Drumont's ideas, and those of his counterparts elsewhere in Europe. Nevertheless, a certain parallelism is discernable in his argument —relying as it did on the assumption that the Jews had themselves always been an exclusive and separate people. In his treatment of the post-emancipation period of Jewish history the influence of Drumont is also apparent, though Lazare was no longer seeking to justify anti-Semitism as a doctrine. Thus he argued that in the period following the French Revolution the Jews had become a valuable ally of the European bourgeoisie. 'As conquerors, not as guests, they came into modern societies. They were like a penned-in flock; suddenly the barriers fell and they rushed upon the field opened to them.'[20]

The early industrialization of Europe was depicted by Lazare in terms reminiscent of Drumont as a kind of 'Jewish conquest', whereby a race of moneylenders and merchant-capitalists with a marvellous power of adaptation had seized their opportunity. Within two generations they had emerged in the forefront of European society as financiers, industrialists, *littérateurs*, politicians and revolutionaries.

> The Jews, it may be said, are situated at the poles of contemporary society. They are found among the representatives of industrial and financial capitalism, and among those who have vehemently protested against capital. Rothschild is the antithesis of Marx and Lassalle.[21]

The anti-Semites had said much the same thing, and Lazare supported their thesis, first proclaimed by Gougenot des Mousseaux, that the Jews were 'breeders of revolutions'.[22] The difference was rather one of evaluating the results of this phenomenon. Catholic, conservative and nationalist circles regarded the Jew as a subversive and destructive element in traditional society. Lazare as a revolutionary anarchist naturally saw the issue somewhat differently, and judged it in the broader context of Jewish history. In his opinion it was the very essence of the Hebrew spirit which had driven many of his emancipated co-religionists to embrace revolutionary causes, just as their distant forefathers had fathered prophetism, messianism and early Christianity. The Jews had always been restless malcontents, seeking immediate satisfaction rather than remote promises of eternal salvation.[23] This pattern had been set by the ancient Hebrews who demanded from Yahweh reciprocity and the fulfilment of mutual obligations. 'The man whom the Jew lauds is not a saint, not a resignee: it is the just man. The charitable man does not exist for the people of Judah; in Israel there can be no question of charity, but only of justice'.[24]

The poor, the humble, the *ebionim* of ancient Israel possessed a concrete ideal of justice, and they dreamed of the day when the wicked would be hurled down. Justice was not something to be realized beyond the grave, but was to be achieved in this life. Moreover, the Israelites had acknowledged no human authority beside Yahweh. They were driven by a fanatical preoccupation with equality, based on the idea that all of Yahweh's children were entitled to an equal share of his joys and blessings.[25] It was this notion which had inspired the communistic precepts of Leviticus, Exodus and Numbers, and the sayings of the Hebrew prophets. The centuries of bondage, humiliation and martyrdom which the Jewish people had undergone in exile reinforced rather than destroyed their invincible belief in the future coming of the Messiah. Bernard Lazare saw the modern Jewish revolutionary as 'the child of biblical and prophetic tradition, that same tradition which animated the fanatic Anabaptists of Germany in the sixteenth century and the Puritan warriors of Cromwell'.[26] In Karl Marx he perceived the 'powerful logic of the ancient rabbis', and in Ferdinand Lassalle 'the passionate thirst for liberty of the ancient Hebrew rebels'.[27] Those who had joined the ranks of the Revolution did not, despite their atheism, cease to be Jews.

> But as a general rule, the Jew, even the extreme Jewish radical, cannot help retaining his Jewish characteristics, and though he may have abandoned all religion and all faith, he has none the less been subjected to the national influence acting through heredity and early education.[28]

For Bernard Lazare, the Jewish revolutionary was not the destructive solvent of anti-Semitic fantasy, bringing disorder and catastrophe, but a fighter for freedom, seeking to realize the ancient Hebrew dream of a terrestrial paradise. It was the Jewish ancestry of Marx, Boerne, Heine and Lassalle that had made them rebels, agitators and controversialists with a unique gift for sarcasm and invective. There was much truth in this analysis, but his conclusion must have seemed like grist to the mill of anti-Semitism.

> The emancipated Jew, being no longer bound by the faith of his ancestors, and owing no ties to the old forms of society in the midst of which he had lived as an outcast, has become in modern nations a veritable ferment of revolutions.[29]

What then was Lazare's answer to the anti-Semitism whose history and causes he had traced from antiquity to modern times? Where did his prognoses fundamentally differ from those of Drumont and his supporters? The conclusion to his book sounded a strangely optimistic note, consonant with his revolutionary and assimilationist perspective but at odds with the general historical trends he had depicted in earlier chapters. In 1894, on the eve of the Dreyfus Affair, he apparently believed that both Judaism and anti-Semitism were on the verge of dissolution. The Talmudic spirit which had preserved the East European Jews in their ghetto was disappearing as their emancipated occidental brethren abandoned 'their ancient prejudices, their peculiar modes of worship, the observance of their special laws'.[30] The Western Jew 'who professes at most a sort of ceremonial deism' was ripe for rationalism. For the free-thinking, anti-clerical Lazare, this was the *sine qua non* of successful assimilation. At the same time, he was convinced that the spirit of national egotism was generally on the wane. A new era of internationalism was emerging, which would sweep away the 'hatred of the alien' at the root of anti-Judaism. The anti-Semites in France, Germany and Austria were unconsciously preparing the road to socialism with their anti-capitalist demagogy. The anti-Semitic movement, in its origin reactionary,

> is now acting to the advantage of the revolution. Anti-Semitism stirs up the middle class, the petty-bourgeois and sometimes the peasant against the Jewish capitalists, but in doing so it leads them gently towards socialism, prepares them for anarchy, drives them to hate all capitalists and more than that, capital in the abstract.[31]

Socialism would inevitably triumph over anti-Semitism—'one of the last, though most long-lived, manifestations of that old spirit of reaction and narrow conservatism'.[32]

The Dreyfus Affair which broke out only a few months after the publication of Lazare's study proved his prognosis to have been tragically naïve. It forced him to re-examine his view of the Jewish problem and completely to revise his opinions. It was evident that anti-Semitism, far from disappearing or preparing the road to revolution, was gaining ground every day. The arrest of a Jewish officer in the

French Army on the charge of high treason had given a new lease of life to Drumont's *Libre Parole* and other organs of anti-Semitic opinion. Lazare's relations with Drumont, which up to this point had been cordial (in spite of their growing divergence of opinion) now rapidly deteriorated.[33] In January 1895 Drumont had still felt able to lavish praise on Lazare's study of anti-Semitism, as being 'dominated from beginning to end by a fine effort at impartiality' and a determination 'not to yield to the impulses of the race'.[34] As late as October 1895, he had published Bernard Lazare's letter in *Libre Parole*, agreeing to adjudicate a competition designed to find the best solution to the Jewish peril! Lazare was prepared to sit on the jury, assuring Drumont of his 'absolute impartiality', and quixotically stating in advance that 'the only logical solution to the problem seems to me a massacre . . .'.[35]

By the time the first meeting of the jury occurred the two men were enemies, and after a number of insults a duel took place in which neither was injured.

The process by which Bernard Lazare emerged as the leading Jewish defender of Dreyfus and the bitterest enemy of the anti-Semites was, however, a complex one. In November 1894, after a closed court-martial had found Dreyfus guilty, Lazare had no more reason than any other future Dreyfusard to doubt the verdict. But he was shaken by the way in which the trial was immediately exploited to whip up a frenzied xenophobic crusade in France. In an article of November 1894 he gave vivid expression to his anxiety at the new *état d'esprit antisémite* which had suddenly surfaced everywhere in French society. Even the most assimilated French 'Israelite' now discovered that he was after all only a pariah, living in a new ghetto surrounded by an impenetrable wall of suspicion. 'This animosity is hidden, and yet the intelligent Jew can perceive it; he has the impression of a wall that his adversaries have built between himself and those in whose midst he lives'.[36] This latent hatred was more shocking for the sensitive, educated Jew than the physical ghetto in which his non-assimilated brethren in Eastern Europe and North Africa still vegetated. It awakened for the first time in Bernard Lazare an understanding of the ambiguity of emancipation and the pariah quality of Jewish existence. Henceforth his activity became one prodigious and misunderstood effort to bring into the light the psychological servitude which afflicted western Jews, and to give political expression to an oppressed nation of outcasts.

Even in civilized France, the land of the Revolution and the Rights of Man, the Jews had discovered the precarious and uncertain character of their citizenship. But with growing lucidity Lazare was also becoming aware that his socialist comrades offered no real solution to the Jewish problem. The Jews could not sit by and passively wait until they were stripped of all their rights in the hope that one day the Revolution would deliver them. In a small pamphlet entitled

Antisémitisme et Révolution (March 1895), which featured an imaginary discussion between two French workers, Lazare for the first time unmasked the pseudo-socialist, demagogic character of Drumont's propaganda. He emphasized that anti-Semitism was essentially an internecine conflict between Christian and Jewish capitalists, in which the Catholic bourgeoisie sought to supplant their rivals. This was also the classic argument of the French Marxists, but unlike the followers of Jules Guesde (or for that matter Drumont), Lazare also added that the Jews in Russia, Eastern Europe and North Africa constituted the most miserable and disinherited proletariat in the world. 'In Russia, Galicia, Rumania and Turkey, in London and New York, even in some areas of Paris, their poverty is dreadful'.[37]

The next stage in Lazare's evolution was a bold press campaign in the radical periodical *Le Voltaire* against Drumont's teachings, originally provoked by Émile Zola's article 'Pour les Juifs' in *Le Figaro* (16th May 1896). In a series of articles later published as a pamphlet entitled *Contre L'Antisémitisme* Lazare sharply took issue with Drumont's assertion that anti-Semitism was a form of class-struggle directed against capitalism and Jewish finance. Decisively rejecting his earlier view that it was smoothing the road to socialism, Lazare frankly admitted that 'I was very naïve at that time'.[38] The only beneficiaries of Drumont's anti-Jewish crusade would be the Christian capitalists: anti-Semitism was therefore a safety valve for capitalism rather than a movement against the status quo. Moreover, it threatened the basic Rights of Man, seeking to deprive all Jews of their freedom and to restore the medieval ghetto. 'It is not only the Jewish banker who is being condemned but the Jewish tradesman, the Jewish lawyer, the Jew in medicine, in the army, in the arts, letters and sciences.'[39] Behind this campaign stood the efforts of the Catholic Church to reassert its authority and to undermine the principles of the French Republic. The war against the Jew was a prelude to the future battle to be waged against the Protestants, the dissenters, free-thinkers, anti-clericals, republicans, anarchists and socialists. By the summer of 1896 it was clear to Bernard Lazare that anti-Semitism aimed to destroy the fundamental values of the French revolutionary tradition by reversing the edict of emancipation and abrogating the Rights of Man. It attacked Jews irrespective of their social class, as the Dreyfus Affair was shortly to illustrate in no uncertain terms.

At first Bernard Lazare had scorned the suggestion of his Gentile publisher Stock that he look into the Dreyfus case, on grounds similar to those put forward by his anarchist colleagues. Dreyfus was a wealthy bourgeois, a Jewish officer—his family would not need Lazare's help! However, by the time Mathieu Dreyfus (brother of the accused) approached him in February 1895 Lazare already had serious doubts concerning the legality of the original trial. His indignation and wrath were aroused by the suspicion that evidence had been forged, that Dreyfus had been the victim of a carefully orchestrated conspiracy. With great tenacity he began to seek out documents, to re-examine testimony, to consult handwriting experts and expose contradictions in the case against Dreyfus. The result of his investigations was the publication in Brussels on 6th November 1896 of the first pamphlet in the Dreyfusard campaign—*Une erreur judiciaire: la vérité sur l'affaire Dreyfus*. Three thousand copies of the pamphlet were sent out to influential personalities in the press, parliament and public life. Lazare argued that Dreyfus's guilt had never been satisfactorily demonstrated, and that illegal methods had been used to secure his conviction. He pointed out that the General Staff had brought extraordinary pressures to bear on the judges, taking advantage of a general climate of hatred and suspicion. Lazare also left little doubt that anti-Semitism had played a substantial role in the case. 'Did I not say that Captain Dreyfus belonged to a class of pariahs? He is a soldier, but he is a Jew, and it is as a Jew above all that he was prosecuted.'[40]

Reaction to Lazare's pamphlet among his anarchist comrades and even such future Dreyfusards as Clemenceau and Jaurès was decidedly cool and even hostile in tone. The socialist paper *La Petite République*, like the rest of the left-wing press, simply did not believe that a wealthy officer could be falsely convicted by members of his own class. The Guesdist militant Alexandre Zévaès even challenged Lazare's personal integrity, describing him as 'the distinguished representative of anarchist *high life*, who is at the same time one of the most faithful admirers of His Majesty Rothschild'.[41] Sarcastically he dismissed his pamphlet as a 'cynical, personal advertisement rather than a sincere attempt to rehabilitate an innocent man'.[42] This comment was of course grotesquely wide of the mark, but it did reflect socialist obsessions with the power of Jewish bankers. This preoccupation with Rothschild was one of the main reasons why the French Left proved so hesitant in taking a stand for Dreyfus, whose cause never won unanimous support among the socialists.[43]

As a result Lazare found himself very isolated within his own political camp during the early days of the Dreyfus Affair. Those who were on the same side of the barricade comprised all shades of opinion, ranging from Colonel Picquart, Mathieu Dreyfus, Scheurer-Kestner, Labori and Joseph Reinach to Clemenceau, Jean Allemane and Lucien Herr on the Left. At the beginning of 1898 they were reinforced by the students and intellectuals of the Sorbonne and École Normale, and above all by the great socialist orator Jean Jaurès. But Lazare's campaign for Dreyfus remained qualitatively different; indeed it was unique of its kind, for in his imagination the prisoner on Devil's Island became a symbol of Jewish martyrdom throughout the centuries, of the tragedy which had befallen a dispersed and disinherited race. 'He has been for me the tragic image of the Algerian Jews, beaten and pillaged, the unhappy immigrants dying of hunger in the ghettoes of New York or of London.'[44]

What a paradox that the misfortune of a rich Alsatian officer should have been the detonator for Bernard Lazare's voyage of Jewish self-discovery! In an open letter published in *L'Aurore* on 7th June 1899 Lazare made it clear, however, that it was precisely this explosion of Jewish self-consciousness which had determined the particular nature of his stand. 'I want it to be said that it was a Jew who first stood up for the Jewish martyr . . . a Jew who knew to what an outcast, disinherited, ill-starred people he belonged, and drew from this consciousness the will to fight for justice and truth.'[45]

Bernard Lazare was the first French Jew fully to comprehend that his origins had a political significance, and that to deny them made any effective struggle against anti-Semitism impossible. Though he stood outside the organized Jewish community and traditional Jewish politics, though he remained totally indifferent to religion and hostile to metaphysical speculations, Lazare was the only important figure to take a conscious stand as a Jew in the Dreyfus Affair. The majority of his co-religionists refused to see that the organized campaign against them demanded something more than passive acquiescence and a prudent silence: they relied for their protection solely on French republican traditions and liberal principles. Far from welcoming Lazare's intercession for Dreyfus, they were embarrassed by it, and eventually succeeded in ostracizing him.

This ingratitude simply reinforced Bernard Lazare's conviction that the politics of assimilation had been a disaster in France. It led him between 1897 and 1899 to formulate what was perhaps the most profound critique by a Westernized nineteenth-century Jew of the dominant assimilationist ideology. Like Theodor Herzl, whose famous pamphlet *Der Judenstaat* (1895) was also written in Paris under the impact of the Dreyfus Affair, he realized that emancipation had not resolved the Jewish problem. Assimilation—this 'spurious doctrine' (*doctrine bâtarde*), as Lazare called it—far from ensuring the security and prosperity of the Jews, had undermined the foundations of their existence.[46] It had left them powerless and incapable of self-defence as soon as they became the focal-point of Gentile hatred. Assimilation had corrupted French Jewry, destroying the natural sentiment of solidarity with their less fortunate brethren; it had dejudaized the community, eroding traditional virtues and substituting the modern vices of mercenary egoism and callous indifference.[47]

The Jewish rich, concerned above all to safeguard their social status and privileges, had abandoned the masses of their impoverished co-religionists to the anti-Semites. The last tenuous link between them and the poor Jews was the organized philanthropy which merely served to perpetuate a rigid class-system within the Jewish community. The real problem was not therefore so much anti-

Semitism as the demoralization of an oppressed nation of pariahs by their own élite. What was necessary was a complete transformation of Jewish life from the bottom upward—to initiate a movement of the Jewish masses that would regain control of their own destiny from a decadent and bankrupt leadership. It is in this revolutionary sense that Lazare's conversion to Zionism must be understood, and it is precisely this perspective which accounts for his isolation within the French Jewish community.

In a lecture given in March 1897 to the Association of Russian-Jewish Students in Paris, Lazare first expounded his nationalist solution to the Jewish problem. He explained that Jewish nationalism did not contradict but rather would complete the emancipation granted by the French Revolution. The latter had failed because it insisted on denationalizing the Jews, thereby reducing them to a state of psychological inferiority. Emancipation had merely made 'a conscious pariah out of an unconscious pariah'.[48] Instead of heralding the end of Jewish misery, it had created a new wave of persecution, and engendered a process of demoralization within the Jewish community. The French Jews had passively acquiesced in the campaign against Dreyfus, thereby becoming accomplices and agents of anti-Semitism. The Algerian Jews who had been granted full citizenship in 1871, had not only been chased from their workshops and factories, but had even their right to exist challenged.[49]

What then did Western emancipation have to offer to the mass of his non-assimilated brethren in Russia, the Balkans and Eastern Europe? Lazare's thesis was that it would remain ineffectual until there was a rebirth of the Jewish nationality which alone would free them from the pressures of anti-Semitism. Freedom could not be granted as a gift from above or preserved for the individual without a collective will to assert national identity. 'Nationalism is for me the expression of collective liberty and the condition of individual liberty.'[50] The Jews would have to take arms against their sea of troubles, and nationalism offered them their only hope of survival. But Lazare's nationalism remained essentially libertarian, social-revolutionary, even quasi-mystical in character. 'For a Jew, the word nationalism should mean freedom.'[51] His nationalism was not exclusivist, it was profoundly internationalist in its support for all oppressed minorities. He sought to find allies for the Jews among other oppressed groups in European society, recognizing that anti-Semitism was part of a broad spectrum of reaction and a general suppression of national liberties. Hence the territorial question was secondary to Bernard Lazare, though he favoured the establishment of a Jewish homeland, without specifying Palestine as its predestined locus. 'A Jew who today may declare "I am a nationalist" will not be saying in any special, precise or clear-cut way, "I am a man who seeks to rebuild a Jewish State in Palestine and who dreams of conquering

Jerusalem.'[52]

Lazare's Zionism was born out of a spirit of revolt against the spiritual and psychological dependence produced by assimilation. It was a defiant reply to the time-honoured role of scapegoat which the Gentile nations had assigned to the Jew: 'We are through with being eternally exploited by all peoples, a troop of cattle of serfs, the butt of every lash, a flock to which men even deny a stable, a horde of people denying themselves the right to have a free soil to live and die in liberty.'[53] The Jews would have to stand up to their enemies and say in a clear voice, 'We are ever the ancient stiff-necked people, the unruly and rebel nation; we want to be ourselves, and we shall know well how to conquer the right which is ours, not only to be men but also to be Jews'.[54]

Lazare saw no contradiction between this right to national freedom and the socialist internationalism to which he was still firmly committed. If socialists demanded autonomy for Cubans, Cretans, Armenians, Finns and other small nationalities, then why should the Jews be any less entitled to their sympathy? In order to be genuinely internationalist the Jews, and especially the exploited, proletarian masses among them, must first possess their freedom to struggle as a nation. 'What do we want? We are constantly saying: give to this nation of the poor, the suffering, the proletarians, consciousness of what it is.'[55] This consciousness involved firstly a clear recognition by the Jews that they could not rely on others if they were to resist oppression. They must consciously assume the burden of their pariahood. 'We must seek what we can extract from ourselves, and to this end we must not Christianize Judaism, but on the contrary, judaize the Jew, teach him to live for, and to be himself.'[56]

In order to achieve this revolution of consciousness the chimerical ideology of assimilation would have to be repudiated. As a result of its influence, French Jews had become more papist than the Pope in their professions of jingoism. With bitter irony, Bernard Lazare characterized their role in the Dreyfus Affair:

> As in all countries where the Jews have been emancipated, they have voluntarily shattered the solidarity which existed among them . . . so that even if some three dozen of them were to be found to defend one of their martyred brothers, thousands would have been found to mount watch around Devil's Island, along with the most devoted champions of the fatherland.[57]

Lazare's unhappy experiences in defending Dreyfus in the teeth of hostility from most of his co-religionists had obviously contributed to this sour verdict. He belonged to the select few like Clemenceau, Zola and Péguy who demanded an unambiguous revision of the original sentence. After the Presidential pardon accorded to Dreyfus, following the second trial at Rennes (where he was again found guilty but 'with extenuating circumstances') Lazare still wished to continue the struggle. As he told Péguy, 'Dreyfus must appear before another court-martial, all his life if need be, but he must be declared innocent like everyone else.'[58]

It was this intransigence on matters of principle which was Lazare's greatest characteristic, but it also accounted for his political isolation. The rich Jews viewed him with special horror, and even made stipulations, according to Péguy, that he should not be allowed to write for any paper that they helped to finance.[59] They were only too glad to let him fade into obscurity and oblivion. For his part, Lazare retained an unquenchable hatred for the Jewish plutocracy in France, which he regarded as a curse for the oppressed masses of his people. 'This Jewish bourgeoisie, rich and not Jewish, is our garbage, our rubbish; we must rid ourselves of it; and if it is unable to protect itself against anti-Semitism, it is not our job to help it.'[60]

Bernard Lazare's fight for Dreyfus, his anarchism, his Zionism and his war on the Jewish bourgeoisie were all part of a self-conscious strain of Hebraic prophetism running through his later writings.

> It is faith in the reign of this justice that has animated my people from the time of the Prophets and the poor poets who sang the psalms to those who, like Marx and Lassalle, have asserted the rights of the proletariat . . . All my ancestors and my brothers desired fanatically that each man be granted his rights, and that the scale never be tipped in favour of injustice. For that they cried out, chanted, shed tears, suffered, despite outrages, despite insults and public contempt.[61]

Bernard Lazare came to Zionism as a modern Jewish prophet convinced that only a great popular movement of the proletarian masses could redeem a downtrodden Israel. In May 1897 he had written to Theodor Herzl, identifying fully with his aim of rallying and strengthening the bonds of the scattered Jewish nation.[62] He had briefly directed the French section of the multi-lingual publication *Zion* produced in Berlin. In 1898 he founded a new Zionist review in France entitled *Le Flambeau* (The Torch) which preached his own social-revolutionary brand of Jewish nationalism. He also contributed to two other French periodicals of social-Zionist character, *Kadimah* and *L'Écho Sioniste*. In 1898 he even participated at the second Zionist Congress, where he was warmly applauded by delegates and served on the Actions Committee. But within less than a year he had resigned, disillusioned by Herzl's *Realpolitik* and the 'autocratic government [which] seeks to direct the Jewish masses as though they were ignorant children'.[63]

In his letter of resignation, published in *Le Flambeau* in March 1899, Lazare explained that he could not identify himself with such a form of government, which ignored the economic, intellectual and moral needs of the Jewish masses.[64] 'It is not the one of which the ancient prophets and humble folk who wrote the psalms have dreamed.'

Lazare recognized the unforgettable services of Herzl to the national movement, and on a personal level he admired the man who 'knew how to stir the depths of Israel'.[65] But differences in temperament, political style, social conviction and general outlook between the two men made a parting of the ways inevitable. In a letter of 4th February 1899 Lazare reproached Herzl with placing the cart before the horse, with instituting 'a government with social and diplomatic commitments' before 'creating a people'.[66] The root of this misconception lay, according to Lazare, in Herzl's failure to understand the social needs of the Jewish masses.

> You are bourgeois in thought, bourgeois in feeling, bourgeois in ideas, bourgeois in social content. And yet you wish to lead a people, our people, a poor, unfortunate, proletarian people. You can only do it in an authoritarian way, leading them to what *you* think is their good.[67]

It was the inevitable revolt of the anarchist against the statesman, of the revolutionary against the diplomat, of *mystique* against *politique*—to adopt Péguy's famous antithesis. Bernard Lazare saw himself as a prophet displaying all the ulcers of the Jewish people to themselves and the world—'poor Job on his dungheap' as he unforgettably put it. Herzl, on the other hand, thought in terms of a state, of high diplomacy, and therefore according to Lazare he distorted the real condition of the Jews. 'Like all governments, you wish to disguise the truth, to be the government of a people which looks clean and the height of duty becomes for you not to display our national shame.'[68]

Above all, Lazare opposed the creation of a Jewish Colonial Trust, a national bank which would organize the colonization of Palestine. 'But a bank is never, and can never be an instrument of national regeneration. What an irony to make a bank the founder of the Jewish nation!'[69] Behind this objection stood Lazare's long-standing hatred of the Jewish plutocracy, his fear that they would ultimately sabotage any genuine popular movement among the Jews. From the beginning he had distrusted Herzl's efforts to woo wealthy philanthropists to support his schemes.

The break between the two men came to a head over the Turkish massacre of the Armenians, an oppressed Christian nationality whose aspirations Lazare had consistently supported. Herzl, still hoping to come to a diplomatic arrangement with the Turkish Sultan, preserved a discreet silence over the issue which made Lazare indignant. He regarded Herzl's negotiations with the Sultan, the German Emperor and the Russian Tsar as utterly irrelevant to the real tasks of the Zionist movement. Nothing could come of deals with the enemies of the Jewish people and the oppressors of other national minorities. Herzl, on the other hand, believed above all in securing the support of Gentile statesmen—even if they were anti-Semites—in order to obtain a national home for the Jews.[70] Nothing was more foreign to Lazare's nature than Herzl's pet idea that Zionism would transform previous enemies of the Jews into friends and allies.

Although Bernard Lazare had broken with the Zionist establishment by early 1899, he continued to fight for the liberation of the Jewish people by means of the pen, and travelling frequently to the Balkans and Eastern Europe. He visited the Jewries of Poland, Constantinople, Worms, Prague and above all Rumania, where his presence almost caused a riot and led to his temporary arrest. He had become a kind of roving ambassador of his oppressed brethren, virtually ostracized in his own country but remembered for his defence of Dreyfus by the poor Jews of Eastern Europe.[71] Charles Péguy, the Catholic poet and Lazare's most faithful friend, left an immortal portrait of him in these last years of increasing poverty and loneliness. He had 'a heart which bled in Rumania and in Hungary, everywhere where the Jew is persecuted, which is, in a certain sense, everywhere'.[72] He described Lazare as a man 'consumed by a fire, by the fire of his people'—an atheist who had 'aspects of a saint, of sanctity'.[73]

The young Péguy, and his *Cahiers de la Quinzaine,* became the only means of solace for the dying Lazare, worn out at the age of thirty-eight by exhaustion, overwork and a terminal illness. It was in Péguy's periodical that his last major study *Les Juifs en Roumanie* was published, and that he carried on his fight against the exploitation of the Dreyfusard victory by an anti-clerical regime.

Péguy and Lazare were united by their common revulsion against this manipulation of the Dreyfusard mystique by opportunist politicians.[74] They shared an uncomprising dislike for the modern world, for parliamentary corruption, political parties and demagogic socialism. Their vision was based on the quasi-religious belief that only an inner revolution, a moral transformation of man, could bring about the new humanity envisaged by socialism.[75] One of the factors which had heightened Lazare's alienation from the mainstream of the French socialist movement was the awareness that it was still tainted by a traditional anti-Semitism. During the Dreyfus Affair most socialists, with the exeption of a few outstanding leaders like Jean Allemane, Herr and Jaurès, had been very reluctant to take a stand. They had either encouraged anti-Semitism by their discreet silence or else in some cases by adopting an anti-Dreyfusard position.

This was pointed out in a little pamphlet entitled *Le Prolétariat Juif,* written in 1898 by the Groupe des Ouvriers Juifs Socialistes Français and addressed to the French socialists. It was signed by Karpel (head of the Jewish hatmakers' union) and Dinner, librarian of the Yiddish Bibliothèque des ouvriers juifs de Paris, but the text shows the unmistakable imprint of Bernard Lazare. We know that by the beginning of 1898 his revolutionary Zionism had found some echo among immigrant Jewish workers and students from Russia and Eastern Europe, living on the margins of Parisian society.[76] These immigrants were sympathetic to his libertarian anarchism, and the pamphlet echoes all Lazare's favourite themes at the time: above all in its insistence on the existence of a world-wide Jewish proletariat living in abject poverty and constantly threatened with persecution and pogroms.[77] It was this proletariat which had to suffer, because of the general hatred for Jewish bankers, and who were always ignored by anti-Semites and even by the socialists. The pamphlet sharply criticized the French Left for its failure to unequivocally condemn the anti-Semitic campaign and for believing that 'class-hatred could be superimposed on to Jew-hatred'.[78]

In an article published in *La Grande Revue* in September 1899 Bernard Lazare expanded this critique into frontal attack on the 'social concept of Judaism' held by most of his comrades on the Left. Already Fourier, Proudhon, Toussenel and Bakunin had denounced the Jews for usury and parasitic middleman activities.[79] This was erroneous enough, but

> it is likewise the view of men who would vehemently protest were you to attribute to them the least hint of prepossession, it is the view of intellectuals enlightened in all things save this, it is even the view of some socialists, notably Jaurès, and that is why it must be answered.[80]

A short time before Lazare's polemic Jaurès had written a reply in *La Petite République* to Edouard Drumont which was highly equivocal in tone. Although himself a leading Dreyfusard, Jaurès spoke of the Jews exercising 'an inordinate and formidable influence in our society': he had further suggested that 'the social concept of the Jew, based on the idea of trade, is in perfect harmony with the mechanism of capital'[81]; if Drumont had only confined himself to pointing this out, then Jaurès would have been with him—'such a socialism, tinted with anti-Semitism, would scarcely have raised any objections among *esprits libres*'.[82]

But the free-thinking revolutionary Bernard Lazare strongly objected to this remark of Jaurès, which he regarded as symptomatic of a whole trend of opinion on the French Left. 'They regard capitalism as a Jewish creation, and just as does Drumont after Gougenot des Mousseaux, so does Jaurès after Marx speak of the judaization of the Christian peoples.'[83] Lazare concentrated his fire on this one-sided, dogmatic stereotype of the Jew which ran like a red thread through modern socialism. Marx, with his call to de-judaize the Jews in order to complete their emancipation, had been the prime culprit. As a logician (added Lazare), Marx 'must have smiled at the empty religio-economic metaphysics which he naïvely displayed in his article ['Zur Judenfrage']. At the time he wrote it he knew nothing about the Jews.'[84] With this critique of Marxism Lazare had come full circle in his spiritual odyssey. The man who had once ignorantly denounced the mercantilism of the Talmud now proceeded to show that the social concept of the Talmudists glorified *manual* work. The great Talmudic scholars and medieval rabbis had all been artisans and anti-mercantile in outlook. The Talmud, like the Bible, regarded agriculture as a pre-eminent activity. One could not find any social concept based on trade in Rashi, Maimonedes or Joseph Caro. Nor was there any basis in the Hebrew Bible for such a concept. On the contrary, the prophets and psalmists consistently defended the poor, the humble and the small freeholders against the encroachments of the wealthy and powerful. It was the Phoenicians and Greeks, not the Children of Israel, who had been the middlemen and carriers of trade in the ancient Middle East.

In more recent times, philosophers and economists of Jewish origin were primarily noted for their opposition or indifference to commerce. Spinoza, in the best rabbinical tradition, had preferred to earn a living grinding lenses rather than seeking fame, honours and wealth in the Courts of Europe. Even David Ricardo's economic theories were scarcely an apologia for capitalism, while Marx and Lassalle, who had based their analyses on his concepts, had arrived at impeccably socialist conclusions. It was non-Jews like Colbert, Turgot, Adam Smith, David Hume and Jeremy Bentham who had laid the foundations of laissez-faire economics, with their advocacy of the profit-motive and utilitarian market philosophies.[85]

Socialists not only forgot all this when they mistakenly identified the Jews with capitalist usury, they completely overlooked the class-struggle within the Jewish communities. In Russia, Poland, Holland, France, England and America, the Jewish worker stood in open conflict with his employers. 'Of all proletarians, the Jewish proletarian is the most wretched, having against him not only the rich and poor of the peoples in whose midst he lives.'[86]

In his last writings, Bernard Lazare emphasized this class-struggle within Jewish society and 'the rottenness of the Jewish upper classes' as a barrier to full national emancipation.[87] More than any other people, the Jews would have to rid themselves of their servility to the rich and cease to be 'revolutionaries in the society of others' instead of their own.[88] This is one of the main themes in *Le Fumier de Job* (Job's Dungheap)—a collection of aphorisms written shortly before his early death in 1903. This little fragment gives one a glimpse of the last stage in Lazare's journey back to the sources of Jewish consciousness.

Though written by an unrepentant atheist and anarchist revolutionary, it contains a moving awareness of the universal, transcendent aspects of the Jewish experience. It belongs with the poems of André Spire and Edmond Fleg's *Écoute Israël!* to that renaissance of French Judaism at the turn of the twentieth century whose midwife was Charles Péguy's *Cahiers de la Quinzaine*.[89]

Lazare's last essay summed up the goal of his tormented struggle to attain self-consciousness, not only as a man, but also as a Jew.[90] It bore witness to the prophet of Israel who had fought for Dreyfus, for the Jews of Rumania, for the wretched of the earth, and for the deliverance of his own soul. Charles Péguy's words may stand as a final testament to this unjustly forgotten defender of freedom:

> Never have I seen a man believe to such a degree, to such a degree be certain that a man's conscience is something absolute, invincible, eternal, something free, that victorious and triumphant stands firm against all the greatness of the earth.[91]

CHAPTER 8

Léon Blum, Frenchman, Socialist and Jew

'The Jews have made a religion of Justice as the Positivists have made a religion of Facts and Renan a religion of Science. . . .'

Léon Blum

'In my eyes he remains an admirable representative both of Semitism and of humanity.'

André Gide

Léon Blum was born in 1872, in the Rue St Denis in the heart of Paris, of middle-class parents. He was the second son of a family of five, whose paternal and maternal ancestors came from Alsace.

On his father's side his origins can be traced to Westhofen, in the district of Hochfelden (lower Rhine), at one time an important Jewish centre. The Napoleonic ordinances of 1808 obliged one of his paternal ancestors to take the name of Moses Blum. Léon's father, Auguste (Abraham) Blum, settled in Paris around 1846, and eventually set up a business in the wholesale ribbons trade.[1] Auguste Blum was a successful merchant, and his children were able to grow up in an untroubled, comfortable atmosphere.[2] However, it was from his mother, *née* Adèle-Marie-Alice Picart, that Léon Blum appears to have inherited some of the traits which distinguished him in later life.[3] She also came from an old Alsatian family, and maintained a strictly orthodox observance of Judaism.

The household was 'kosher', and religious festivals were celebrated in traditional fashion: although Léon Blum abandoned these customs once he left home, his orthodox upbringing was undoubtedly a major source of his deep feeling for and pride in the Jewish people. At the same time, Blum imbibed from his mother's side of the family a hatred of injustice and oppression and an early appreciation of the French liberal-revolutionary tradition. The milieu in which he grew up encouraged progressive republican sentiments which reflected the prevailing ideology among the assimilationist Jewish bourgeoisie in nineteenth-century France.[4] Attachment to French culture, to the Great Revolution of 1789 which had emancipated the Jews, and to the liberal tradition went hand in hand for Léon Blum with his ancestral heritage.[5]

Blum was an exceptional student at the Lycée Charlemagne, and then at the Lycée Henri IV, and in 1890 he entered the École Normale Supérieure—the training-ground for France's political, administrative and cultural élite. Blum was not happy at the École Normale, and left after a year, for reasons which have never been entirely clarified, but which most probably derived from his rebellious temperament.[6]

He took up law, and at the same time embarked on a successful career as a drama critic. His first literary efforts appeared in *La Revue Blanche*, an avant-garde publication, which perfectly captured the cosmopolitan, *fin-de-siècle* individualism of the period.[7] It was a time when Maurice Barrès's novels and his introspective *culte de moi* were all the rage, and until the Dreyfus Affair divided them, Blum felt the greatest admiration for Barrès.[8] The director of *La Revue Blanche* was a Polish Jew, Thadée Nathanson, and its literary editor, Lucien Muhlfeld, was also of Jewish origin. Several co-religionists of Léon Blum such as Julien Benda, Marcel Proust (a half Jew), Daniel Halévy and Tristan Bernard were among its contributors.[9] Like most of the collaborators to the little review, the young Blum was more attracted by anarchism than by socialism, though his political views were as yet far from ripe. The dilettante anarchism which *La Revue Blanche* exuded was essentially a revolt against the positivism and scientism which had dominated French intellectual life since Renan and Taine.

In the early 1890s the young Léon Blum lived the life of an elegant man about town; he felt at home in the Parisian salons, he was curious about everything, he regularly reviewed books, plays and contributed a monthly sporting and racing column for the review. Significantly, his first article in 1892 (dedicated to Barrès) described the 'progress of apolitics in France', the mood of political disillusion which had overtaken the country in the wake of abortive revolutions throughout the nineteenth century.[10] In his early writings there was as yet little to suggest his future conversion to socialism. Nevertheless, influences were already at work which helped to crystallize Blum's social and political convictions by the end of the decade.

In spite of his worldly allure of refined aesthete and Parisian dandy, there was in Blum a moral earnestness and devotion to justice which made him receptive to the new creed of socialism. His consciousness of belonging to a people which had for so many centuries been persecuted and oppressed undoubtedly played a role in this transition: more immediate, however, was the personal influence of Lucien Herr, the socialist librarian of the École Normale, who in Blum's own words 'achieved a reorientation of my individualistic and anarchistic nature in the direction of socialism'.[11] Lucien Herr made of him a Dreyfusard and introduced him to Jaurès—the man who was to exercise a magnetic attraction and lasting influence on the young Blum. There was nothing surprising in Blum's receptivity to an idealistic republican socialism, for a whole generation of students at the Sorbonne and the École Normale (including Jaurès, Péguy and many others) were to be converted by Herr's charismatic powers of persuasion.[12]

In the case of Léon Blum, the process of commitment to the life of a socialist militant was, however, slower than usual. By temperament, background and life-style, he still identified with the bourgeois world of the salons, for which he felt no consuming hatred or resentment. He continued to love the theatre, and to believe in a cultivated aristocracy of the spirit, long after his intellectual conversion to socialism. This dualism in Blum's outlook was later to create many difficulties, but he always remained true to his own inclinations and never made any concessions to the conventional image of a socialist leader.[13] Indeed, it is open to question whether Blum would have opted for a political career had it not been for the assassination of Jaurès in 1914.

Blum's intimate association with Jaurès was the decisive factor in his evolution, and it developed during the Dreyfus Affair.[14] The events associated with this period of French history proved to be as much a baptism of fire for Blum as for most of his contemporaries. The conviction of the Alsatian Jewish captain for high treason in 1894 did not initially trouble public opinion in France. Not until late 1896 did Bernard Lazare's pamphlet on the case bring to the attention of a still indifferent public the possibility that there had been a serious miscarriage of justice. Although Blum knew and admired Lazare as '*un juif de la grande race*', imbued with the ancient Hebrew prophetism, he felt as little persuaded by Lazare's assertions as did such future Dreyfusard leaders of the stamp of Clemenceau and Jaurès.[15]

It was again Lucien Herr who convinced Blum, in the autumn of 1897 while he was holidaying in the countryside outside Paris, that Dreyfus was indeed innocent.[16] Within a few months Blum had become active in the Dreyfusard struggle, working conscientiously at sifting the evidence and preparing briefs for Labori, the defence counsel of Dreyfus. His legal acumen (Blum was by this time an accomplished jurist) proved extremely useful, though he was content to leave the political action to others. In 1898 he contributed a detached, analytical article to *La Revue Blanche* on the Zola trial which summarized the results of the proceedings and expressed his optimism that the 'truth' would triumph.[17] The article was signed 'Un juriste', and, avoiding all references to the dramatic demonstrations and riots which had accompanied Zola's trial, confined itself to demonstrating logically the necessity for revising Dreyfus' original conviction. Curiously enough, Blum as yet felt no compulsion to comment on the virulent anti-Semitic campaign which was developing in opposition to calls for precisely such a revision. In order to understand this surprising omission, one must consider the general attitude of French Jews to the case, and also Blum's self-image at this time. In his *Souvenirs sur l'Affaire*, written nearly forty years later, Blum himself observed that the French Jewish community had reacted with extreme caution and defensiveness to the Dreyfus case.

> They did not speak of the Affair among themselves; they avoided the subject, rather than bringing it up. A great sorrow had fallen upon Israel. One submitted to it, without saying anything, hoping that time and silence would efface its effects.[18]

Blum was in retrospect highly critical of this passive attitude, which he attributed to egoistic prudence. He understood that his co-religionists remained silent for fear of casting doubt on their own loyalties, and thereby further inflaming anti-Semitism. Since the defence of Dreyfus was equated by nationalists with an assault on the honour of the French Army, any stand on his behalf threatened the very touchy patriotism which French Jews shared with their Catholic countrymen.[19] Moreover, as Blum pointed out, the French Jewish community 'did not want it believed that they were motivated by any form of racial or religious solidarity'.[20]

Blum, however, argued that the struggle for truth and justice transcended the narrow-minded human reflex which generally adopts for security and tranquillity. He drew a parallel between Jewish timidity at the time of the Dreyfus Affair and reluctance actively to combat French fascism in the 1930s. 'The wealthy Jews, the middle bourgeois Jews, the Jewish functionaries were all afraid of engaging in a struggle for Dreyfus, just as they are afraid of engaging today in the struggle against fascism.'[21] Blum, although no less assimilated than most of his co-religionists, was convinced by Herr, Clemenceau and Jaurès that the Dreyfus Affair was indeed a great moral struggle for human rights and Jacobin principles. It was in this broader context that he supported the Dreyfusard cause, not because Dreyfus was a Jew, but because he was the symbol of an injustice which if it was not redressed would threaten the integrity of republican institutions.[22]

On the issue of anti-Semitism, however, Blum's position was much less convincing, and lacked the historical perspective of Bernard Lazare, or the intuitive vision of Theodor Herzl. One cannot attribute this defect solely to Blum's assimilationism, though his attitude was characteristic of many liberal and socialist Jews. Rather it stemmed from his genuine incapacity to comprehend that the anti-Dreyfusard agitation was founded on deep-rooted, irrational motives which were not susceptible to reasoned argument and debate.[23] The young Léon Blum too flippantly dismissed French anti-Semitism as an affair of the clubs and the racecourses which was not likely to be dangerous.[24] His almost casual underestimation of this phenomenon comes out clearly in his remarkable *Nouvelles Conversations de Goethe avec Eckermann*.

Blum had composed these dialogues for *La Revue Blanche* between 1894 and 1901, and they give one a fascinating picture of the mental world which the young socialist philosopher, aesthete and literary critic had fashioned for himself. With remarkable maturity and intellectual daring, Léon Blum transplanted the 'universal' German poet and thinker Goethe into his own time and place, and made him the mouthpiece for a very French sensibility and outlook. Written at the time of the Dreyfus Affair, the *Nouvelles Conversations* cover a whole multitude of subjects. They also contain some of Léon Blum's most interesting observations on the position of the Jews in French society, on their past and future role.

The shallowest part of these reflections consist of Blum's oversanguine conviction that there was no ground for fearing an outbreak of real persecution in France, despite the mounting anti-Semitic hysteria. He regarded the latter as an ephemeral reaction to an external stimulus, rather than as a natural development of French society and thought.[25] In 1899 he accordingly counselled the French Jews not to be so touchy about their exclusion from the salons of the aristocracy and from certain careers in the army or civil service.[26] They should cultivate a proud independence of spirit instead of complaining at their treatment.

> If the Jews are courageous, if instead of inflating the effect of those acts which wrong them, they absorb and minimize them, if instead of complaining they smile at it, if they are quietly confident like their ancestors that every injustice is temporary and that civilization never retraces its steps, then none will be able to say that they are persecuted.[27]

Persecution, in the opinion of the young Léon Blum, was a subjective state of mind which could be overcome by assuming a dignified posture. Doubtless this over-simplified judgment reflected the fact that Blum did not feel personally discriminated against as a Jew. Though proud of his origins, he was above all attached to French culture, and thoroughly imbued with a faith in its republican traditions and humanist values. He saw no contradiction between his French patriotism, with its messianic Jacobin universalism, and what he took to be the eternal values of Judaism.[28] The genuine affinity which Blum felt between French and Hebraic rationalism explains more than anything else his optimism about the situation of Jews in France and his tendency to ignore the historical roots of anti-Semitism.[29]

Léon Blum's fidelity to Judaism, unusual as it was among assimilated Jewish intellectuals in *fin-de-siècle* France, was never isolationist or particularist. It had nothing to do with religious orthodoxy, but it did lay stress on certain 'innate' characteristics of the Jewish race, and on the messianic universalism which Blum considered common to both Judaism and socialism.[30] In his *Nouvelles Conversations* the 27-year-old Blum remarked:

> In so far as I can discern the collective impulse of their race, it leads them towards revolution; their critical powers (and I use the word in its highest sense) drive them to destroy every idea, every traditional form which does not agree with the facts or cannot be justified by reason. . . .

These were the qualities which, in Blum's opinion, made them the Jews admirably suited to become apostles of socialism.[31]

This statement seemed uncannily to presage Blum's future role as a socialist leader. His assessment of Judaism also cast an interesting light on his upbringing and attitude to religion in general:

> I have never encountered people so free from religious notions or traditions—to the point that it is impossible, as you know, to formulate the Jewish dogma. Among the people religion is only a collection of family superstitions which are observed without any

conviction, purely out of respect for the ancestors who conformed to them for 2500 years; for enlightened people, it means nothing.[32]

At the same time, Blum emphasized that such rationalism was profoundly *religious* in a this-worldly sense, that the 'prophetic' ideal expressed by the founders of socialism was that of a just, harmonious society.[33] Though emancipated from traditional beliefs and prejudices, the Jews had not lost their faith in humanity, in social justice, and in a better future.

> The Jew has made a religion of Justice as the positivists have made a religion of Facts or Renan a religion of Science . . . the idea of inevitable justice is the one thing which has sustained and united the Jews in their long tribulations . . . It is this world . . . which must one day be ordered according to Reason, to make one rule prevail over all men and to give to everyone his due. Is that not the spirit of socialism? It is the ancient spirit of the race.[34]

For the young Blum, Hebraic messianism 'is nothing else than the symbol of eternal justice which may doubtless forsake the world for centuries, but which cannot fail to rule over it one day'.[35] Judaism, unlike the Christian Gospels, valued justice in *this world*, not personal immortality in world to come. Blum added, 'If the Christ preached charity, Jehovah demanded justice. The Bible says a just man, where the Gospels say a saint'.[36] He drove home his point by observing that 'it is not by an accident of Providence that a Marx and a Lassalle were Jews'.[37]

These reflections on the affinity between Judaism and socialism reveal much about the political direction in which the young Léon Blum was already moving, and about his own self-understanding as a Jew. Before the Dreyfus Affair he had felt no special compulsion to come to terms with this aspect of his heritage; as he modestly put it, four decades later, he had 'no more obvious calling than any other to receive the Dreyfusard grace'.[38] The Affair had provided the first serious rupture with his comfortable *salonnard* existence, it had brought him into contact with French socialism and the small circle of militant Dreyfusard intellectuals who fought for integral justice and universal moral ideals. The Librairie Georges Bellais, founded by Charles Péguy and located near the Sorbonne, had become the *front line* for those who like Léon Blum were resolved to follow Jaurès in his fight to salvage the Rights of Man against the assaults of the clerico-military oligarchy.[39]

Blum had joined the Dreyfusards not as a Jew but out of genuine republican convictions and high moral principles. Similarly, he joined the Groupe de l'Unité Socialiste in 1899 and the Parti Socialiste Français in 1902, not out of 'a hereditary messianic deviation', as

Léon Daudet claimed, but as a logical consequence of his Dreyfusard rationalism.[40]

The Dreyfus Affair had profoundly influenced Blum's sense of personal identity, convincing him that the Jews in France would have to face up to anti-Semitism and combat it in the name of universal principles. At the same time his encounter with Jaurès made of him a socialist of the heart as well as the head, persuaded that the cause of justice and of humanity was identical with the realization of socialist ideals. In 1899 he joined Lucien Herr as one of the five directors of the Société Nouvelle de Librairie et d'Édition, a short-lived publishing venure intended to popularize socialist literature.[41] Blum's own history of working-class and socialist congresses from 1876 to 1900 appeared the following year, and already showed him to be thoroughly familiar with the internal evolution of French socialism.[42]

Nevertheless, before 1914 Blum was content to remain in the shadows as a counsellor and adviser of Jaurès and as a critic and observer of social and political events. Although instrumental in the founding of *L'Humanité* in 1904, he confined his contributions in Jaurès's newspaper to literary essays and dramatic criticism.[43] His home became a meeting-place for the élite of French society and his professional career as a jurist at the Conseil d'État continued undisturbed. Twice Jaurès proposed that he stand as a Socialist candidate to the Chamber of Deputies (in 1902 and 1906), but each time Blum declined, preferring his role of social critic and reporter on political affairs. This curious reticence was only ended by the outbreak of the First World War and the assassination of his great friend and mentor, Jaurès, in 1914. This traumatic event seems to have awakened latent guilt feelings in Blum, that he had thus far played an insufficiently active role in the socialist movement. But by 1918 the mantle of the great pre-war leader of French socialism had fallen on his shoulders, and he was to become the guardian of its democratic traditions in a most difficult and testing atmosphere.[44]

Blum's evolution as a Jew at this time seems to have undergone an important change which it is difficult precisely to document. There is, however, a highly ambivalent portrait of Léon Blum in 1914 by his long-standing friend, the novelist André Gide.[45] The latter attributed to Léon Blum the belief in a future 'age of the Jew', when his coreligionists would penetrate all areas of culture, industry and politics, dominating those who had once been their persecutors. According to Gide, Blum was convinced of the 'superiority' of his own race, of its greater adaptability and logical capacities. While admiring Blum's 'precise kind of mind', his 'lucid brilliance' and the 'nobility, generosity and chivalry' of his character, Gide declared himself irritated by his friend's 'apparent resolve always to show a preference for the Jew'.

In Gide's estimation, Blum considered 'it is his duty to work towards its triumph [the triumph of the Jewish race] with all his strength'.[46] There can be little doubt that this was a gross misinterpretation of Blum's outlook, but is interesting not only because Gide was a senstitive student of human psychology, but also because it contains a half-truth which is worth analysing.

Already in his *Nouvelles Conversations* of 1899 Blum had indeed endowed the Jews with a superior clairvoyance which made them better adapted to perceive the inevitability of socialism. In his view even Jewish millionaires and capitalists would resign themselves to eventual expropriation, because the 'natural law of their race' encouraged them never to vainly fight against the stream.[47] At the same time, despite this dubious invocation of supposedly 'racial' characteristics, Blum clearly rejected the mentality of the Jewish bourgeoisie which had forgotten the Hebraic command to realize social justice. 'The life of the race is not seated there. Go seek for it in the proletariat among skilled workers, among the industrious and bighearted youth of the lower middle classes. It is from there that the sap rises'.[48]

Blum emphasized that Jewish bankers and finaciers were not representative of the prophetic ideals with which he identified socialism. The essential point, however, was that the Jews would bow to historical necessity, because bitter experience had taught them to accept the loss of worldly goods. They had already lost their fatherland and their temple, they had endured dispersion, persecution and hatred—therefore, Blum reasoned, 'Nobody will accept better than they the equitable redistribution of tasks and the common law of labour'.[49]

This was Blum's rather bizarre explanation of the paradox that Jews had helped create capitalism, just as they had founded the socialism which would one day also expropriate their wealth. The effects of Jewish history had not yet been exhausted; Blum held that they still had an important part to play in the building of a new society. Precisely for this reason, he criticized those of his contemporaries who were concerned at the possible exclusion of Jewish officers from the army. In his view, too many Jews sought entrance to careers which 'were poorly adapted to the fundamental character of their race'.[50] They lacked the requisite docility, mechanical precision and intellectual dullness to become servants of the State—whether in the bureaucracy, the army or similar occupations! Exclusion from such avenues of advancement would actually be beneficial, since 'their real nature will be preserved; they will know that joy of independence which a defective social organization generally refuses to superior beings'.[51]

These passages in Blum's writings seem to reflect a certain élitist esotericism in his approach to the Jewish problem. Gide was not totally wrong to suggest that Blum thought the Jews 'superior', but he misinterpreted the nature of this sentiment. Belief in a chosen mission of the Jewish people did not imply any desire for domination, but rather the acceptance of a moral burden to advance humanity. It was Gide, not Léon Blum, who exhibited an unconscious racism when he declared that 'the qualities of the Jewish race are not French qualities'.[52] Gide never retracted 'the rather harsh passages' of his 1914 *Journal* about Blum, for as he put it in 1948, 'I continue to think them utterly correct'.[53] But he did come to see in Léon Blum 'an admirable representative both of Semitism and of humanity' and a personality 'much more utopian and mystical than I am willing to be'.[54]

The tragic events of the Second World War gave Gide and many of his compatriots a new esteem and admiration for the courage of Léon Blum. It showed them a different side of that 'marvellously organized, organizing, clear and classifying intelligence' which between the wars was to render Blum so needlessly sinister and suspect to his political enemies and opponents.

During the First World War Léon Blum became the *chef de cabinet* of Marcel Sembat's Ministry of Public Works, and gained his first experience of the workings of government. He also set out to restore the shattered unity in the French socialist ranks and to formulate a programme of action for the party in the post-war period. Already in his late forties, he abandoned in 1919 a brilliant legal career at the Conseil d'État, as well as the salon world of the literary dilettante, to become the leader of a working-class party. He carried with him into the new era much of the republican heritage of the pre-1914 French labour movement, with its emphasis on the democratic road to socialism, on orderly evolution and peaceful progress towards the final goal.[55] He had never been a Marxist, in the sense of accepting historical materialism and the exclusive primacy of the class-struggle; nor did Blum have any sympathy with Bolshevism, which he regarded as an anarcho-Blanquist deviation that had turned the seizure of power into an end in itself.[56]

In the tradition of Benoît Malon, Lucien Herr and Jean Jaurès, he saw socialism as the incarnation of universal morality, and gave an ethical, rationalist colouring to the teachings of Marx. He believed that a long period of evolution was necessary before the social revolution could substitute a collectivist system of production and property. Having matured in the pre-war mould of Jaurèssian humanism, Blum's socialism was inevitably republican and reformist, patriotic yet internationalist in the classic French tradition. At the Congress of Tours (1920), which witnessed the schism of the French labour movement under the impact of the Bolshevik Revolution in Russia, Blum defended this tradition against the Communist idea of a proletarian dictatorship.[57] In his opinion, Bolshevism was inapplicable to France, and he consequently led the opposition to the conditions of membership demanded by Moscow for adhesion to the Third International. Blum's twenty years of service in the Conseil d'État, which endeavoured to protect individual rights against encroachment by the State, had left him with a fine feeling for democratic legality and the value of civic freedoms. As director of *Le Populaire* and president of the parliamentary socialist group in the 1920s and 30s, Blum never wavered in his opposition to the use of violence and terror as a political weapon, whether by the Left or the Right.

His patient rebuilding of socialist strength after the break-away of the French Communists earned him their marked hostility and even hatred, which was only partially restrained during the period of Popular Front government in 1936–7.[58] In the inter-war period Blum was frequently abused from the extreme Left as an 'agent of the bourgeosie' and a 'traitor to the working class'. His elegant appearance, which made no concessions to working-class taste, his evident intellectual superiority, his Jewishness and bourgeois background, were seized on by his Communist opponents.[59] Their malicious hostility to Blum had many sources, and was a factor in their refusal to participate in his Government of 1936, though they had supported and even initiated the principle of the Popular Front. It was not that the PCF was explicitly anti-intellectual or anti-Semitic, though there can be little doubt that they did not welcome a Jewish middle-class intellectual as leader of the French labour movement; rather, they saw in Blum an *inclassable*, a leader whose sophistication and independence of mind was alien to their whole outlook and an obstacle to their ambitions to gain exclusive hegemony over the working-class movement. Even by Communist standards, the abuse directed at Blum was however quite exceptional. A leading French Communist, André Marty, on 7th October 1939, in an 'open Letter to Léon Blum', probably composed in Moscow, wrote:

> You vulgarly, vilely insult Stalin, Monsieur le Conseiller d'État imperialiste—you thereby expose yourself still more in attempting, you a pygmy, to match a giant of humanity . . . you, Blum, intimate of the biggest cosmopolitan financiers, hate the man who has made out of the old socialist dream a reality . . .[60]

In another open letter, in February 1940, Maurice Thorez, the Secretary-General of the French Communist Party, made Blum personify all the evils represented by such diverse enemies of Stalinism as Millerand, Pilsudski, Mussolini, Noske and Trotsky. Thorez observed:

> The working class cannot fail to nail this moral and political monster to the pillory of infamy. It cannot fail to condemn and reject with horror and disgust Blum the bourgeois, Blum the noninterventionist . . . Blum the assassin of Clichy, Blum the police inspector, Blum the warmonger. This is a condition of the victorious struggle for peace, for socialism.[61]

Blum's ancestry was of course more significant for the political Right, who used it unscrupulously and with extraordinary virulence to reinforce hostility to his political programme. His opposition to the French occupation of the Ruhr, in January 1923, had aroused a storm of violent anti-Semitic invective from Rightist deputies in the French Parliament. Blum regarded French Government attempts to re-establish hegemony on the Continent as an anachronistic utopia, and its attempt to enforce German reparations as grist to the mill of monarchist and military reaction across the Rhine.[62] His plea for moderation led Léon Daudet of the Action Française to abuse him as a representative of '*la finance juive*', Ybarnegaray as a 'Jewish Protestant' and Lieutenant-Colonel Josse to refer to him as a German patriot![63] In reply to Daudet's taunt 'À Jerusalem!', Blum answered with characteristic dignity, 'I am indeed a Jew, in fact, it is no insult to remind me of the race into which I was born, which I have never renounced and towards which I feel only gratitude and pride'.[64] Blum always defended himself against anti-Semitic slurs, not only as a socialist, but also as a conscious Jew. Even in the mid-1930s, when he became the first Socialist and Jewish Premier in France, and the verbal attacks from the Rightist Press, especially *Gringoire* and *Je Suis Partout* reached a new height of scurrility and viciousness, Blum maintained an extraordinary serenity.

For the Action Française and the rapidly mushrooming fascist leagues in France, Blum symbolized the danger from *within*, and his personality and appearance were mercilessly pilloried.[65] When Blum presented his Government to the Chamber of Deputies in June 1936, Xavier Vallat, future Commissioner for Jewish Affairs under the Vichy regime protested 'For the first time this old Gallo-Roman country is to be governed by a Jew . . . it would be better to have someone ruling France whose origins, however modest, blend into our soil, than a subtle talmudist'.[66]

A flood of pamphlets and articles focused on Blum's allegedly 'corrupting' intelligence, his pacifism, his over-subtlety, nervousness, attachment to doctrine—all so-called 'Semitic' characteristics which were made responsible for French divisions and impotence.[67] Blum stood up with great courage and dignity to this sudden wave of hostility, which also included Jews fearful of the growth of anti-Semitism, who demanded his resignation.[68]

Even within his own party in the early 1930s an anti-Semitic current had appeared among the 'Neo-Socialists' led by Marcel Déat, Renaudel and Marquet. They called for a militant 'socialism of action' and a preventive coup against the fascists; their socialism was national, authoritarian and sought to win the mass of petty-bourgeois *déclassés* to the party through demogogic slogans. Blum's style of leadership was characterized by them as 'Byzantine', doctrinaire and sterile, in an era of triumphant National Socialism and dynamic mass movements.[69]

Blum in reply to this challenge used the same arguments as he had against the Bolsheviks, rejecting the either-or policy of collaboration or outright opposition to the bourgeois regime, proposed by the Neo-socialists. He pointed out that in their impatience Déat and his supporters copied fascist methods, and confused a purely political with an authentic social revolution.[70] Blum was basically correct in his appraisal of Neo-Socialist tactics, but he showed much less perception with regard to the menace of Hitlerism. He mistakenly regarded Hitler's racism as a simple form of nationalism, underestimating its attraction and power in the wake of the German economic crisis. He was convinced after the elections of November 1932 in Germany that Hitler's road to the Chancellorship was blocked and his star in eclipse. Even after the Nazis came to power, he clung for some time to the view that their triumph was ephemeral, and that working-class unity and a disarmament conference would effectively neutralize their success.[71]

The urgent need for solidarity in the face of fascism proved, however, a major factor in the formation of the Popular Front which came to power in France on a wave of popular enthusiasm in June 1936. As Prime Minister, Blum was able, during his single year of office, to extract substantial benefits for the working class—including collective contracts, holidays with pay, a forty-hour week and a system of industrial arbitration. This was an impressive achievement, but the Government foundered in its non-intervention policy during the Spanish Civil War (provoked by political opposition inside France and Blum's alliance with England) and through the loss of confidence by financial circles in its policy. The Left was alienated by Blum's inability to save the Spanish regime and the French bourgeoisie by fear of his socialist policies. Ever conscious of the limits of his mandate and the restraints on his exercise of power in a constitutional, capitalist framework, Blum preferred to resign when the Senate refused to give him full powers to stop the flight of capital. Thus ended the most promising experiment in social change, undertaken in the inter-war period of the Third Republic.[72]

Léon Blum's prominence as a socialist leader in the 1930s inevitably made him a focal point of racial hatred, but though never indifferent to these aspersions, he developed a protective armour which enabled him calmly to face his detractors. He always made a point of stressing his origin, even greeting Schacht (Hitler's envoy to the Popular Front Government) by announcing '*Je suis marxiste, je suis juif*'—a fact of which the German Economics Minister was doubtless well aware.[73]

In the 1930s anti-Semitism had become an international issue involving the domestic and foreign policies of the various European governments. In France the immigration of Jewish refugees had set alight the old xenophobia that Blum had already experienced at the time of the Dreyfus Affair. The socialist leader was very critical of the egoistic attitude adopted by his co-religionists and their communal representatives.[74] Instead of requesting that the doors of France be opened to the victims of Nazi persecution, the official leadership of French Jewry, beginning with the Chief Rabbi, emphasized their agreement with the appeasement policy practised by the French Government at Munich. The preservation of peace seemed to them all important; in their reluctance to denounce Hitlerian racism, French Jewish leaders were pathetically trying to demonstrate their loyalty to France![75] Léon Blum condemned such tactics as undignified, foolish and morally reprehensible. In a speech of 26th November 1938 to the *LICA* (Ligue Internationale contre l'Antisémitisme), he declared:

> There is nothing in the world so painful and so dishonourable as the sight of French Jews occupying themselves today in closing the doors of France to the Jewish refugees of other countries. Do they imagine that they will thus preserve their own tranquillity and security? There is no example in history that anyone has ever gained security through cowardice . . .[76]

These were prophetic words, though they were scarcely appreciated at the time by official representatives of the Jewish community; they were the confession of one of those rare socialists who could say in all sincerity, 'I am a Jew who has never blushed because of his origin, a Jew who has always borne his name'.[77]

Only in 1940, after the crushing defeat of France, did Blum experience a momentary despair, and consider completely withdrawing from political life. By this time his vulnerability as a scapegoat for the deep dissensions in France, and the unpopularity which his name evoked, made him seriously reflect whether he was not in fact damaging the cause for which he had fought so courageously.[78] But Blum, ever true to himself, preferred to stand his ground, and in June 1940, when Churchill tried to persuade him to leave France, he refused on grounds which for anyone else would have been reason enough to flee. '*Je suis français, je suis socialiste, je suis juif.*'[79] Blum was too profoundly patriotic to abandon his country in danger, whereas his rabidly nationalist detractors proved to be more than willing collaborators with the Nazis.

Imprisoned by order of Marshal Pétain, and virtually condemmned by the Vichy regime before he had been tried, Blum put up a spirited defence of his past record at the trial in Riom. Nevertheless, he was eventually handed over to the Germans and made a political prisoner at Buchenwald. There he met and married his third wife, Jeanne Levilliers, also a political prisoner and a Jewess, like Léon Blum's two previous spouses, Lise Bloch and Thérèse Péreira.[80]

Throughout the war years Blum continued to write and reflect on events and to face his situation with remarkable stoicism. Despite his treatment at the hands of the Vichy French and the Germans, and the death of his brother in a concentration camp, Blum was devoid of all desire for vengeance. In June 1944, he wrote in his diary 'I do not believe in fallen or condemned races. I believe it no more for the Germans than for the Jews. I feel cruelly what is happening every day.'[81] After 1945, he called on Jews to overcome their feelings of hatred and vengeance and rejected the notion of collective German guilt.

When Léon Blum was deported to Germany on 10th November 1943 a colony called Kfar Blum was established in his honour in far-off Palestine. At the dedication ceremony homage was paid to the French workers' leader and Moshe Sharett (later Foreign Minister of Israel) recalled that few Jews in the West had understood as early as Léon Blum, the positive significance of Zionist efforts in Palestine. Sharett added that Blum had spoken at the Zionist Congress in Zürich (1929) as a convinced and enthusiastic Jew.[82] This was no exaggeration, for Blum had been a sympathizer with Zionism ever since Chaim Weizmann had drawn his attention around 1918 to the pressing problems of poverty and persecution confronting world Jewry.[83]

It appears that after the Balfour Declaration Blum had even used his influence to counteract French opposition to a British mandate over Palestine.[84] In the 1920s Léon Blum, together with Jean Longuet (the grandson of Karl Marx) and Vincent Auriol, was the most active of French socialist supporters for a Jewish Workers' Palestine and the idea of a *national home*. He saw Zionism above all as a response to the needs of homeless Jews who could not find peace and security in their native lands. At the same time, as a socialist, he saw in Jewish Palestine a 'wonderful experimental laboratory' for social progress which deserved the admiration of humanity.

Blum's positive attitude to Zionism, both as a socialist and as a Jew, was relatively unusual in the 1920s. At a banquet in honour of Dr Chaim Weizmann, held in Paris on 16th December 1924, he paid glowing tribute to the Zionist leader's energy, perseverance and powers of persuasion which had first awakened his own interest in Jewish colonization of Palestine.[85] Blum used the occasion to comment extensively on his own feelings as a Jew, and on the attitude of his co-religionists towards Zionism. He observed that French Jews felt very lukewarm and reserved towards Zionist efforts out of motives which were 'not very heroic and also not very sympathetic'.[86] Their indifference 'derived from egoism', from the security and civil equality which they enjoyed as French citizens, and their reluctance to do anything which might endanger this status. Blum added that French Jews feared above everything the nationalist reproach of dual loyalties which might be reinforced by a declaration of Zionist sympathies.

> What was always being said in France during periods of anti-Semitism? It was said: "A Jew can never be a full, complete, indivisible Frenchman; in the bottom of his heart he always remains a Jew, that is someone who is different, alien, not assimilable to true French ways.[87]

Blum naturally rejected this argument, but he equally emphatically repudiated the assumption that Zionism conflicted in any way with loyalties to France. He told his audience that he felt profoundly French by background, education and language, that 'there was no nuance of French sensibility, honour or culture which was alien to him'.[88] Nevertheless, he felt himself a Jew as much as a Frenchman, and had never perceived 'the slightest contradiction' between these two parts of his consciousness. National feelings did not need to be exclusively related to a single human group; one could simultaneously be an excellent Frenchman, a good Jew and a convinced Zionist.

Assimilation did not entail the abandonment of individual identity, still less did it imply that French Jews should forget their less fortunate brethren in other lands. It was in this latter sense that Léon Blum was a Zionist, and he forcefully reminded his audience of their duty to aid their persecuted co-religionists. In any case, Zionism was a reality, and it could not be in the Jewish interest that it should disappear, or in the French interest that French culture, arts and sciences played no role in the development of Palestine. French Jews who refused to support the Zionist project out of timorous fear of anti-Semitism had, according to Léon Blum, failed to understand the true causes of the latter phenomenon in France. Recalling the Dreyfus Affair, Blum suggested that its origins lay in social resentment at the tactless efforts of wealthy 'parvenus' to penetrate high society in France. The Jewish upper classes by their ostentatious display of wealth, snobbery and desire to conceal their origins had created antagonism among the very people they tried so hard to resemble.[89]

Blum tended to underestimate the vitality and strength of anti-Semitism in France in 1924, as he had done a quarter of a century earlier. Nevertheless, there was a profound truth in what he constantly told his fellow-Jews in France—that they would gain little by renouncing their heritage. For his part Blum confessed, 'I have never understood how one can be anything other than a Jew, who openly and proudly acknowledges the race, the people and the religion to which he belongs'.[90]

It was this natural feeling of solidarity with the Jewish people which led Blum to support passionately the Zionist cause in Palestine. Weizmann's influence on Blum's attitude, as we have pointed out, had been paramount, ever since they first met during the First World War. Blum himself admitted, 'I have never been able to refuse him anything. I knew nothing about Zionism when I met him. He informed me about the work and he won me over.'[91] (*Il me fit connaître l'oeuvre et il m'y gagna*). Blum added, 'It was a great source of pride and satisfaction to me that I could help him'.[92] The friendship between Blum and Weizmann was of considerable importance in the post-1945 period in securing French support for the cause of Palestinian Jewry in its struggle against the British occupation. But however persuasive Weizmann's appeals, they would have been unavailing if Blum had been indifferent to the achievements of Jewish labour in Palestine. As a socialist, Blum felt a strong affinity with the institutions and spirit of co-operation among the Jewish working class in Palestine, especially with the powerful trade-union organization (the Histadrut). There was, moreover, a long tradition of friendship and contacts between the SFIO (Section Française de l'Internationale Ouvrière) and the Jewish labour movement in Palestine, which Blum had played his part in developing.

The most important single factor in Blum's post-war sympathy with Zionism was, however, the trauma of the Holocaust and the widespread opposition in almost all sectors of French public opinion to British policy in Palestine.[93] Blum recognized that the terrible sufferings of the Jews under Nazism and the condition of the survivors in displaced persons' camps required an immediate solution. He was indignant at the British policy of restricting Jewish immigration and intercepting desperate refugees from Europe off the Palestine coast in order to take them back to Cyprus. This policy reached its abysmal climax with the case of the refugee ship symbolically named *Exodus*, which sailed from France in May 1947. It was turned away from Palestine by the British, who conveyed the passengers back to France, and then took them on to Germany when they refused to disembark. French public opinion was outraged by the callous insensitivity of the British Government, and Blum likewise strongly disapproved of its behaviour over the Exodus Affair.[94] He was doubly disappointed because of his long-standing admiration for English democratic institutions, and because it was a Labour Government in Britain which was executing decisions in flagrant contradiction to its declared policy in opposition.[95] In April 1944 the Labour Party executive in its pro-Zionist enthusiasm had exceeded even Weizmann's hopes and intentions. Labour's landslide victory in 1945 seemed therefore to open up the promise of fulfilling the dream of a Jewish homeland, which had never seemed more necessary than after the massacre of six million Jews in Europe.

In an article in *Le Populaire* on 21st August 1946 (and many times afterwards) Léon Blum asked how the British could possibly deny Palestine as a refuge to the survivors of the death-camps, who had nowhere else to go. He considered the behaviour of the British Foreign Secretary, Ernest Bevin, as particularly shocking, both as a trade-union leader, a socialist and a Cabinet Minister.[96] Bevin wholeheartedly accepted the Foreign Office view that Britain must placate the Arabs, and his statements also revealed him to be increasingly anti-Semitic in his attitudes. Blum could not forgive the Labour Cabinet for acceding to this policy and to the advice of the Foreign Office, which if successfully implemented would have closed the last door of hope to the remnants of the Jewish people.

This was the fundamental reason why Blum acceded to Weizmann's requests and used all his influence with Vincent Auriol, President of the Republic, and other leading personalities to help the cause of Palestinian Jewry. In *Le Populaire* he blamed British intransigence for the wave of terrorism which was unleashed in Palestine between 1945 and the proclamation of an independent Jewish State in May 1948. Blum strongly favoured the creation of the Jewish State, even when others (including some Zionist leaders) wavered and hesitated. At the time of the debate on the partition of Palestine in the United Nations, when a positive French vote was important because of its possible impact on undecided nations, the French Socialist Party played a considerable role in influencing public opinion. The Quai d'Orsay was still opposed to the creation of an independent Jewish state, but in the end the French voted in favour of the partition plan.[97] Blum, as the elder statesman of the French Socialist Party, had played a major part in rallying public opinion during this crucial period. Blum's sympathies for Zionism were a natural outcome of his emotional make-up, his fidelity as a Jew, his political outlook as a democratic socialist and his perception of the French role in the world. Shortly before his death in 1950, he sent a message to Guy de Rothschild on the occasion of the inaugural meeting of the Fonds National Juif Unifié, which exemplified his feelings of solidarity with the Jewish State.

> French Jew, born in France of a long line of French ancestors, speaking only the language of my country, nourished principally with her culture, refusing to leave her even at the time when I ran the most danger, I participate with all my soul in this effort, so admirably transported from the world of dreams to the world of historic reality, that will henceforth assure a homeland worthy of that name, free and equal, to all Jews who have not had the good fortune, as I have had, to find that in their native lands. I have followed their effort ever since President Weizmann made me understand it. I have always felt and now feel more than ever solidarity with you.[98]

It was a fitting personal testament to the career of a socialist politician, whose exceptional honesty and fidelity to his own principles triumphed over the vicissitudes of fortune.

The Pale of Settlement at the beginning of the twentieth century

Russia

Julius Martov and Leon Trotsky

> **'It is difficult to be a Russian; it is difficult to be a proletarian. It is difficult to be a Jew, to belong to a persecuted and disgraced race; but to be simultaneously a Russian proletarian and a Jew—that means suffering beyond endurance, that means exposure to every insult, to every torture that can be inflicted by a stupid omnipotence, by a greedy baseness, by a wicked idiotism.'**
>
> **Karl Kautsky**

Before 1914 about a half of world Jewry was concentrated in the gigantic, sprawling land-mass controlled by the Russian Tsars. According to the 1897 census, there were 5 189 400 Jews in the Tsarist Empire (4·13 per cent of the total population), over 90 per cent of them concentrated in the so-called Pale of Settlement. This territory, stretching from the shores of the Baltic to those of the Black sea, covered approximately a million square kilometres. Jews were in a minority in every one of its provinces, constituting 11·6 per cent of its mixed population, which included Ukrainians, Poles, White Russians, Lithuanians and Russians. But in such cities as Warsaw, Lódź, Bialystok, Minsk, Pinsk, Vilna, Berdichev they formed a very high percentage (often the majority) of the urban population. They were especially densely concentrated in Russian Poland (1 316 576 Jews in 1897—i.e., 14·1 per cent), Lithuania and White Russia (Belorussia). In the Pale of Settlement there was a large Jewish proletariat by the end of the nineteenth century, consisting mainly of impoverished craftsmen, artisans and their apprentices. The desperate economic conditions of this proletariat and the draconian laws to which the Jews were subject by the Tsarist authorities especially after 1882, gave birth to an important Jewish labour movement which enjoyed a large mass following. The Bund (General Jewish Workers Union in Lithuania, Poland and Russia) as it came to be called, was founded in Vilna in 1897 as a Jewish socialist party committed to defend the special interests of the Jewish masses. It had originated in the Lithuanian-Belorussian provinces, but later spread to Poland and the Ukraine. It played an important part in founding the all-Russian Social Democratic Party in March 1898, and for some years remained the best-organized mass movement within its ranks. But it failed in its efforts to persuade the all-Russian party to restructure itself on a national-federal basis, and its Yiddish-oriented secular Jewish nationalism was increasingly attacked by the Russian Marxists.

The spearhead of these attacks against the Bund was the assimilated Jewish intelligentsia within the Russian and Polish revolutionary movements, which opposed any form of Jewish separatism as reactionary. Two of the most representative examples of this socialist assimilationism, Martov and Trotsky, are discussed in the concluding chapters. Neither of them was strictly speaking a product of the Pale of Settlement, nor did they learn its language, which was overwhelmingly Yiddish. Martov was born into the privileged class of the Russian-Jewish bourgeoisie which could reside in the capital cities of Moscow and St Petersburg (though special permission from the authorities was required, and this could always be revoked). Trotsky, the son of a Jewish farmer in the Southern Ukraine was schooled in Odessa, a town with a very heterogeneous population, where a freer atmosphere prevailed than elsewhere in Russia.

These assimilated Jewish intellectuals had little to do with the mass of poor Jews in the Pale, concentrated in crafts and petty trade. Nevertheless, they also suffered from the oppressive despotism of the Tsarist regime and its hatred of the Jews. The pogroms of 1881, the May Laws of 1882, the *numerus clausus* (restricting the number of Jews at high schools and universities to a minimum), the prohibitions on freedom of movement (within and without the Pale), the police harassment, the poverty and backwardness of the Empire—all these pressures radicalized Jewish youth in Russia. The ferocious anti-Semitism of the Black Hundred gangs (organized under the name of Union of the Russian People) the pogroms of 1903 and 1905, the blood-libel trial of Mendel Beilis in Kiev (1913) demonstrated beyond doubt that Jew-baiting was an official State policy. In this situation there were essentially three options open to the mass of Jews—emigration, Zionism or belief in a socialist revolution. Between 1881 and 1914, two million Jews voted with their feet for emigration, mainly to the United States. Zionism also found a considerable response among the Russian-Jewish masses in the Pale, though only a thin trickle of pioneers went to Palestine in those early years. Nevertheless, the Russian Zionists were the backbone of the World Zionist organization, the basis of its mass support, its Palestinian orientation and of its increasingly socialist outlook.

The third choice, with which we are mainly concerned, lay between the Bund and the all-Russian Social Democratic Workers' Party, between a specifically Jewish socialism based on the Jewish masses and the universalist ideology of Marxism adapted to general Russian (or Polish) conditions. For the assimilated Jewish intelligentsia, the Russian and Polish revolutionary movements offered a kind of melting-pot in which all ethnic particularism, racial and religious differences would eventually be overcome. For the Bund and the Zionists' on the other hand, there was no other road to liberation except through the auto-emancipation of the Jews. Both movements in their opposing ways sought to regenerate the Jewish 'nationality', and this was why they were strongly opposed by the Russian Marxists, whether Bolshevik or Menshevik.

On 16th March 1917 the Provisional Government installed by the first Russian revolution, which had swept away the Tsar, abolished all restrictions on the Jews, beginning with the Pale of Settlement. In October 1917 the Bolshevik party seized power in Petrograd. Its theoretical attitude to the Jewish question was assimilationist, favouring the rapid integration of the Jews. There can be no doubt that it fought hard in the early years of Lenin's rule to wipe out anti-Semitism in Russia by legal means. But the new regime never adopted a single, consistent policy—sometimes favouring the creation of a national Jewish culture (in Yiddish), but later seeking to completely extirpate Jewish institutions from Soviet life. The activities of the Yevsektsiya (Jewish section of the Communist Party) in the 1920s reflected these contradictory policies. At the same time that the Yevsektsiia was carrying on a ruthless war against Judaism, Zionism and the Hebrew language, some Soviet leaders conceived the idea of settling the Jews on the land and giving them an autonomous region called Birobidzhan, near the Chinese frontier. The latter policy proved a fiasco, with the Jewish population of this Siberian 'Palestine' never rising above its peak in 1937 of 18 000 (24 per cent of the population), and steadily declining since.

Although individual Jews had been prominent in the Bolshevik Party at the time of the October Revolution (Trotsky, Sverdlov, Zinoviev, Kamenev, Radek, Uritsky, Volodarsky, Litvinov, Lozovsky, etc.) all without exception believed that the Jewish masses should completely merge with their Russian environment, and that there was no room for a separate Jewish identity. Ironically, few of them were to survive Stalin's purges of the Old Guard in the 1930s.

Leon Trotsky, who had been exiled at an earlier date, was profoundly shocked to discover that anti-Semitism could also be used by the Russian Communists as a political weapon. This was doubtless one factor in his belated realization that total assimilation was in the short term impossible for the Jewish people as a whole. Had he lived longer he would have witnessed the resurgence of Russian nationalism within the ruling Communist élite, and with it the traditional anti-Semitism which for so long had been a hallmark of Russian State policy. It was one of the tragedies of the Russian-Jewish intelligentsia that the revolution which it helped to make ended by destroying the internationalist Westernizing principles for which it stood.

CHAPTER 9

Julius Martov, the Revolutionary Conscience

'The Jewish labour movement was relegated to the background; we looked upon it with a superiority complex which was reflected in the fact that our work is conducted in the Russian language. We have inherited from the Jewish bourgeoisie a feeling of mistrust towards our masses, and as a result we idealized the Russian masses and neglected the growth of the actual Jewish movement.'

Julius Martov

'His first reaction to great events always revealed a revolutionary aspiration. But after every such effort his thought, not being sustained by the mainspring of will-power, disintegrated and sank back. . . .'

Leon Trotsky

Iulii Osipovich Zederbaum (Julius Martov), the founder of Russian Menshevism, was born in Constantinople in 1873. His grandfather Alexander O. Zederbaum was one of the leading champions of the Russian Jewish *haskalah* (enlightenment) in the 1860s. He had founded and edited journals in Hebrew, Yiddish and Russian, such as *Ha-meliz* (The Mediator) and *Rassvet* (The Dawn), which aimed at preparing Russian Jewry for emancipation. Alexander Zederbaum sought to overcome the enormous gulf between the ghetto and Russian society, from which all but a handful of privileged Jews were excluded.[1] Iulii's father, Osip, was similarly a man of the *haskalah*, and for a time assisted A. O. Zederbaum in publishing his Yiddish newspaper in St Petersburg. When Iulii was born, Osip was working for a Russian steamship company in Constantinople, and also as a part-time Eastern correspondent of two leading Petersburg journals, *Petersburgskaya Vedomosti* and *Novoe Vremya*.[2]

Iulii's mother, Viennese by birth and of Sephardi extraction, had been brought up in a convent school in Constantinople. Neither she nor her husband were religiously inclined. Their son consequently grew up without a positive sense of Jewish identity during his early childhood. The household was cosmopolitan, polyglot and privileged, with numerous servants; typically, Iulii's parents addressed their son in French, the favoured language of the Russian élite.

In 1877 his parents moved to the thriving Black Sea port of Odessa, which contained a colourful heterogeneous mixture of national groups and a very substantial Jewish population. Iulii's early years seem to have been marked by a sense of loneliness, a premature introversion and tendency to flee from his surroundings into books; perhaps this was due to the absence of his father in St Petersburg, or to the pronounced limp and fragile health which afflicted him throughout his life.[3] When Iulii was seven years old an event occured which was to leave a profound imprint on his consciousness. The Odessa pogrom erupted in May 1881, not long after the assassination of Alexander II. The mobs swept through the city streets, systematically pillaging shops and houses owned by Jews. Iulii's home was spared by chance, but he vividly recalled the sense of panic generated among relatives and servants, who vainly begged his mother to hang ikons by the windows to protect themselves from the fury of the crowd.[4]

It was Iulii Zederbaum's first taste of primitive Russian anti-Semitism, and it left a permanent mark on his impressionable mind. Though he came from a privileged household, although he rose to be leading figure in the Russian revolutionary intelligentsia, Zederbaum never wholly forgot what it meant to be a downtrodden Jew in a hostile environment. Many years later he recalled the graphic account by an old Jew, on the train to St Petersburg shortly after the Odessa pogrom, of similar happenings in Elizavetgrad.[5] In his memoirs the ageing Martov underlined the connection between this childhood experience and his subsequent revolutionary career:

> Would I have become what I became if the Russian reality had not imprinted her coarse fingers on my plastic, youthful soul in that memorable night and carefully planted under the cover of that burning pity which she aroused in my childlike heart, the seeds of a redeeming hatred.[6]

The sensitive, frail young Zederbaum, with his passionate hatred of injustice and persecution, was shaken to the depths of his being by the pogromist barbarity of Tsarist Russia. He had been brought up in a liberal, cultured family; such savagery heightened his sense of horror at the treatment of his poorer, oppressed brethren.

After the Odessa pogrom, Zederbaum's family left for St Petersburg. Iulii entered a Russian *gymnasium* where he encountered Jew-baiting teachers and students at first hand. In his memoirs he recounts how a geography teacher asked him to indicate the capital of Russia on the blackboard. Zederbaum correctly pointed to Moscow, and then to the medieval capitals of Kiev and Novgorod. The teacher turned to the class with a cynical sneer, remarking, 'And I thought he would point to Berdichev'—a city in the Jewish Pale.[7] The incident was typical enough of the prejudices that were rife in Russian secondary schools in the 1880s. As Martov later recalled

> We, the few Jewish students, were confronted on all sides by a spontaneous view of ourselves as an 'inferior' race rather than with anti-Semitic hatred. The others, sons of petty bourgeois Jews, carried this burden passively, attempted to survive unnoticed. . . . I, who had been brought up in a Russified and liberal milieu, was incapable of surrendering without a struggle. Exacerbated by the whole order of school life, my sensitiveness became a disease.[8]

The seeds of Zederbaum's revolt against his society were sown in this brutal atmosphere of discrimination. He felt acutely the vulnerability which was a consequence of his Jewishness, accentuated by his own physical weakness. The obedient, conscientious schoolboy ceased to study diligently, and only the intervention of his father saved him from expulsion. Iulii began to withdraw into himself, into the world of romantic and epic literature which offered him spiritual nourishment and a shield against this harsh and ugly environment. He read Schiller, Victor Hugo and above all the great Russian writers like Turgenev, Lermontov and Herzen. They inspired in the fourteen-year-old boy dreams of a revolution which would remake Russian society. In 1889 Yuri enrolled again in a Petersburg high school after a dispute over the family's legal right to reside in the

Imperial city. They had not been troubled by the Tsarist authorities, until the police temporarily revoked their right to remain in Petersburg. Only his father's connections prevented the carrying out of the deportation order.[9]

At his new school the sixteen-year-old Iulii found himself for the first time among like-minded students impassioned by revolutionary ideals. These sons of the Russian intelligentsia were as estranged from existing society as the Jewish intellectual élite;[10] the spiritual affinity was cemented by the solidarity of youth and comradely ties as well as by the clumsy tactics of a repressive regime. In a few years Iulii Zederbaum would bring his own emotional fervour, subtle intellectuality and great polemical gifts to the ranks of the Russian intelligentsia.

In 1891 he entered the University of St Petersburg, and soon became involved in underground student activities. His revolutionary initiation was completed by his arrest in February 1892 for proclaiming extreme Jacobin views. He remained in prison for three months, and after his release was expelled from the University. He began to read Marx's *Das Kapital*, and the works of Plekhanov and Axelrod. With the foundation of what came to be called the Petersburgskaya Gruppa Osvobozhdenii Truda (Petersburg Group for Emancipation of Labour), Zederbaum took the decisive step towards identifying himself with the revolutionary movement. In December 1892 he was rearrested, and after his release in May of the following year sent into administrative exile for two years, a fate which was by no means as unpleasant then as it has since become.

Zederbaum selected Vilna as his retreat, an industrial centre on the Polish-Lithuanian border which had an active working-class movement. He was invited to take over a study circle of garment-workers, and soon made contact with the local labour leaders.[11] Vilna was a pioneering centre in the early 1890s for new methods of class struggle which did not as yet exist elsewhere in Russia. The Jewish craftsmen and workers of Vilna had initiated an important strike movement in 1893 for shorter hours and better working conditions.[12] A network of mutual aid funds had been established throughout the local garment industry. Though the strike had failed, the Jewish Social Democratic leaders in Vilna discovered the importance of economic agitation for creating a broader social and political mass movement.[13] This was to be an important tactical lesson, pointing to the next stage in the development of Russian social democracy. Zederbaum, who played a significant role in this evolution, later wrote, 'We decided that the centre of our activity should be transferred to the sphere of agitation and that all propaganda and organizational work should be subordinated to this basic task'.[14]

Previously the local Jewish artisans had passed through study circles conducted in Russian which had given them the possibility of bettering themselves and eventually rising out of their class. Zederbaum and his colleagues began to realize that the 'circles' merely reinforced the petty-bourgeois aspirations of the tailors, dressmakers and seamstresses whom he was trying to educate towards proletarian class-consciousness. Jewish garment-workers in Vilna could not, he noted, identify with Marx's portrait of a venal, dissolute, egoistic and dominating Western bourgeois class:[15] in their more restricted experience, the bourgeoisie was patriarchal, civilized, industrious and free thinking, while the industrial proletarian was considered drunken, disorderly and dissolute.

The change in policy initiated by Jewish social democrats in Vilna was designed to overcome the apparent gulf between the workers and the radical intelligentsia.[16] Participation in proletarian organizations was henceforth necessary for admission to the study circles; the courses were to be conducted in Yiddish, rather than in Russian. The new strategy was formulated in an important pamphlet *Ob Agitatsii*, published in 1896.[17] It was written by Samuel Gozhansky and Arkady Kremer, future leaders of the Bund, and edited by the 22-year-old Zederbaum, under his new pseudonym of Julius Martov. Essentially, the pamphlet emphasized the importance of *economic* agitation and of a worker-centred political programme. It sought to link the theories of the intelligentsia to the spontaneous needs and demands of the working-class in their everyday conflicts with employers.[18] The Vilna period was thereby to provide Martov-Zederbaum with a new programme of action and invaluable practical experience in organizing a workers' movement.

It was also crucial for understanding Martov's attitude to the Jewish problem. Vilna, the multi-national 'Jerusalem of Lithuania', was the centre of a specifically *Jewish* labour movement, which was to culminate in the foundation of the Bund in 1897. There were a number of regional and historical features in the Lithuanian environment (which only marginally concern us here), that favoured this development;[19] the essential point being that Jewish workers were cut off from their Russian, Polish and Lithuanian 'class-comrades' by national traditions, language, customs and religion. Moreover, far from being an appendix of Russian social democracy (which in 1895 was at a very embryonic stage) Jewish workers constituted its avant-garde element. Only the Polish workers could claim an older revolutionary tradition of organization and struggle, but their dream of a restored Poland was wholly alien to the Jewish proletariat. As Martov put it, 'We were oriented to Petersburg and Moscow, they to Warsaw'.[20]

Although he was a Russified Jew and a newcomer in Vilna, who did not even speak Yiddish, Martov showed a remarkable aptitude in 1894–5 for grasping the aspirations of the Jewish workers. He was one of the first to formulate the central idea of Bundism—in Marxist terms that the Jewish proletariat had specific national interests which necessitated its organizational autonomy. His famous address of 1st May 1895 in Vilna, to a group of some thirty or forty agitators, emphasized the importance of *auto-emancipation* and the national dimension in the political struggle of Jewish workers. The young Martov's speech was in effect virtually a foundation-charter of Bundism.[21] This probably explains the sharpness of his subsequent polemics against the Bund.[22] Having been himself so deeply implicated in the evolution of this movement, Martov, once he changed direction, was all the more unrelenting in his attacks on it. But in May 1895 Martov, like Gozhansky, Mill and Kremer (future leaders of the Bund), was convinced that neither socialist internationalism nor the class-struggle could by themselves solve the particular problems of the Jewish masses.

> We have to state openly and clearly that the aim of the Jewish Social Democrats consists in the founding of a special Jewish workers' organization, which should be the leader and teacher of the Jewish proletariat in its struggle for economic, civic and political liberation.[23]

This special organization would strive, in Martov's words, 'for liberation from civic inequality'; one of its main objectives would be to awaken the masses from their lethargy by emphasizing the national character of the struggle.

> The national indifference of the Jewish masses is a hindrance in the awakening of their class consciousness. Our task should be to arouse them from both their national and class indifference. . . . We have to endow our movement with a definitive Jewish character, in the certainty that thereby we shall not cease participating in the world-wide movement in general and in the Russian in particular.[24]

Martov's stress on the national dimension of the Jewish workers' movement strongly influenced the future leaders of the Bund, thereby inadvertently contributing to their future conflict with Russian social democracy. The Russian workers were still relatively passive in 1895, which was one of the main factors underlying Martov's argument. 'We are no longer able to expect that we shall receive everything from the Russian proletariat, as our bourgeoisie expects to receive everything from the Russian liberals and the Russian bureaucracy.'[25] He pointed out that the Jewish bourgeoisie were incapable of securing civil and political rights for their oppressed co-religionists. The rich Jews sought to improve their own situation by relying on a weak and cringing Russian liberalism, or else circumventing discriminatory legislation by means of bribery. The assimilationist intelligentsia had also contributed little to Jewish emancipation in Russia. Like the Russian and Polish revolutionaries, they would tend to sacrifice what mattered most to the Jews—namely, religious freedom and national equality—to further their desperate struggle for political rights. Hence, young Martov argued, Jewish workers could only rely on themselves; they would even have to liberate the Jewish capitalists 'who sit on our backs and oppress us through their weight of their moneybags'.[26] The fight for emancipation was simultaneously directed against capitalism and against Jewish lack of civil and national rights.

> As workers we suffer under the yoke of capital; as Jews, we languish under the yoke of illegality. These obstacles oppress us, enslave us, hold us down and make the struggle against the capitalists difficult.
>
> They prevent us from selling our labour in the most favourable conditions, drive us into the Pale of Settlement, cause hectic competition and worsen our lot. They make every gendarme our sovereign and further prevent us from improving our position.[27]

The dual nature of this struggle for auto-emancipation necessitated a socialist and national component in the movement. As long as national oppression existed, as long as the Jews were an oppressed 'race', they could not liberate themselves as an oppressed class. For this reason Martov accepted the legitimacy of a Yiddish-oriented labour movement to awaken the national (and ultimately the class) consciousness of the Jewish proletariat. His advocacy of agitation in Yiddish, like the rest of his 'Bundist' programme, had little to do with Jewish nationalism. It was simply a logical and utilitarian deduction from his experience among the Vilna social democrats.

After his return from exile to St Petersburg, Martov was soon able to experiment with agitational techniques he had learnt in Vilna. Together with Vladimir Ulyanov (Lenin), he helped to found the St Petersburg Union of Struggle (1895), which sought to conduct economic agitation in the Petersburg naval shipyards and textile factories.[28] The strike movement of 1895–6 among Russian workers gave some encouragement to these hopes; but within three months of his return Martov had been arrested, and was eventually banished to an Arctic outpost in Siberia. It was during the last few months of 1899 that Lenin, Martov and Potresov began to plan for the future, from their respective places of exile in Siberia. In 1900 the new 'Troika' established *Iskra* abroad, as a bi-weekly newspaper intended to give a previously lacking ideological cohesion to Russian social democracy.

Under Lenin and Martov *Iskra* carried on a remorseless war against 'Economists', Revisionists and Bundists.[29] Between 1900 and 1903 Martov was as much a centralist and a determined opponent of socialist 'opportunism' and reformism as Lenin. The bald-headed, stocky

Great-Russian Vladimir Ilyich Ulyanov, with his narrow Tartar eyes, and the bespectacled, pale-faced, intellectual-looking Jew, Martov, with his inexhaustible gregariousness, were seemingly inseparable; Lenin regarded Martov as his most reliable friend and his most gifted collaborator. This affection for the slightly younger man never completely left him, despite all their future political conflicts. For his part, Martov until 1903 accepted Lenin's organizational views and his stress on the need for a single, united and effective fighting force to represent the emerging Russian proletariat.[30]

This more than anything explains why Martov revised his earlier views on the Jewish question; once he had committed himself to the all-Russian movement Martov felt that the revolutionary energy and talent of the Jews should be harnessed to the Russian workers' cause. The Pale of Settlement now seemed to him too narrow a field in comparison with the seemingly limitless perspectives of an all-Russian revolution. The Bund was no longer the only mass workers' organization in the Tsarist Empire; Moscow, Petersburg and Kiev had become as important as Vilna and Minsk.[31] Moreover, Martov had abandoned his earlier scepticism concerning the readiness or ability of the Russian revolutionary movement to secure civil rights for the Jews.

Martov's break with his former comrades was sealed after the Fourth Congress of the Bund (1901) had proposed cultural-national autonomy for Jewish workers and a federal organization of Russian social democracy. In an article for *Iskra* (August 1901) Martov described this as a nationalistic blunder: the basic problem of the Jewish masses was their isolation from the surrounding population.[32] In order to overcome this handicap, a strengthening of the ties between the Jewish and the all-Russian labour movement was necessary. Martov also rejected the Bundist demand for cultural-national autonomy in a future socialist Russia; the Jews, he now argued, had no specific national tasks, since they were a minority even within the Pale of Settlement and lacked a territory of their own.[33]

Martov's complete reversal of position on this issue undoubtedly encouraged Lenin to adopt his intransigent attitude to the national 'separatism' of the Bund. It was Martov who had led the way in urging Jewish socialists to 'assist the organization of the vast majority of the (Russian) proletariat' instead of wasting their energies on their 'own little corner' of the Pale. It was also Martov who insisted that Bundist separatism (and especially Zionism) obstructed the common struggle against chauvinism and anti-Semitism; indeed, he even asserted that they were more dangerous to the revolutionary cause than anti-Semitism, which affected backward rather than progressive elements of the Russian proletariat.[34] Martov also stressed that the claims of the Bund would weaken the all-Russian revolutionary movement in regions such as Southern Russia, where Jews were the most active agitators and represented the avant-garde of the workers' movement. Finally, Martov agreed with Lenin that the Bund's organizational principles would lead to a federated rather than a centralized party, which would threaten the internal cohesion of Russian social democracy.

The historical irony was not merely that Martov had been a founding-father of the movement whose existence he now completely negated, it was that by leading the onslaught against the Bund at the second Congress of the Russian Social Democratic Workers' party (1903) he ultimately ensured Lenin's future majority and his own demise. By attacking the Bund's federal principle in the name of *Iskra*'s centralism, he helped clear the road for the hypercentralization which the Bolsheviks represented. A prisoner of his own past, Martov played into Vladimir Ulyanov's hands and compounded his tragedy by being unable to make a complete rift with Leninism. All the implications of Martov's behaviour at the historic second Congress of the RSDWP lay admittedly far in the future, but they were no less poignant for that.

It was the 30-year-old Martov who presented the resolution signed by twelve delegates (all Jews), opposing the Bund's demand for recognition as a national organization of Jewish workers within the Russian party. He urged the closest unity of the Jewish workers with the nationalities among whom they lived, and their complete fusion with the all-Russian party.[35] This ignored what Martov had understood much better eight years earlier—that the masses in the Pale could not simply throw off their national identity at will.

Their situation was quite different from that of the Russified Jews in the revolutionary movement who advocated assimilation. In 1903, however, Martov attacked the Bund with the zeal of a neophyte; he accused it of pursuing an egoistic and futile policy, contrary to socialist internationalism. This would only nourish an artificial antagonism between Russian and Jewish workers. In his opinion, the overriding fact was that the Jewish masses lived outside those areas where the decisive future battles of the Russian Revolution would be fought. The net result of the onslaught against the Bund led by Martov was to provoke its secession from the second Congress of the RSDWP. This greatly helped Lenin in the next round against Martov when the issues of organization and the conditions of party membership were discussed.[36] The departure of the Bund and the dissolution of the *Rabochee Delo* (*Workers' Cause*) group enabled Lenin to transform a 28–22 vote against his views on this issue into a majority of two votes. Henceforth his 'hard' faction was to enjoy the considerable psychological advantage of being called *Bolsheviki* (Majorityites) in contrast to Martov's 'softs', who ineptly accepted the designation of *Mensheviki* (Minorityites).

What was the main stumbling block which divided Mensheviks

from Bolsheviks after 1903, despite their agreement on many issues, including the Jewish question? Essentially, Martov stood for a broad party open to all workers and intellectuals rather than a narrow élite of professional revolutionists. Russian social democracy in his view was to be organized as a mass party of the proletariat, 'the conscious expression of an unconscious process'; he opposed the draconian powers of control which Lenin demanded for the party, ostensibly in order to root out opportunism and wavering. Instead Martov favoured the West European concept of a social-democratic class party engaged in open political struggle. Inevitably under Russian conditions there were severe disadvantages connected with this democratic ideal.

During the 1905 Revolution in Russia these differences crystallized around concrete issues; Martov, Plekhanov and Axelrod saw the goal of the Revolution as being the establishment of a bourgeois-democratic republic, rather than a socialist order, which they considered impossible in backward Russia for a very long time to come. Martov envisaged the socialist task to be that of a reformist opposition under a bourgeois regime, until such time as conditions were ripe for a proletarian revolution.[37]

Martov's theory presupposed *abstention* from seizing power during the bourgeois revolution; his conception of the social-democratic party was based on the 'elective' principle, and a profound belief in the initiative of the working class.

During his period of exile (mainly in Paris) between 1906 and 1912, Martov edited the Menshevik paper *Golos Sotsialdemokrata*, but continued to co-operate with the Bolsheviks on most issues. He did, however, criticize the terrorist methods of the Russian underground, the bank robberies and expropriations indulged in by the Bolsheviks. Nevertheless, between 1908 and 1911, when his rivals were split and seemingly discredited, Martov missed his best chance of securing Menshevik domination of the Russian workers' movement.[38] He waited too long to expose Bolshevik terrorism in his pamphlet *Spasiteli ili uprazdniteli?* (Saviours or Destroyers?) (Paris, 1911) out of a scrupulous desire to avoid an open split in the movement. Lenin would never have suffered from such inhibitions.

Martov paid little attention to the Jewish question after 1903, convinced since his confrontation with the Bund that international socialism would solve the problem. He agreed with the views of Kautsky and Lenin about the desirability of a rapid process of assimilation, but he continued to feel involved in the struggle against anti-Semitism in a way that was more personal than that of Trotsky or Rosa Luxemburg. Martov was particularly shaken by the terrible Black Hundred pogroms of 1905–6, and later by the Beilis trial of 1913. In 1908 he even wrote a little book entitled *Russki narod i evrei* (The Russian People and the Jews) which testified to his sensitivity about the pogroms and the persecution of Russian Jews. He remained to the end of his life acutely aware of the disabilities which Russian Jewry suffered, and never abandoned his feelings of solidarity with the persecuted race from which he descended. Two personal details concerning Martov's Jewishness are significant in this respect. First he signed his private correspondence with his family name 'Zederbaum' and not with his revolutionary pseudonym 'Martov'—a step inconceivable for Trotsky.[39] Secondly, he preferred to live illegally in Petersburg after his return to Russia in 1913 rather than accept a fictitious baptism for reasons of expediency.[40]

But Martov's reluctance to break his last links with the Jewish people does not alter the fact that he became a typical example of the assimilated Jew in the revolutionary Russian intelligentsia. In 1914, when the First World War broke out, Martov's initial reaction was almost identical to that of Lenin, Trotsky, Rosa Luxemburg and other revolutionary internationalists. He regarded the imperialist war as a senseless, tragic carnage, but at the same time as a golden opportunity to overthrow capitalism. However, he opposed Lenin's bid to destroy the Second International, favouring instead an organized socialist peace movement. On his return to Petrograd on 8th May 1915 he led the Menshevik internationalist faction, seeking the establishment of a Popular Front government.[41] He opposed the official Menshevik line of coalition with the Provisional Government, but baulked at any formula for seizing power against the bourgeois coalition. On the crucial peace issue, Martov favoured breaking with the Allies if they refused to change their war policies. But he advocated continuing the war if Russia was attacked by Germany. It was a typical compromise solution, and as a result of it Martov found himself isolated even in his own Menshevik camp.

The October Revolution proved to be Martov's personal tragedy, for he played only a minor role, not only in comparison with Lenin and Trotsky, but even with such lesser figures as Kerensky, Dan and Tseretelli. He was unable fully to grasp the desperation and revolutionary mood of the masses, their hunger for firm leadership and for a way out of the destructive war, famine and chaos.[42] Lacking the support of his own Menshevik party, he had no other power-base from which to influence events. He found himself caught between the fear of Bolshevik revolution and the threat of counter-revolution from the militarist, conservative and neo-monarchist Right. Opposed to Bolshevik methods of terror, and also to the Menshevik alliance with Kerensky, he wavered in the middle.

On the first day of the second Congress of Soviets (25th Oct. 1917), after the Bolshevik coup, Martov still sought a compromise solution and a coalition of all the socialist parties in a democratic government. He saw clearly the evils which would flow from a Bolshevik minority dictatorship, but sadly, as with so many of his proposals, it came too late. It was the arrogantly self-confident Trotsky who now pilloried Martov and his Mensheviks, with whom he had once been closely associated. 'You are pitiful isolated individuals, you are bankrupts; your role is played out. Go where you belong from now on—into the dustbin of history!'[43] Martov walked out of the Congress hall, and with him went perhaps the last hope of a socialist democracy emerging in the new Russia.

Martov continued to act in the first three years of the Soviet regime as the 'conscience of the Revolution', criticizing the Bolshevik terror and censorship, the pseudo-socialism of the barracks and the primitivization of life.[44] But hopes for a democratic transformation of the Bolshevik regime soon faded. Nevertheless, he bravely raised his voice against the indiscriminate shooting of prisoners, the reintroduction of the death-penalty and the suppression of free opinion. Such criticism carried little weight, however, even when the Menshevik press was still legal. On 14th June 1918 Martov and his colleagues were expelled from the Central Executive Committee, and the Menshevik newspapers were closed down. Despite these actions, Martov supported the Bolsheviks against Kolchak and Denikin during the Russian Civil War, and later during the intervention.[45] Interestingly enough, when rejecting the arguments of a Bundist critic who proposed a neutral stand between Reds and Whites during the Civil War, Martov referred with great passion to the 'White' pogroms. The virulent anti-Semitism of the White counter-revolutionaries was one of the decisive tests for Martov of how should he act in the given situation.[46]

In 1920 Martov was allowed to leave Russia unmolested as a last act of generosity by Lenin towards the comrade for whom he still felt a very special affection. The Bolsheviks always recognized Martov's stature as one of their most intelligent and sincere opponents. Lenin's wife Krupskaya observed in her memoirs how every time Martov 'even in the slightest degree, showed signs of taking the correct line', Lenin felt strangely gratified. After the Revolution he told Gorky: 'I am sorry, deeply sorry, that Martov is not with us. What a splendid comrade he was, what an absolutely sincere man!' On his deathbed Lenin still thought fondly of his former friend: 'They say Martov is dying, too. There was in his voice a note of tenderness'.[47]

Martov has been well described by his most recent biographer as the 'Hamlet of democratic socialism', a man of great intellectual gifts whose failure was essentially one of will-power.[48] This was also the verdict of Karl Radek, Charles Rappoport, Trotsky and many others who supported the Bolshevik cause. Trotsky was especially uncharitable in denigrating his former comrade's lack of revolutionary decisiveness and will. He wrote:

> There scarcely is or could be at any time another socialist politican who could exploit Marxism with such talent to justify deviations

> from and direct betrayals of it. In this respect Martov could be called without any irony a virtuoso.[49]

Trotsky unfairly accused Martov of twisting dialectics into 'the most refined casuistry'; he was for Trotsky, 'the most refined, the most elusive and the most incisive politician of the stupid, banal and cowardly petty-bourgeois intelligentsia. And the fact that he himself did not see nor understand this indicates how mercilessly his Mosaic incisiveness was laughing at him'.[50]

But Martov's tragedy was not merely a result of certain personal deficiencies, notably his over-refined intellectualism and a tendency to irresolution in crises. It was also a product of the insoluble dilemma of classical Marxism operating in a semi-feudal, absolutist system that could not be transformed overnight into a modern communist society. Martov remained a democrat in theory and practice, who correctly foresaw the pitfalls of the Bolshevik attempt to impose socialism by force on a reluctant, underdeveloped society. But he had no clear alternative to offer, and his moral scruples weakened his position against far more ruthless opponents. Hampered by his own Marxist determinism and fatalistic view of dialectics, Martov, like Otto Bauer, could not arrive at a convincing socialist critique of Lenin's actions. Nor did he realize until far too late the fundamental incompatibility between his evolutionary socialism and the policies implicit in Leninism. Instead he clung to a mirage of Russian socialist unity which had already collapsed well before the Bolshevik coup.

Martov's failure was ultimately that he could not face up to the challenge of power. A humane Marxist and cosmopolitan Jewish intellectual, utterly alienated from 'pogromist' Russia, he longed for a just society which could one day be governed by reason and logic.

Martov's Menshevism was doomed to political futility.[51] His love hate relationship with Lenin, and his total commitment to classic Russian Marxism, blinded him to the real gulf between Bolshevism and his own democratic credo of socialism. As a consequence he felt obliged to accept Lenin's putsch as a 'historic necessity'. It was only after the Revolution that Martov's moral stature was revealed by his unequivocal denunciation of the Red Terror, and the abuses of the Cheka in the name of socialism. Sadly by that time, the power-shy father of Menshevism was a lonely prophet crying in the wilderness of the new Russia.

CHAPTER 10

Leon Trotsky, Bolshevik Neophyte

'"You consider yourself, I suppose, either a Russian or a Jew". "No", Trotsky responded, "you are wrong. I am a Social Democrat and only that."'

Vladimir Medem

'He was the neophyte who wanted to outdo in zeal and ardour the Bolsheviks themselves, the neophyte who wanted to be forgiven the many crimes against Bolshevism he had committed in the past—by becoming more intransigent, more revolutionary, more Bolshevik than any of them.'

Angelica Balabanoff

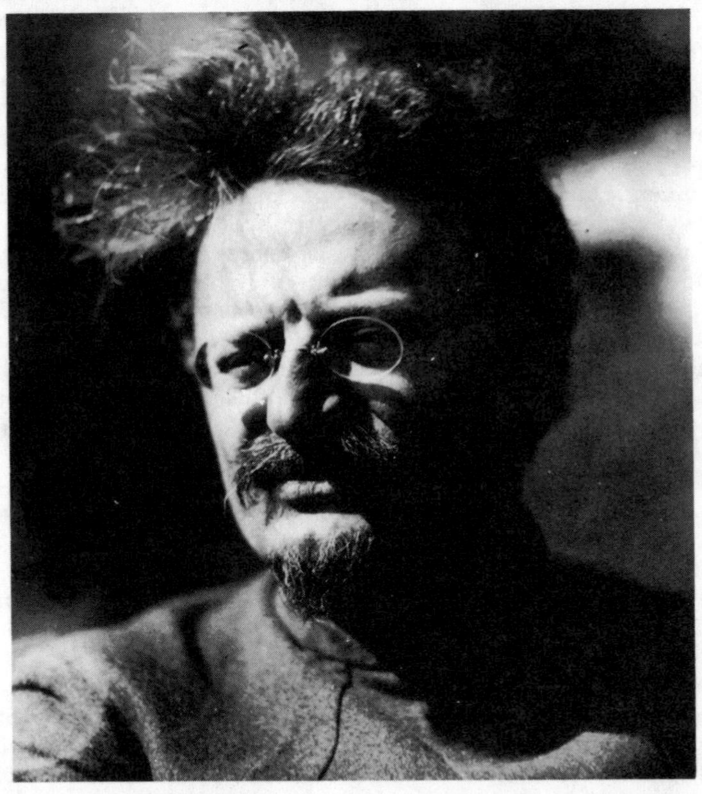

More than any contemporary, Leon Trotsky personified the twentieth-century attitude of the revolutionary Jew as a cosmopolitan, in flight from what he considered a parochially confining milieu. No other Russian revolutionary more obviously symbolized the paradox of being an alien to the Jews and a Jew to the Gentiles. Vladimir Medem recalled that after a debate in Switzerland in 1903 Trotsky told him that he regarded himself as neither a Russian nor a Jew, but as a *social democrat.*[1] The verdict of his environment was different, although it took the victory of Hitlerism and Stalinism to make Trotsky belatedly and somewhat confusedly aware of the fact. For the understanding of Trotsky's ethnic background and its influence on his career, his autobiography for all its obvious reticences, omissions and silences remains an indispensable source. From Trotsky's own pen, we learn how he viewed his family, his milieu and early years in Yanovka, a small village on the steppes of Southern Russia.

Born in 1879 in this obscure corner of the Tsarist Empire the son of a hard-working farmer, Trotsky subsequently depicted this environment as decidedly 'petty-bourgeois' in habits and dominated by the acquisitive instinct.[2] His father David Leontievich Bronstein was a thrifty, grafting man, who had left his home in Poltava for the free steppes of the South. Trotsky noted that there were about '40 Jewish agricultural colonies in the province of Kherson and Ekaterinoslav, with a total population of about 25 000 souls',[3] and it was from this same background that he came. The Bronstein family was different from the typical ghetto Jews of the Russian Pale of Settlement, and in his illiterate but enterprising father one can already perceive the outlines of a frontier type, made sturdy by physical labour. The Bronsteins were 'Am Haaretz' (people of the soil) in the traditional Yiddish sense of the word, considered by their urbanized coreligionists as uneducated, boorish, ill-mannered and uncultured. They might be shrewd, but they were held to be ignorant: more specifically, rabbinical wisdom stigmatized such Jews as people who did not respect the law, who did not educate their children in religious practices, and who tended to take on the character of the surrounding population. Such a description would perhaps not entirely fit David Bronstein, who, we learn from Trotsky, made some vain efforts to have his son acquainted with the Hebrew and Yiddish which was no longer in everyday use at home.[4] These attempts were not likely to succeed in a household where tradition was very laxly observed.

Trotsky records, 'Father did not believe in God from his youth and in later years spoke openly about it in front of mother and the children. Mother preferred to avoid the subject, but when occasion required, would raise her eyes in prayer'.[5] Although on holy days his parents journeyed to synagogue and his mother abstained from sewing, ceremonial observance declined with the years into religious inertia and indifference. Nevertheless, David Bronstein wanted his son to know the Hebrew Bible in the original language.

When Lev Davidovich was seven he was sent to a Yiddish-speaking *heder* (Jewish religious school) in Gromokley, a few miles from Yanovka. This was an unhappy experience for young Bronstein, who, unfamiliar with Yiddish, could not understand either his teachers or classmates.[6] He was repulsed, moreover, by the sight of the Jews of Gromokley humiliating a woman of loose morals, whom they had driven out of one of the main village streets.[7] This unpleasant memory of Jewish squalor and intolerance contrasted strikingly for Lev Davidovich with his recollection of the tidy, neat cottages of the German colonists in Gromokley.

From Trotsky's reminiscences we learn that in 1888 he went to Odessa to stay with his cousin Moissei Filipovich Spentzer, a cultivated middle-class liberal who polished his manners, taught the boy Russian and sent him to St Paul's Realschule. Bronstein lost a year because of the *numerus clausus* which limited the number of Jewish pupils in Russian secondary schools to 10 per cent, but on this subject he was distinctly reticent. What made a deep impression on him was rather the cosmopolitan atmosphere and heterogeneous national composition of his Lutheran *gymnasium*, with its Russians, Germans, Poles, Ukrainians and Jews. Religious education was given in the Greek Orthodox, Roman Catholic, Lutheran and Jewish faiths. Trotsky recalled that 'a good-natured man by the name of Ziegelman instructed the Jewish boys in the Bible and the history of the Jewish people. These lessons, conducted in Russian, were never taken seriously by the boys'.[8]

Young Lev Bronstein was equally dismissive in his comment on the private lessons he received in the Bible from an elderly Hebrew teacher in Odessa: 'My studies lasted only a few months and did little to confirm me in the ancestral faith'.[9]

Bronstein, who was 'always at the top of the grade', felt unaffected by any restrictions which existed on the Jews at his *gymnasium*. Altogether his account of life in a Russian secondary school in the early 1890s differs markedly from that of his socialist comrades Martov and Axelrod, who vividly recalled the anti-Jewish persecution to which they were subjected. Not that the young Bronstein was totally indifferent to the nationality question; his eye was caught by the indignities to which Germans, Ukrainians and Poles were subjected. Thus he singled out the baiting of a Polish Catholic boy by a Russian Orthodox priest as an example of national inequality: this, he reflected, 'was one of the underlying causes of my dissatisfaction with the existing order, but it was lost among all the other phases of social injustice. It never played a leading part—not even a recognized one—in the list of my grievances.'[10] Although one cannot rule out the possibility that here, as elsewhere, Trotsky may have suppressed his vulnerability as a Jew, his account of his school experiences in the more tolerant, multi-racial atmosphere of Odessa is not necessarily implausible. What emerges is that for the self-image of the young Bronstein, Jewish experiences played little if any role at this stage of his life. But his intellectual brightness and general sophistication, encouraged by his model showing as a pupil in Odessa, rapidly alienated him from the coarseness and narrow horizons of life on the farm in Yanovka. Already, before his conversion to socialism, he began to see his family, and especially his father, as a privileged 'kulak', a 'hoarder' who mistreated the servile labourers on the farm.[11]

As a proud, sensitive adolescent, Bronstein was pushed by circumstances rather than a predestined 'Jewish' fate, towards socialism. Like Marx, he was momentarily repulsed by the 'socialist utopia', distrusting what he felt to be a formula for 'mob rule'; but it was not long before he abandoned class, religion and upbringing for the revolutionary cause. It was in the Black Sea port of Nikolayev that he first made contact with radical students and working-men and was exposed at the end of 1896 to Populist doctrines. His progress was rapid, and by the end of 1897 Bronstein had become a Marxist and helped to organize the Southern Russian Workers Union in Nikolayev, which had some two hundred members. From this revolutionary initiation—which earned him the customary punishment of imprisonment and later exile to Siberia—Trotsky never looked back.

Neither his religion or nationality as such influenced his conduct in becoming a revolutionary: with regard to both, Trotsky remained an unrepentant rationalist. 'Even in my early youth, the national bias and national prejudices had only bewildered my sense of reason, in some cases stirring in me nothing but disdain and even a moral nausea.'[12]

If we are to believe his own account, anti-Jewish discrimination was therefore a minor and quite unimportant episode among the many social injustices which drove Trotsky to join the Russian revolutionary movement.[13] Young Lev Bronstein's approach to all problems was to the end governed by a comprehensive, all-embracing rationalism, deepened by his Marxist education and acquaintance with different political systems and cultures. 'The feeling of the supremacy of general over particular experience, of law over fact, of theory over personal experience, took root in my mind at an early age and gained increasing strength as the years advanced.'[14] Marxism was attractive as a universal, (scientific) solution to the problems of mankind as a whole. Here was a class doctrine which transcended national and religious frontiers, and which was interpreted by Trotsky as an inevitable outcome of the dialectic of history.

In Trotsky's militant, defiant optimism—so often found in Jewish revolutionaries—there was nevertheless a voice which echoed from the depths of a millennial experience. The 21-year-old

Lev Davidovich greeted the twentieth century from his Siberian exile with fighting words that could well have been the epitaph for his stormy career. 'As long as I breathe I shall fight for the future, that radiant future in which man, strong and beautiful, will become master of the drifting stream of his history. . . .'[15]

Bronstein—now known under his pseudonym of Trotsky—first confronted the Jewish problem at the Second Congress of the Russian Social Democratic Workers' Party in London in 1903. The conflict with the Bund which emerged there was to have important repercussions on the history of Russian social democracy. The struggle between the *Iskra* board and the Bund brought to a climax a series of problems involving the Jews and their role in the Russian revolutionary movement.[16]

Were the Russian Jews to assimilate, or did they require a separate Yiddish culture and an independent organization to represent their interests? Was the Bund to have a special autonomous status in the party and the right to frame its own policy with regard to the Jewish proletariat? Was it justified in demanding schools in the Yiddish language and cultural-national autonomy for Jewish workers? Finally, could the Russian Social Democratic Party accept that the Bund was the sole representative of the Jewish working class in Russia?[17]

Beyond these specific demands raised by the Bund lay a crucial problem for Lenin. Was the Russian revolutionary party to be a centralized, disciplined, cohesive unit or a federation of autonomous national groupings as for example in Austria-Hungary? On the former issue it was the assimilated Jews around Lenin, led by Martov, Axelrod and the 23-year-old Trotsky who opposed the Bund and tabled their signatures to a resolution rejecting its demands. Trotsky was already sufficiently established to play an important role in the debate.

Representing the makeshift Siberian Social-Democratic Workers' Union, he was in fact Lenin's hatchet-man in forcing the Bund to abandon the London Congress—thereby, unintentionally helping, with Martov, to forge a Bolshevik majority at the proceedings. Trotsky particularly provoked the Bundist delegates by his aggressive manner and insistence on speaking as a *Jew* in order better to refute their demands. He accused the Bund of endangering the cohesion of the anti-Tsarist forces and encouraging Jewish workers along the path of nationalism and separatism. He supported Martov's resolution, calling for the 'closest unity of the Jewish proletariat with the proletariat of those races among whom it lives',[18] and took the floor ten times to speak in the debate. He declared that the twelve Jewish comrades who signed Martov's resolution 'while working in the all-Russian party regarded and still regard themselves also as representatives of the Jewish proletariat.'

This claim, coming from a revolutionary who had previously disdained all affiliation to the Jewish people, not surprisingly made the Bundist delegates indignant. Mark Liber, the young Bundist spokesman, described Trotsky's statement as a piece of 'gross tactlessness' and demanded its retraction.[19] This was refused by Plekhanov, the Chairman of the conference, no admirer of Trotsky, but even less sympathetic to the Bund.

Bolsheviks and Mensheviks alike rejected the claim of the Bund to a special place in the Russian party, although they did not wish to undermine its local work among the Jewish proletariat. Trotsky regarded the Bund as a parochial organization whose leaders had undeniably achieved much in the past, but who would obtain better results in the future if they looked beyond the Pale of Settlement. In his opinion, instead of representing the Social Democratic Party among Jewish workers, the Bund sought to defend the latter's interest against it, thereby casting a vote of no confidence in the Russian party. The Bund had allowed a national viewpoint to predominate over class-interest. But this parochialism had been rejected by the Second Congress, which in Trotsky's words was a triumph for *Roman* universalism against *Greek* provincialism![20]

Trotsky essentially never went back on this harsh judgment of the specifically Jewish labour movement, which he regarded with a certain disdain and hauteur. Like Rosa Luxemburg, who held remarkably similar views (although expressed for various reasons with less arrogance), he regarded the Bund as a nationalistic outgrowth of Jewish isolation and of an outmoded ghetto psychology. But there was a deeper principle at stake in Trotsky's polemic against the Bund, which also extended to his rejection of Zionism. Not merely was the notion of a Jewish 'nationality' unacceptable to him, it directly offended his self-image as a Russian revolutionary and as a progressive Marxist.

Chaim Weizmann recalled that Lenin, Trotsky and Plekhanov all exuded contempt for the Zionist students in the Russian colonies of Switzerland who were moved by a love of Jewish tradition and concern for the fate of the Jews. '*They* could not understand why a Russian Jew should want to be anything but a Russian. *They* stamped as unworthy, as intellectually backward, as chauvinist and unmoral, the desire of any Jew to occupy himself with the sufferings and destiny of Jewry.'[21] Lenin himself had written in October 1903 that the 'idea of a Jewish nation was Zionist in inspiration and therefore false and reactionary'.[22]

Young Trotsky was no less scathing than his Russian comrades in taking both the Bund and Zionism to task. In an article in *Iskra* (January 1904) on 'The Decomposition of Zionism and its Possible Successors', he asserted that the Sixth Zionist Congress was proof that Herzl's movement was about to collapse.[23] In this article, ironically enough, Trotsky repeated the opinions of the Bundist leader Vladimir Medem who had also attended the Sixth Congress in Basle (1903) when the British offer of Uganda for Jewish settlement had indeed nearly wrecked Zionism.[24] Trotsky outdid even Medem in his vituperative attack on Herzl for seeking 'the aid of the princes of the world' on behalf of 'his' people. Herzl was in Trotsky's eyes a 'repulsive figure' and a 'shameless adventerer' who had the impudence and perfidy to try to obtain a fatherland for the Jews.[25] It was transparent to Trotsky that Zionism was a reckless adventure doomed to defeat, and he sarcastically described the cries of betrayal among delegates, angry at Herzl's acceptance of the Uganda project as 'hysterical sobbings of the romanticists of Zion'. What interested Trotsky was whether or not social democracy would benefit from the inevitable (!) collapse of Zionism in Russia. He predicted that the Zionist-Left would be driven by police repression and the need for self-defence against pogroms, into the Russian revolutionary ranks, rather than towards the nationalist Bund.[26]

Trotsky's initial reaction to the Kishinev pogrom of 1903 was typical of other Marxist revolutionaries. In the student colonies of Switzerland, he argued that there was no necessity for a specific struggle against anti-Semitism, since this was a temporary product of the lack of socialist consciousness among the Russian masses.[27] Anti-Semitism would fade automatically once the masses were enlightened by social democracy. Even the terrible pogroms of 1905 were a secondary issue to Trotsky, a diversion by the Tsarist regime against mass discontent, strikes and a revolutionary mood following the Russian defeat by Japan. Nevertheless, his descriptions of the pogroms—the murder, rape and arson practised by drunken bands in the name of the Tsar, God and fatherland were certainly an impassioned indictment of the regime. Trotsky eloquently depicted the horrors of the 'black October bacchanalia', in which 'hundreds of towns suffered from 3 500 to 4 000 dead and up to 10 000 maimed'[28] and mentioned the fear and panic of the Jewish population, even in St Petersburg. In a famous speech of October 1906, defending his role the previous year as leader of the Petersburg Soviet, Trotsky cited the pogroms as proof that the Tsarist regime was 'an automoton for mass murder', cutting the living flesh of the people to pieces.[29] But the style of his indictment indicated that the pogroms did not exert the same traumatic effect on him as they did on Martov, nor did Trotsky react with the same severity and fierce resolution as Lenin in seeking during the Civil War to crush the pogroms. Like Rosa Luxemburg, he did not want Jews to be singled out as the special victims of the pogrom policy of the Tsarist regime. The assertion that he was 'obsessed' by the pogroms or touched to the core by the butchery of defenceless Jews in Russia seems, therefore, unwarranted by the evidence.[30]

There are, however, two examples of Trotsky's reaction to virulent anti-Semitism before 1914 which do reveal his basic attitude. In November 1913 he devoted an essay in the Viennese publication *Die Neue Zeit* to the Beilis case in Russia. Trotsky had no doubt of course that the monstrous blood-libel was a staged affair, backed by the Tsar, the police, the Black Hundreds and the clergy. He vividly depicted the proceedings as being reminiscent of a medieval trial court presided over by monarchist reactionaries in an atmosphere of the vilest pogromist nationalism. He observed that the accusation against Beilis, a simple irreligious Jewish worker, who had been accused of draining the blood of a Christian child for ritual purposes, made the Dreyfus case pale by comparison.[31] This calculated, barbaric incitement of atavistic prejudices and medieval superstitions revealed to Trotsky the nadir of Russian justice and the imminent doom of the Tsarist regime.

In 1913, as Balkans correspondent in Vienna for the liberal Russian paper *Kievskaya Mysl*, Trotsky also wrote a few articles on the Jewish problem in Rumania. He observed that almost 300 000 Jews were not recognized as Rumanian citizens, although they themselves and their fathers were born in the country. 'Any Jew can at any moment be thrown out of the country, like a roaming vagabond . . . although they are excluded from citizenship, the government nonetheless imposes on them the whole burden of civic obligations' including taxes and military service.[32]

The Jewish question in Rumania appeared to Trotsky symptomatic of a corrupt feudal society dominated by a 'Boyar' clique who lorded it over 'servile' peasants. The ruling class in Rumania hated the Jews, but could not survive without them—as a leaseholder, moneylender, middleman, hired journalist, the Jew was indispensable. He was the intermediary between landlord and peasant, the agent of feudal exploitation, instructed to 'fulfil the dirtiest assignments of Purishkevich'.[33] Trotsky's conclusion was very much to the point. 'Anti-Semitism appears as a State religion, the last psychological cement of a completely decadent feudal society, covered up with a gold leaf—the strictly qualified constitution.'[34] He also observed that despite the miserable lot 'of the unhappy pariahs, inhabiting the filthy suburbs of Moldavian villages', the Rumanian ruling class had a healthy respect for the influence of high finance and the 'Jewish' press in Western Europe. Was it not Bismarck, the Iron Chancellor, who had personally taken the cause of Moldavian Jews to heart, under proddings from his Jewish financial adviser, Bleichröder? Trotsky ironically described how as a result of these machinations the fate of Rumanian Jewry had become a pawn in the game of European diplomacy.[35]

The outbreak of the First World War found Trotsky in Vienna, and in disbelief he watched festive crowds in the Ringstrasse, greeting the news of mobilization with hope and joy. The war was in his opinion a struggle for imperialist hegemony between Germany and England. The task of the proletariat was to create 'a new, more powerful and stable fatherland—the republican United States of Europe, as a transition to the United States of the World'.[36] Trotsky anticipated a Russian Revolution which would be 'an integral part of the social revolution of the European proletariat'.[37] The latter would have to liquidate the old socialist International, whose national party framework had bound it to the defence of conservative state structures and of 'social-imperialism'.

Returning to Russia in 1917, Trotsky was to play a decisive role in the October Revolution, as its foremost orator and mass spellbinder.[38] Between 1917 and 1924 the architect of the Bolshevik insurrection and creator of the Red Army paid very little attention indeed to the Jewish question.[39] During this brief era of internationalist euphoria, Trotsky doubtless believed that assimilation would prove a viable solution for the Jewish masses. His immediate problem was to overcome his lack of an organizational base in any faction of Russian social democracy. Trotsky's position in the Bolshevik hierarchy was by no means secure, despite his central role in planning the insurrection. This had nothing to do with his Jewish origin, but went back to his disagreements with Lenin in 1903–4.

The proceedings of the Second Congress of the RSDWP in 1903 had ended by convincing Trotsky that in matters of organization and political philosophy Lenin was a 'dull caricature of the tragic intransigence of Jacobinism'; he was a Bolshevik parody of Maximilien Robespierre, whose outlook could only lead to a form of dictatorship *over* the proletariat.[40] The logic of Bolshevism would lead to the guillotine and terror and 'Marx's lion head would be the first to fall' wrote Trotsky, more prophetically than he could realize, in 1904.[41] The young Trotsky at that time veered towards the Menshevik views of Paul Axelrod, to whom his venomous attack on Leninism was dedicated. He felt alienated by what was specifically Russian in Bolshevism—its links with the native autocratic, violent tradition and its distrust of democratic methods. Trotsky was a Westerner in outlook who felt oppressed by the conspirational atmosphere of the Russian revolutionary movement and the intrigues, squabbles and splits of party politics in exile.[42] He preferred the free initiative of the West European socialist parties, and between 1905 and 1917 had remained aloof from the Bolshevik party. During the 1905 Revolution, as Chairman of the Petrograd Soviet, the twenty-six-year-old Trotsky had nevertheless been the only Marxist leader of note to play a major directing role.

On the basis of his practical experience, he had evolved with the help of Parvus (another Russian-Jewish revolutionary) a novel theory to describe the future tasks of socialist revolution. The next uprising in Russia would have to be a 'permanent revolution' which would telescope together in one unbroken continuum the aims of both the bourgeois and socialist revolutions. The theory of permanent revolution turned Russian backwardness into a springboard for mass action, under proletarian leadership. Lenin had come round to a similar point of view from a different starting-point. Both Lenin and Trotsky encouraged an immediate link and transition from the bourgeois-democratic to the proletarian-socialist order in Russia.[43]

The October Revolution brought Lenin and Trotsky together, despite their past differences. Unlike other Bolsheviks who resented Trotsky's sudden rise to eminence as that of an upstart and former adversary, Lenin was ready to forgive and forget the past. Trotsky's Jewish origin seemingly played little role at this stage in his differences with other Bolshevik leaders. This does not mean, however, that anti-Semitism had disappeared or ceased to play any part in the dramatic events which followed the October uprising. Trotsky himself seems to have been well aware that his Jewishness might be held against him. In his autobiography he wrote, 'If, in 1917 and later, I occasionally pointed to my Jewish origin as an argument against some appointment, it was simply because of political considerations'.[44]

The question first arose when Lenin offered him the post of Commissar for Home Affairs in the new Soviet Government: he declined on the grounds that this would play into the hands of the 'White' counter-revolutionaries, whose anti-Semitism was proverbial. Lenin regarded this as an unjustified concession to the 'socialism of fools'.[45] But he backed down and accepted Sverdlov's suggestion that Trotsky should head the new Soviet Foreign Ministry. Ironically enough, Trotsky, who had seen his Jewishness as a complication with regard to suppressing internal disorders, was able as commander of the Red Army to summon the Russian people to prodigious efforts during the Civil War against the White Armies. As the embodiment of the October insurrection, he was able to rally war-weary workers and peasants to the defence of Russia, and to act as an inspiring catalyst of dormant revolutionary energies. In his autobiography he quotes from a White Guard writer, reporting a Cossack's defiant reply to taunts that he had accepted the command of the 'Jew' Trotsky . 'Trotsky is not a Jew, Trotsky is a fighter. He's ours, he is Russian! . . . It is Lenin who is a communist, a Jew, but Trotsky is ours, a fighter, a Russian.'[46]

Trotsky in the flush of victory must subjectively have seen himself as a Russian, for all his cosmopolitan internationalism. What did *he* have in common with the Jewish masses in Russia, to whom he devoted a mere four sentences in his *History of the Russian Revolution*? Only much later when he had lost power did he remark, 'Anti-Semitism raised its head with that of anti-Trotskyism. They both derived from the same source—the petty bourgeois reaction against October.'[47] Although a Jew, Trotsky showed far less insight into this question than did Lenin—just as the latter showed greater realism and sensitivity on the national problem in general.

For the mass of Russian Jewry—merchants, traders, shopkeepers and peddlers—the new regime meant economic ruin. The Jewish masses only began to swing towards the Bolsheviks in 1919 out of an instinct of self-preservation against the murderous pogroms of the White armies.[48] Jewish assessments of Trotsky at this time were compounded of mixed feelings of pride and fear; on the one hand, he seemed like an avenger of Jewish humiliations under Tsarism, bringing fire and slaughter to their worst enemies. On the other hand, in the Ukraine where Trotsky's Red Army had put down aspirations for national independence and peasant revolts, as well as the anarchist Makhnovite bands, resentment and hatred was rife. The pogroms of 1917–19 in the Ukraine, fed by White propaganda, were at least in part a reaction against the *Zhid* Trotsky and the Bolshevik armies under his command.[49]

The prominence of other Jews not only in the Bolshevik political leadership in the period from 1917 to 1922 (15–20 per cent of the delegates at party Congresses were Jews) but especially in the Cheka, nourished anti-Semitism. Jews were suddenly conspicuous as local Commissars, bureaucrats, and tax officers, as well as secret police officials. Trotsky himself appears to have been worried at this, and favoured a greater number of Jews at the battle front—to counter 'chauvinist agitation' among Red Army men.

> 'I suggest that the Jewish battalions enter those regiments where there are also battalions of other nationalities. In this way we can avoid the chauvinism which results from the estrangement of the different nationalities, and which unfortunately arises when entirely independent national military units are formed.'[50])

But he remained wholly indifferent to the plight of the Jewish masses in Russia, whom he identified with the despised petty-bourgeoisie. At the pinnacle of his power he invariably sent Jewish delegations away, repeating that he was an internationalist and a social democrat, unconcerned with their problems.[51] This indifference extended even to his own father, who, at the height of the Civil War found himself menaced by the Whites because of his son, and by the Reds because he was a rich kulak. Having lost all his savings during the Revolution, David Bronstein (who was too illiterate to read any of his son's works) had to walk hundreds of miles to find shelter in Odessa. In his autobiography Trotsky showed a chilling lack of respect for his father, laconically observing, 'My father died of typhus in the spring of 1922, at the very moment when I was reading my report at the Fourth Congress of the Communist International'.[52]

Trotsky's revolutionary career had totally alienated him from his family, religion and national origin. During the Civil War he only concerned himself with the administrative and propaganda aspects of the Jewish question which occasionally arose with regard to the recruitment of Jewish youth to the revolutionary forces. Trotsky suspected that these recruits joined the Bolsheviks for national rather than class reasons, but he encouraged them, if only to counter the widespread belief that Jews shirked military service.[53]

As long as Lenin was alive, Trotsky's star remained in the ascendant, although his role in suppressing the Kronstadt rebellion, in advocating the militarization of labour, and bureaucratic centralism, made him enemies. A latecomer among the Bolsheviks, he had nevertheless emerged after 1917 as Lenin's trusted lieutenant and hero of the Revolution. Why then did he lose his power? Was it his defects of character, his incapacity for intrigue, his pride and 'colossal arrogance', and the fear of his colleagues that he might establish a military dictatorship? Or was it the mood of the Russian people, grown weary of sacrifice and adventure, who had no more taste for his dramatic, messianic style of politics? Did anti-Semitism play a role in his downfall, as even he subsequently appeared to suggest?

The political forces ranged against Trotsky, allied with his tactical errors and personal failings, were probably reason enough for his fall. Moreover, he undoubtedly underestimated the exhaustion of the Soviet working class, the demoralization and chaos caused by the collapse of the Russian economy. He initially failed to see that Stalin appealed to a general craving for peace, stability and safety: by contrast, Trotsky seemed to be a heroic 'saviour' who would further involve Russia in unwanted new adventures and dangers. He was convinced that backward Russia alone would never achieve socialism; the Soviet fortress existed to spark off an international revolution, without which world capitalism would inevitably destroy the socialist island in its midst. Salvation could only come from a revolutionized West. This view offended against the Russian idea of their unique socialist destiny (with its sources in Russian Slavophilism and messianism) and ignored the real isolation of the Soviet Union in the 1920s.[54] Stalin's slogan of 'socialism in one country' was an emotionally compelling reaction to the seemingly impossible burdens of revolutionary internationalism conducted in a void. It appealed to the popular mood, it was rooted in the socio-economic realities of an exhausted nation, and it was nourished by ancient reflexes of Russian self-centredness and self-sufficiency. The apathy of a post-revolutionary period did not favour Trotsky's activism, his impatience with anything but global revolution, his indifference to Russian national symbols and traditions. It was not difficult for Stalin and his allies to accuse him of defeatism, of underestimating the peasantry, of lack in faith in the Soviet proletariat and irresponsible adventurism.[55] Trotsky also underestimated Stalinism, which he denounced as a counter-revolutionary process of de-radicalization, the triumph of self-satisfied mediocrity. Stalin was to him merely the creature of the upstarts, kulaks, bureaucrats, careerists and Nep-Men who had risen in the post-revolutionary order of the mid-1920s.[56]

What part, if any, did Trotsky's Jewishness play in the struggle for power? Winston Churchill had no doubt that it was central to his defeat.

> He was still a Jew. Nothing could get over that. Hard fortune when you have deserted your family, repudiated your race, spat upon the religion of your father, and lapped Jew and Gentile in a common malignity, to be baulked of so great a prize for so narrow-minded a reason![57]

Was the choice between Stalin and Trotsky ultimately that between a Great-Russian nationalist of Georgian background and a Jewish international Marxist? Was anti-Semitism a factor in routing the supporters of Trotsky? Certainly the tactic appears to have been used in clandestine fashion by Stalin and his followers against the 'Trotskyist' and 'Zinovievist' opposition.

In a letter to Bukharin on 4th March 1926 Trotsky incredulously protested against anti-Jewish undertones in the whispering campaign against him. 'Is it true, is it possible, that in *our party*, in MOSCOW, in WORKERS' CELLS, anti-Semitic agitation should be carried on with impunity?!'[58]

He raised the same protest two weeks later, at a Politburo meeting, but his colleagues merely shrugged and professed to know nothing. Stalin's campaign gathered momentum, and in 1927 the 'Jews' in the opposition led by Trotsky, Zinoviev and Kamenev were calumniated as agitating against Leninism. Trotsky openly challenged this campaign before the Presidium of the Central Control Commission, which was considering his expulsion, together with that of Zinoviev. He observed that questions worthy of Black Hundred anti-Semitism were being posed in 'workers and peasants' cells' about the 'opposition'. In his *Platform of the opposition*, written in 1927, Trotsky for the first time publicly linked this issue with careerism and bureaucratism in the party. Later, in his 'Thermidor and Anti-Semitism', Trotsky was to develop the idea that Stalin's bureaucracy was actively promoting anti-Semitism in the USSR, despite the legal ban on it imposed during Lenin's rule.[59]

It was only in defeat and exile that Trotsky came to glimpse something of the reality of anti-Semitism, which he had so cavalierly dismissed in the past. But this did not lead him to rediscover his personal identity as a Jew, in a religious, an ethnic or an existential sense.

For example, in the 1930s Trotsky came into contact with the immigrant Jewish workers' organizations in France and America which published Yiddish-language newspapers. Characteristically,

Trotsky affirmed that the most important task of Jewish workers in France, as elsewhere, was 'to participate in the workers' movement of the land in which they live, work and struggle'.[60] He added, 'Sixty thousand Jewish workers in Paris is a great force'(!) and could contribute to shake up 'the country's strong conservatism'. As foreigners sharing the bottom layers of society with the indigenous proletariat, they were 'of an immigrant spirit, more mobile, more receptive to revolutionary ideas!'[61] Their historic mission was an international obligation to fructify in a revolutionary manner the French working class.

Trotsky's greetings to Jewish workers in America were conceived in a similar spirit. He affirmed that

> Historical conditions have made the Jewish workers susceptible to the ideas of scientific Communism. The very fact of the dispersement of the Jewish workers in a number of countries should instill in them, and does instill in them, the ideas of *internationalism*. In view of this alone, the Communist Left opposition has every reason to count on a big influence among the Jewish proletarians in the United States.[62]

The Jewish workers, because of their 'pariah' status, their lack of civil rights and economic situation were 'a weak link of the proletariat'. Trotsky evidently hoped that this fact would make them receptive to the Left opposition which he was seeking to rally against the Stalinist policies of the Comintern.

Trotsky's view of Zionism was, however, only slightly modified by the menacing situation facing the Jews in the 1930s. He was of the opinion that the rise of Nazism and the Arab-Jewish struggle in Palestine proved 'that the Jewish question cannot be solved within the framework of capitalism'.[63] The material conditions 'for the existence of Jewry as an independent nation could be brought about only by the proletarian revolution'.[64] He appeared to believe that large-scale Jewish immigration to Palestine, and the establishment of a territorial base there, could only happen 'either on the basis of a mutual understanding, or with the aid of a kind of international proletarian tribunal which should take up this question and solve it'.[65]

This naïve proposal confirms Trotsky's own admission that he was 'not thoroughly familiar with the facts' about Palestine. Asked to comment on official Communist policy, following the Jewish-Arab clashes in Palestine in 1929, he tentatively suggested that there were mixed elements behind the Arab riots—'such as national liberationists (anti-imperialists) and reactionary Mohammedans and anti-Semitic pogromists'.[66] The essence of Trotsky's position remained, however, clear, and did not involve him in any major re-evaluation about the need for a Jewish 'homeland' in face of the Nazi persecution. 'The blind alley in which German Jewry finds itself as well as the blind alley in which Zionism finds itself is inseparably bound up with the blind alley of world capitalism as a whole.'[67]

In 1934, in *Reply to a Question about Birobidjan*, Trotsky for the first time appeared—perhaps unconsciously—to be reversing his earlier position on the Jewish question. Predictably, he again condemned Zionism because it 'draws away the workers from the class struggle by means of unrealizable hopes of a Jewish state under capitalist conditions'.[68] But he affirmed that 'a workers' government is duty-bound to create for the Jews, as for any nation, the best circumstances for cultural development'.[69] This included, by Trotsky's own definition, Jewish schools, press, theatre and a 'separate territory for self-administration and development', if they so desired.

After his arrival in Mexico, in January 1937, Trotsky answered a further series of questions from correspondents of the JTA (Jewish Telegraphic Agency) and *Der Weg* about his attitude to Birobidjan, anti-Semitism in the Soviet Union, assimilation and the Palestine problem. The revision of his previous standpoint was much clearer, although it did not imply a change in his opposition to Zionism. Thus he accepted that his original belief in the 'quasi-automatic' disappearance of the Jewish question had proved unfounded: decaying capitalism had everywhere (and especially in Germany) 'swung over to an exacerbated nationalism, one part of which is anti-Semitism'.[70] Moreover, the rise of a Yiddish language culture had led to the development of a *Jewish nation* which still lacked a territorial base. Zionism had sprung from this lack of a common territory, but it was incapable of solving the Jewish question. Against the background of the Arab revolt in Palestine, Trotsky added, 'The conflict between the Jews and the Arabs in Palestine acquires a more and more tragic and more and more menacing character. . . . I do not at all believe that the Jewish question can be resolved within the framework of rotting capitalism and under the control of British imperialism'.[71]

At the same time Trotsky emphasized that the 'Jewish nation' was a reality with which one must reckon 'for an entire epoch to come'. But what could revolutionary socialism offer the Jews? All that Trotsky proposed was the 'grand historical perspective' of socialism under the condition 'of the most developed technique and culture'.[72] In this ideal world there would be no compulsory migrations or displacement of nationalities, no 'creation of new ghettoes' but a freely consented reassemblage of peoples as 'part of the planned economy'. Only with the context of 'the complete emancipation of humanity' would the Jewish question be solved. 'To work for international socialism means also to work for the solution of the Jewish question.'[73]

On the issue of Soviet anti-Semitism Trotsky was, however, much more realistic. He stressed that the omnipotent bureaucracy in the

USSR did not hesitate

> to resort in a scarcely camouflaged manner to chauvinistic tendencies, above all the anti-Semitic ones. The latest Moscow trial, for example, was staged with the hardly concealed design of presenting internationalists as faithless and lawless Jews who are capable of selling themselves to the German Gestapo.[74]

Trotsky himself had been demonologized *in absentia* at the Moscow Show-Trials, and this must have strengthened his personal revulsion at the tactics of Stalin's henchmen. He traced the emergence of anti-Semitic demagogy in the USSR back to 1926, emphasizing that it was camouflaged and manipulated 'with a cunning skill in order to canalize and to direct especially against the Jews the existing discontent against the bureaucracy'.[75]

This plain statement of the facts aroused strong resentment in some left-wing American Jewish quarters! B. Z. Goldberg, a columnist on the New York Yiddish daily *Der Tog*, objected to Trotsky's sudden discovery of anti-Semitism after he had lost power and been removed from the Kremlin. The USSR, he asserted, did not oppress its nationalities, nor was there any anti-Semitism in the Soviet State.[76]

Trotsky's views on this issue were, however, more perceptive than those of his critics. In an article entitled 'Thermidor and Anti-Semitism', written in February 1937, Trotsky accused his detractors of 'vulgar non-dialectical thinking'.[77] In their eagerness to counterpose a 'kingdom of national harmony' in Stalin's Russia to the 'absolutist kingdom of anti-Semitism' in Hitler's Germany they mistook their illusions for reality.[78] Trotsky recalled that the October Revolution had abolished the outlawed status of the Jews without eliminating the national prejudices deeply rooted in the backward social strata of 'Mother' Russia. It was naïve to think that in less than twenty years the Soviet regime could wipe out the legacies of Tsarism, the 'national and chauvinist prejudices, particularly anti-Semitism'.[79]

Trotsky again related the emergence of Soviet anti-Semitism to the bureaucratic deformation of the workers' state. Hatred of the bureaucracy by workers and peasants was 'a fundamental fact in Soviet life', and it was all too common to deflect this against the Jewish officials. Fearful of its privileges, the Soviet bureaucracy exploited 'the most ingrained prejudices and the most benighted instincts'.[80] For Trotsky the new anti-Semitism was a symptom of the general corruption of the Stalin regime, one of its means 'to divert the indignation of the working masses from itself to the Jews'.[81] He traced its origins to the struggle of Stalin against the opposition in the late 1920s.

After 1926 Stalin's clique 'purposely emphasized the names of Jewish members of casual and secondary importance', and once

Kamenev and Zinoviev joined with Trotsky the situation had worsened. Jews were removed from responsible party positions even if they supported the general line, and the opposition was depicted as being led by three 'dissatisfied Jewish intellectuals'.[82]

Trotsky stated that the baiting of the opposition in Moscow, Leningrad and elsewhere 'often assumed a thoroughly obvious anti-Semitic character', and that he had received hundreds of letters deploring this fact. The slogan 'Beat the opposition' took on, in Trotsky's own words, the complexion of the old slogan 'Beat the Jews and save Russia' as Stalin's campaign gathered intensity.[83] It was in Trotsky's view a carefully calculated and premeditated campaign—and even sought to divide the opposition into 'orthodox' and 'Jewish' factions. Trotsky also emphasized Stalin's exposure of the real (i.e., Jewish) names of his opponents Zinoviev (Radomislyski) and Kamenev (Rozenfeld), at the time of the Moscow show-trials. This was in his opinion deliberately intended to foster an anti-Semitic mood. He was particularly sensitive to the use of such tactics against his own son, Sergei Sedov, whose 'real' name was 'unmasked' by the Soviet press as Bronstein. Trotsky bitterly complained at this fact, exaggerating its importance and thereby revealing his own unconscious 'Jewish' complex.

> If these falsifiers wished to emphasize the connection of the accused with me, they would have called him Trotsky, since politically the name Bronstein means nothing at all to anyone. But they were out for other game; that is, they wished to emphasize my Jewish origin and the semi-Jewish origin of my son. I paused at this episode, because it has a vital and yet not an exceptional character. The whole struggle against the opposition is full of such episodes.[84]

In reply to critics who attacked him for 'suddenly' raising the Jewish question, Trotsky conceded that in the past it had 'never occupied the centre of my attention'; but this was no argument for silence and blindness to a problem 'which exists and demands solution'. In what he called the transitional historical period, he was prepared to envisage an 'independent Jewish republic' in the USSR on the lines of a free and independent Ukraine. But he dismissed Birobidjan as 'a bureaucratic farce' which could never succeed, since it was organized by Stalinist methods.[85] Only under a Soviet democracy and 'completely *voluntary* migrations' within a federal socialist regime could a territorial solution to the Jewish problem have any chance of success.[86]

Toward the end of the 1930s Trotsky had also become aware for the first time that the situation of European Jewry, facing the threat of Nazism, was increasingly untenable. In contrast to the Stalinists and Social Democrats, he had shown a sensitive awareness of the strength of the Nazi movement and of Hitler's abilities as an organizer, agitator and tactician. He seemed to sense the impending disaster, and this caused him more than anything else to modify his internationalism in favour of a more immediate remedy for the Jewish question. Trotsky noted with horror in 1938 that 'the number of countries which expel the Jews grows without cease', while those ready to accept refugees was decreasing.[87] In a remarkable prediction of the approaching Holocaust, he added, 'It is possible to imagine without difficulty what awaits the Jews at the mere outbreak of the future world war. But even without war the next development of world reaction signifies with certainty the *physical extermination of the Jews*'.[88]

But Trotsky's clairvoyance on this point (impressive as it was compared with that of his detractors) was not matched by any convincing practical proposals. His appeal to American Jews menaced by fascism and anti-Semitism called for the 'audacious mobilization of the workers against reaction, creation of workers' militia, direct physical resistance to the fascist gangs, increasing self-confidence, activity and audacity on the part of all the oppressed'[89] to stop world fascism. Unfortunately, the Fourth International set up by Trotsky in 1938 was far too weak and impotent to do anything about the impending catastrophe. His appeal to the Jewish people 'to come to the help of the revolutionary vanguard' was too vague and unrealistic to make any difference.[90]

Trotsky's last comment on the Jewish problem came after the Second World War had already begun. In May 1940 he drafted a manifesto to the world proletariat, presented at an Emergency Conference of the Fourth International which briefly analysed among other things, the relation between imperialism and anti-Semitism.

In the 'monstrous intensification of chauvinism and especially of anti-Semitism' Trotsky saw the final bankruptcy of decaying capitalism.

> Today decaying capitalist society is striving to squeeze the Jewish people from all its pores; seventeen million individuals out of the two billion populating the globe, that is, less one per cent, can no longer find a place on our planet! Amid the vast expanses of land and the marvels of technology, which has also conquered the skies for man as well as the earth, the bourgeoisie has managed to convert our planet into a foul prison. . . .[91]

Hitler's 'zoological' anti-Semitism was for Trotsky a 'chemically pure distillation of the culture of imperialism'; he quoted the old Marxist slogan (which he mistakenly attributed to Engels), that anti-Semitism was the 'socialism of idiots'! Trotsky also noted that since the Nazi-Soviet pact there had not been a 'single word of condemnation about the destruction of Czechoslovakia and Poland, the seizure of Denmark and Norway and the shocking bestialities inflicted by Hitler's gangs on the Polish and Jewish people!'[92]

In July 1940, only a month before his assassination, Trotsky also expressed his views on the Palestine problem following the British White Paper restricting Jewish immigration.

> The attempt to solve the Jewish question through the migration of Jews to Palestine can now be seen for what it is, a tragic mockery of the Jewish people. Interested in winning the sympathy of the Arabs who are more numerous than the Jews, the British government has sharply altered its policy toward the Jews, and has actually renounced its promise to help them found their 'own home' in a foreign land. The future development of military events may well transform Palestine into a bloody trap for several hundred thousand Jews. Never was it so clear as it is today, that the salvation of the Jewish people is bound up inseparably with the overthrow of the capitalist system.[93]

A month later he was struck down by an ice-pick aimed at the back of his skull by one of Stalin's agents in Mexico.

In the course of his remarkable career Trotsky had slowly come to realize that, in the light of Nazism, assimilation was no longer a valid answer to the Jewish question. But he was equally convinced that Zionism was impractical and a lost cause, as a result of British Government policy. He remained faithful to the classic Marxist belief that 'within the framework of rotting capitalism' the Jews would find no answer to their plight. Their salvation could only occur once conditions for a fully developed international socialism had ripened. This was the *idée fixe* to which his followers have tenaciously clung, despite Trotsky's mistaken predictions.

Leon Trotsky died an unrepentant revolutionary with an 'unshaken faith in the Communist future'.[94] Though he would have repudiated with horror any 'national messianic pride' in his origins, there was in his last Testament despite its militant atheism, an echo of the defiant belief in humanity which represents perhaps the best in the Jewish tradition.

> This faith in man and in his future gives me now such power of resistance, as cannot be given by any religion.[95]

Notes

INTRODUCTION

1 See Werner T. Angress, 'Juden im politischen Leben der Revolutionszeit', in *Deutsches Judentum in Krieg und Revolution* (Tübingen, 1971) ed. Werner E. Mosse and A. Paucker.

2 L. Schapiro, 'The Role of the Jews in the Russian Revolutionary Movement', in *Slavonic and East European Review* (1961–2), Vol. XL.

3 Robert Michels, *Political Parties: A Sociological Study of the Oligarchical Tendencies of Modern Democracy*, translated by Eden and Cedar Paul (New York, 1959), 260.

4 Nicolas Berdyaev, *The Russian Revolution* (Ann Arbor, 1961), 69–70.

5 See J. L. Talmon, 'Jews between Revolution and Counter-Revolution', in *Israel Among the Nations* (London, 1970), 17–26.

6 See Jacob Toury, *Die Politische Orientierungen der Juden in Deutschland* (Tübingen, 1966).

7 Kurt Lewin, 'Self-hatred among Jews', in *Contemporary Jewish Record* (New York, 1941), Vol. IV, No. 3, 219–32.

8 Theodor Lessing, *Der jüdische Selbsthass* (Berlin, 1930).

9 See Jean-Paul Sartre, *Réflexions sur la question juive* (Paris, 1954).

10 Isaac Deutscher, *The Non-Jewish Jew and Other Essays* (London, 1968), 25–41.

11 Ibid., 33.

12 See Walter Laqueur, 'Zionism, the Marxist Critique, and the Left', in *Dissent* (December 1971), 566–74.

13 V. I. Lenin, 'The Position of the Bund in the Party', in *Collected Works* (Moscow/London, 1961), Vol. VII, 100 ff.

14 V. I. Lenin, 'Critical Remarks on the National Question', in *Sochineniya*, Vol. 20 (4th. ed.), written October-December 1913.

15 Elias Tscherikover, *The Pogroms in the Ukraine* (New York, 1965) in Yiddish.

16 See C. Abramsky, 'The Biro-Bidzhan Project, 1927–1959', in *The Jews in Soviet Russia since 1917*, edited by L. Kochan (London, 1970), 62 ff.

17 Quoted in *The Golden Tradition*, edited by Lucy S. Davidowicz (London, 1967), 410.

18 Bebel–Kautsky, 4th September 1901, in Victor Adler, *Briefwechsel mit August Bebel und Karl Kautsky* (Vienna, 1954), 137.

19 *Protokoll über die Verhandlungen des Parteitages der Sozialdemokratischen Partei Deutschlands*, Lübeck 22–28 September 1901 (Berlin, 1901), 195.

20 Gustav Noske, *Erlebtes aus Aufstieg und Niedergang einer Demokratie* (Offenbach-am-Main, 1947), 27.

21 See Eduard David, *Das Kriegestagebuch des Reichstagsabgeordnete Eduard David 1914 bis 1918*, edited by Erich Matthias and Susanne Miller. (Düsseldorf, 1966).

22 Paul Lafargue, 'L'Opinion du Parti Socialiste sur les Juifs', in *Le Cri du Peuple*, 2nd October 1886.

23 'Kautsky on the Problems of the Jewish Proletariat in England', in *Justice* 23rd April 1904.

24 Friedrich Engels, 'Uber den Antisemitismus', in *Arbeiter-Zeitung* (Vienna) 9th May 1890.
25 V. I. Lenin, *Sochineniya*, Vol. XIX (Moscow, 1929). 2nd. ed., 354–5.
26 Robert Michels, *Political Parties*, 261.
27 *Rosa Luxemburg im Kampf gegen den deutschen Militarismus* (East Berlin, 1960), 97.
28 Peter Nettl, *Rosa Luxemburg* (London, 1966). Vol. II, Appendix II, 861.
29 Isaac Deutscher, *The Non-Jewish Jew and Other Essays*, 36.
30 Ibid., 40–1.

KARL MARX

1 For further details on Marx's geneology, see E. Lewin-Dorsch, 'Familie und Stammbaum von Karl Marx', in *Die Glocke* (Berlin, 1923) Jg. IX, Vol. I, 309 ff., 340 ff. Also the family tree given in Albert Massiczek's *Der menschliche Mensch. Karl Marx' jüdischer Humanismus* (Vienna, 1968), 627.
2 See Massiczek, ibid., 129–85; Werner Blumenberg, *Karl Marx* (London, 1972), 6–11, 59–60; and David McLellan, *Marx before Marxism* (London, 1972), 43–9.
3 On Heinrich Marx's conversion see Adolf Kober, 'Karl Marx' Vater und das Napoleonische Ausnahmegesetz gegen die Juden', 1808, in *Jahrbuch des kölnischen Geschichtsvereins* XIV (1932) IIIff. Also Lewis S. Feuer, 'The Conversion of Karl Marx's father', in *The Jewish Journal of Sociology*, Vol. XIV, No. 2 (December 1972), 149–66.
4 Kober, ibid., 124.
5 See Heinz Monz, 'Die soziale Lage der elterlichen Familie von Karl Marx', in *Karl Marx 1818–1968. Neue Studien zu Person und Lehre*. (Mainz, 1968), 71–74.
6 Ibid., 75. See also the letter of Henriette Marx to Lion and Sophie Philips, dated 14th April 1853, in Werner Blumenberg, 'Ein unbekanntes Kapitel aus Marx' Leben', in *International Review of Social History*, Vol. I (1956), Pt. I, 5 ff.
7 Ibid. Letter of Eleanor Marx to Henri Polak, 31st October 1893.
8 See Arnold Künzli, *Karl Marx. Eine Psychographie* (Vienna, 1966), 117–29, 199–202 for a psychoanalytic interpretation of Marx's anti-Judaism and resentment against his mother.
9 Künzli, ibid., 147; Blumenberg, op. cit., 107.
10 David McLellan, *The Young Hegelians and Karl Marx* (London, 1969), 48 ff.
11 See Moses Hess, *Briefwechsel* (The Hague, 1959), 80, edited by E. Silberner.
12 Eleanore Sterling, *Er ist wie Du. Aus der Frühgeschichte des Antisemitismus in Deutschland 1815–1850* (Munich, 1956), 50. Also Jacob Toury, *Die Politische Orientierungen der Juden in Deutschland* (Tübingen, 1966), 31–3.
13 *Marx-Engels Gesamtausgabe* (MEGA) Vol. I (i), 2, 308, Marx-Ruge 13th March 1843 (Berlin/Moscow, 1927–35). Also Helmut Hirsch, 'Karl Marx und die Bittschriften für die Gleichberechtigung der Juden, in *Archiv für Sozialgeschichte VIII* (Hanover, 1968), 233–49.
14 MEGA, I (i), 2, 308.
15 Ibid.

16 See the French edition of Karl Marx, *La Question Juive*, followed by Bruno Bauer, *La Question Juive* (Paris, 1968). Despite its misleading introduction, this edition by placing the two texts together facilitates comparisons.
17 MEGA, op. cit., Marx–Ruge.
18 See Nathan Rotenstreich, *The Recurring Pattern. Studies in Anti-Judaism in Modern Thought* (London, 1963).
19 See Dietmar Scholz, 'Politische und menschliche Emanzipation—Karl Marx' Schrift "Zur Judenfrage" aus dem Jahre 1844', in *Geschichte im Wissenschaft und Unterricht*, Jg. VIII, Heft I, January 1967.
20 Franz Mehring, *Aus dem literarischen Nachlass von Karl Marx* (Stuttgart, 1902), Vol. II, 356; Otto Heller, *Der Untergang des Judentums: Die Judenfrage, Ihre Kritik, Ihre Lösung durch den Sozialismus* (Berlin/Vienna, 1932), 16; Abraham Léon, *La Conception Matérialiste de la Question Juive* (Paris, 1968), 15–16; and István Mészáros, *Marx's Theory of Alienation* (London, 1970), 29–30.
21 On Bauer's development into a racial anti-Semite, see *Bruno Bauer. Studien und Materialen* (Assen, 1972), edited by Ernst Barnikol.
22 See Robert Misrahi, *Marx et la Question juive* (Paris, 1972), 168–204.
23 See Zvi Rosen, 'The Anti-Jewish Opinions of Bruno Bauer (1838–143), their sources and significance' (in Hebrew), in *Zion*, Vol. XXXIII (1968), 59–76; and David McLellan, *The Young Hegelians and Karl Marx*, 58–9, 77–8.
24 *Marx-Engels Werke* (MEW), Vol. I, 348 (East Berlin, 1964).
25 Ibid., 377.
26 See Moses Hess, *Philosophische und Sozialistische Schriften* (1837–1850), edited by A. Cornu and W. Mönke (Berlin, 1961), 334–45, for his essay *Ueber das Geldwesen*, which was first published in 1845. For a textual comparison with Marx's aricle, see McLellan, 154–8.
27 *MEW*, I, 376.
28 See Robert S. Wistrich, 'Karl Marx and the Jewish Question', in *Soviet Jewish Affairs*, Vol. 4, No. I (Spring 1974), 53–60.
29 *MEW*, I, 377.
30 Ibid., 373.
31 See Helmut Hirsch, 'Marxiana Judaica', in *Cahiers de L'Institut de Science Économique Appliquée* (August 1963) 5–53.
32 *MEW*, I, 373.
33 Bruno Bauer, *Die Judenfrage* (Brunswick, 1843), 144, quoted by Marx in *MEW*, I, 373.
34 See Robert S. Wistrich, *Socialism and the Jewish Question in Germany and Austria 1880–1914* (University of London, Ph.D. thesis, 1974), 13–45.
35 *MEW*, I, 372.
36 See Arthur Hertzberg, *The French Enlightenment and the Jews* (New York, 1968).
37 *MEW*, I, 372.
38 Edmund Silberner, 'Was Marx an Anti-Semite? *Historia Judaica* (New York) Vol. XI, No. I (April 1949).
39 *MEW*, I, 374.
40 Ibid.
41 Ibid., 376.
42 Ibid., 377.

43 Ibid., 372.
44 See Karl Marx, *Early Writings* (London, 1963), edited by T. B. Bottomore.
45 R. Misrahi, op. cit., 71–89.
46 Ibid., 86–91.
47 *The Holy Family* has been strangely ignored by commentators on Marx's attitude to the Jews. Even Silberner scarcely mentions it, and it is also overlooked by Gustav Mayer in his interesting essay 'Early German Socialism and Jewish Emancipation, in *Jewish Social Studies* Vol. I (1939), 409–22.
48 'Die Judenfrage No. 3', in: Karl Marx, *Die Heilige Familie*. See *Aus dem literarischen Nachlass* (Stuttgart, 1902), edited by Franz Mehring Vol. II, 213.
49 Nathan Rotenstreich, 'For and Against Emancipation: The Bruno Bauer Controversy, in *Leo Baeck Year Book* (1959), IV, 3–36.
50 Karl Marx, 'Die Judenfrage No. 3', in: Mehring (ed.) op. cit., II, 213.
51 Ibid., 214.
52 Ibid.
53 See Shlomo Avineri, 'Marx and Jewish Emancipation', in *Journal of the History of Ideas*, Vol. XXV (July–September 1964), No. 3, 445–50. In my view Avineri mistakes the nature of Marx's support for Jewish emancipation.
54 See Roman Rosdolsky, *Cahiers de L'Institut de Science Économique Appliquée* (August 1963), 53–72.
55 Karl Marx, 'The Russian Loan, 4 January 1856', quoted in Silberner, *Historia Judaica* (1949), 35 ff.
56 For example, by Silberner, Isaiah Berlin and Daniel Ben-Nachum, 'Ha-Nekudah ha-Yehudit Ve' Ha-she-elah ha-Leumit etzel Marx', in *Ba'Shaar* (June 1968), 449–56.
57 Reproduced in *Karl Marx on Colonialism and Modernization*, edited by Shlomo Avineri (New York, 1968), 134–43.
58 César Famin, *Histoire de la Rivalité et du Protectorat des Églises Chrétiennes en Orient* (Paris, 1853), 52 ff.
59 *Marx Nachlass*, International Institute of Social History (Amsterdam), B. 59, Notebook, 13–14.
60 Famin, op. cit., 55.
61 Karl Marx, *Herr Vogt* (London, 1860), 143–44.
62 MEW, Vol XXX, 165.
63 Ibid., 259. Marx–Engels, 30th July 1862.
64 *MEGA* Vol. 2 Part III (Berlin, 1930), 122. Engels–Marx, 7th March 1856.
65 Arthur Prinz, 'New Perspectives on Marx as a Jew', in *Leo Baeck Year Book* (1970), 17–25.
66 See his famous letter first published in the Viennese *Arbeiter-Zeitung* (9th May 1890), and reprinted in Victor Adler, *Aufsätze, Reden und Briefe* (Vienna, 1922–9) Vol. I, 6–8.
67 See Chapter 10 in Friedrich Engels, *Anti-Dühring* (Moscow, 1962), 3rd. ed., 312–46, written by Marx.
68 Mikhail Bakunin, *Gesammelte Werke* (Berlin, 1921–4), Vol. III, 208–9.
69 The first anti-Semitic pamphlet directed against Marx was written in 1850 by a former collaborator, Edouard von Müller-Tellering. He had been the Viennese correspondent of the *Neue Rheinische Zeitung* in 1848–9.

See Werner Blumenberg, in *International Review of Social History* (Amsterdam, 1951), 178–97.

70 *MEW*, Vol XXXV, 241. Also in Boris Nicolaievsky and Otto Maenchen Helfen, *Karl Marx, Man and Fighter* (London, 1973), Appendix I, 408 ff.

71 Arthur Prinz, op. cit., 121.

72 Max Beer, *Fifty Years of International Socialism* (London, 1935), 72.

73 Eleanor Marx–Aveling–Karl Kautsky, 28th December 1896 (*Marx Nachlass*, Amsterdam).

74 Max Beer, op. cit., 72.

75 C. Tsuzuki, *The Life of Eleanor Marx* (1855–1898) (Oxford, 1967), 253. See also Wilhelm Liebknecht, *Briefwechsel mit Karl Marx und Friedrich Engels* (The Hague, 1963), edited by G. Eckert, 458–60. Eleanor Marx–Natalie Liebknecht, 14th January 1898: 'What *do* you say to the infamous Dreyfus business? It is not a pleasant fact that the one clear, honest note has been struck not by one of our party, but by Zola! The whole thing is utterly sickening.'

76 *MEW*, I, 375.

77 See Robert S. Wistrich, 'Karl Marx, German Socialists and the Jewish Question', in *Soviet Jewish Affairs* (1973), Vol. 3 No. I, 92–7.

FERDINAND LASSALLE

1 Gustav Mayer, 'Ferdinand Lassalle und die jüdische Reformbewegung', in *Der Jude* (Berlin), V, April 1920.

2 Alex Bein, 'Lassalle als Verteidiger Geigers und des jüdischen Lehr und Lesevereins in Breslau—Zwei Jugendarbeiten Ferdinand Lassalles', in *Bulletin des Leo Baeck Instituts* 36, Jg. IX (1966), 330–41.

3 *Ferdinand Lassalles Tagebuch*, edited by Paul Lindau (Breslau, 1891), 85–6, 2nd February 1840.

4 Ibid.

5 Ibid., 160–1.

6 Ibid.

7 Ibid.

8 Ibid., 181.

9 Ibid., 190–1, 26th August 1840.

10 Ibid., 180.

11 Dr Adolf Kohut, 'Ferdinand Lassalle und seine Mutter', in *Allgemeine Zeitung des Judentums*, Jg. 78, Nr. 35 (28 August 1914).

12 David Footman, *The Primrose Path. A Life of Ferdinand Lassalle* (London, 1946), p. 31.

13 Ferdinand Lassalle, *Nachgelassene Briefe und Schriften* (Stuttgart, 1921), Vol. I, 75 (edited by Gustav Mayer). Also, *Juden und Judenthum in Deutschen Briefen aus drei Jahrzehnten*, edited by Fritz Kobler (Vienna, 1935), 282 ff.

14 Gustav Mayer, 'Lassalle und das Judentum', in *Der Jude*, VIII (1924), 733.

15 *Nachgelassene Briefe*, I, 75 ff.

16 Ibid., 90.

17 Shlomo Na'aman, *Ferdinand Lassalle, Deutscher und Jude* (Hanover, 1968), 34 ff.

18 *Nachgelassene Briefe*, I, 109.
19 Ibid.
20 Ibid., 110.
21 Quoted in Shlomo Na'aman *Lassalle* (Hanover, 1970), 64–5.
22 Ibid.
23 Footman, op. cit., 53.
24 For a psychoanalytic interpretation of Lassalle's relationship with the Countess von Hatzfeldt see Erwin Kohn, *Lassalle: Der Führer* (Leipzig-Vienna-Zürich, 1926), 62–70.
25 P. B. Axelrod, *Perezhitoe i peredumannoe* (Berlin, 1923), Vol. I, 73–4.
26 *Marx–Engels Gesamtausgabe* (MEGA) Vol. 2, Part III, 258–9, 282–4, 366–9: Marx–Engels 22.12.1857, 1.2.1858 and 25.2.1858.
27 See Susanne Miller, *Das Problem der Freiheit im Sozialismus. Freiheit, Staat und Revolution in der Programmatik der Sozialdemokratie von Lassalle bis zum Revisionismusstreit* (Frankfurt-am-Main, 1964), for a detailed discussion.
28 Shlomo Na'aman, op. cit., 622–34.
29 Quoted in Bertrand Russell, *German Social Democracy* (London, 1965), 61–2.
30 See Robert Michels, *Political Parties* (New York, 1959), translated by Eden and Cedar Paul, 191.
31 See Georg Brandes, *Ferdinand Lassalle. Ein literarisches Charakterbild* (Berlin, 1877) for some vivid descriptions of the enthusiasm which Lassalle aroused in the masses.
32 Ferdinand Lassalle, *Nachgelassene Briefe*, Vol. VI (Stuttgart, 1925), 21st October 1856, 'Reisebericht aus dem Orient', 218–19.
33 *Une page d'amour de Ferdinand Lassalle: Récit. Corréspondance. Confessions* (Leipzig, 1878), 47–50. Also quoted in Na'aman, *Lassalle*, 503–10.
34 Ibid.
35 Ibid.
36 Ibid.
37 Na'aman, op. cit., 93.
38 See Hermann Oncken, *Lassalle. Eine politische Biographie* (Stuttgart, 1912), 13, for an exaggerated picture of the backwardness of Lassalle's social and family milieu. Also the remarks of Edouard Rosenbaum, 'Ferdinand Lassalle. A Historiographical Meditation', in *Leo Baeck Yearbook* (1964), 122–30.
39 *MEGA* Vol. 3 Part III (Berlin, 1930), 188.
40 Ibid., 190, Marx-Engels, 7th September 1864.
41 Ibid., 188.
42 Karl Marx, *Lettres à Kugelmann* (Paris, 1971) 34–8. Letter of 23rd February 1865.
43 Na'aman, op. cit., 664–5.
44 Eduard Bernstein, *Sozialdemokratische Lehrjahre* (Berlin, 1928), 26.
45 Na'aman, op. cit., 664.
46 See Isiah Berlin, Benjamin Disraeli, 'Karl Marx and the Search for Jewish Identity', in *Midstream* (July 1970) for an interesting comparison. Unfortunately, Sir Isaiah Berlin does not mention Lassalle in this essay.
47 Ferdinand Lassalle, *Aus Seinen Reden und Schriften* (Vienna-Cologne-Stuttgart-Zürich, 1964), 39. Introduction by Ernst Winkler.

EDUARD BERNSTEIN

1 See Eduard Bernstein, *Die Voraussetzungen des Sozialismus und die Aufgaben der Sozialdemokratie* (Stuttgart, 1899), 130 ff; Peter Gay, *The Dilemma of Democratic Socialism: Eduard Bernstein's challenge to Marx* (New York, 1952); Pierre Angel, *Eduard Bernstein et L'Évolution du Socialisme Allemand* (Paris, 1961), 231–83. Bernstein challenged the status quo within the SPD by exposing the discrepancy between its revolutionary theory and in reformist practice. He wished the party to recognize openly that the emancipation of the working classes within capitalist society was an accomplished fact, and to revise certain presuppositions of Marx in the light of a changing reality.

2 *Bernstein Nachlass* (International Institute of Social History), A. 57, 'Herkunft und Eltern', 4.

3 Eduard Bernstein, *Von 1850 bis 1872. Kindheit und Jugendjahre* (Berlin, 1926), 40–1.

4 *Bernstein Nachlass*, op. cit., 8, 96–7.

5 Eduard Bernstein, op. cit., 40 ff.

6 Aron Bernstein, born in Danzig, the son of a rabbi, had gone to Berlin of the age of twenty, teaching himself the German language. His nostalgic affection for Jewish ghetto life created a new literary genre. He also wrote many essays on science, published in twenty-one volumes in 1855–6, as *Naturwissenschaftliche Volksbücher*. In addition he contributed countless political editorials to the *Berliner Volkszeitung*, and was a historian of the 1848 Revolution. See his *Revolutions- und Reaktionsgeschichte Preussens und Deutschland von den Märztagen bis zur neuesten Zeit* (Berlin, 1882) and *Die Jahre des Reaktion* (Berlin, 1881).

7 Eduard Bernstein, *Entwicklungsgang eines Sozialisten* (Leipzig, 1930), 8.

8 Eduard Bernstein, *Sozialdemokratische Lehrjahre* (Berlin, 1928), 26.

9 See *Bernstein Nachlass* (I.I.S.H.), B. 8; August Bebel, *My Life* (London, 1912), 37; Peter Gay, *The Dilemma of Democratic Socialism*, 137–9.

10 Gay, ibid., 83–92.

11 Eduard Bernstein, *Entwicklungsgang eines Sozialisten*, 11.

12 Eduard Bernstein, 'Wie ich als Jude in der Diaspora aufwuchs', in *Der Jude* II (1917–18), 194.

13 Eduard Bernstein, *My Years of Exile* (London, 1921), 45 ff, 64 ff., for an interesting picture of Karl Höchberg. Also, Angel, *Eduard Bernstein et L'Évolution du Socialisme Allemand* 57–8.

14 See Robert S. Wistrich, *Socialism and the Jewish Question in Germany and Austria (1880–1914)* 173–8.

15 *Der Sozialdemokrat*, 6th February 1881.

16 See Robert S. Wistrich, op. cit., 107–15 on 'The Jewish Community and social democracy'. It is revealing to observe how Eduard's famous uncle, Aron Bernstein, in an article entitled 'Ein Wort zur Judenfrage' (1881), expressed the reaction of many German Jews to Stoecker's anti-Semitic campaign: they would, he suggested, have preferred to see the Jew-baiting as a 'socialistic' phenomenon, rather than as a movement supported by the 'educated' classes. A leading Jewish liberal like Ludwig Bamberger

had no doubt at all that revolutionary Marxism was more dangerous to the national interest than (anti-Semitic) Christian-Germanic conservatism.

17 See the classic study by Jacob Toury, *Die Politische Orientierungen der Juden in Deutschland* (Tübingen, 1966) 168–9.

18 *Eduard Bernsteins Briefwechsel mit Friedrich Engels* (Assen, 1970), edited by Helmut Hirsch, 27–8. Bernstein-Engels, 23rd July 1881.

19 Ibid., 28–29. Engels-Bernstein, 17th August 1881.

20 Ibid., 37. Bernstein-Engels, 9th September 1881.

21 Ibid.

22 Ibid.

23 Ibid., 228. Bernstein–Engels, 10th November 1883.

24 Ibid.

25 Ibid., 123 Bernstein–Engels, 1st September 1882.

26 Ibid., 293 Bernstein–Engels, 18th August 1884 (?). See also Eduard Bernstein, *Geschichte der Berliner Arbeiterbewegung* (Berlin, 1907), Vol. II, 239.

27 *Eduard Bernsteins Briefwechsel mit Friedrich Engels* 299, Bernstein–Engels, 24th September 1884.

28 See *Der Sozialdemokrat* 27 September 1890.

29 See Friedrich Engels, Paul et Laura Lafargue, in *Corréspondance* Vol. II 1887–90 (Paris, 1956), 419.

30 Pierre Angel, op. cit., 91–6, 103–9; Eduard Bernstein, *My Years of Exile*, 174 ff. Also James W. Hulse, *Revolutionists in London. A Study of Five Unorthodox Socialists* (Oxford, 1970), 141 ff.

31 Eduard Bernstein, 'Das Schlagwort und der Antisemitismus', in *Die Neue Zeit* (1893–4), II, 233.

32 Ibid., 232.

33 Ibid.

34 Ibid.

35 Ibid.

36 Ibid., 236–7.

37 On the Centralverein, see Ismar Schorsch, *Jewish Reactions to German Anti-semitism 1870–1914* (New York, 1972), 118–148.

38 See George L. Mosse, 'German Socialists and the Jewish Question in the Weimar Republic', in *Leo Baeck Year Book* (1971), 130–1.

39 Eduard Bernstein, *Die Voraussetzungen des Sozialismus*, 47–50.

40 Ibid. 70–3, 148. Bernstein pointed to the factors which Marx had neglected in his theory of crises. Above all, he emphasized the adaptive power of capitalism and the gradual integration of the proletariat into bourgeois society.

41 Theodor Herzl, *Der Judenstaat* (Jerusalem, 1946), 11th. ed., 23–4.

42 Eduard Bernstein, *Die Neue Zeit* (1897–8), Vol. II, 232.

43 Eduard Bernstein, 'Eleanor Marx', in *Die Neue Zeit*, ibid., 122.

44 Ibid.

45 Ibid.

46 *The Letters and Papers of Chaim Weizmann*. Vol. I (London, 1968), 389. Letter No. 302, dated 29th August 1902, originally written in Russian.

47 *Bernstein Nachlass* (I.I.S.H.) D. 341, 23 October 1902, Kasteliansky-Bernstein; Ibid. D. 505. A. Nossig-Bernstein 17 October 1903; ibid. D. 857 Zlocisti–Bernstein, 6th June 1902.

48 *Motteler Nachlass* (I.I.S.H.) 2222/1. Kautsky–Motteler, 9th January 1903.

49 *Stenographische Berichte über die Verhandlungen des Reichstags X Legislaturperiode, II Session 1900/03*, Vol. 10 (March 10–April 30), 8756–9.

50 See *Dokumente des Sozialismus* Vol. II/III (Stuttgart, 1903), edited by Eduard Bernstein, 344–6, 563–569.

51 Ibid, 344–6. Review of Sarah Rabinowitsch, *Die Organisationen des jüdischen Proletariats in Russland* (Karlsruhe, 1903).

52 *Dokumente des Sozialismus* Vol. V (1905), edited by Eduard Bernstein, 298–9. Review of Mathias Acher (Birnbaum), *Das Stiefkind der Sozialdemokratie.*

53 Ibid, 537. Review of David Balakan, *Die Sozialdemokratie und das jüdische Proletariat.*

54 Eduard Bernstein, 'Der Schulstreit in Palästina', in *Die Neue Zeit* (1913–14), Vol. I, 745–52.

55 Ibid., 752.

56 *Bernstein Nachlass* (I.I.S.H.), A. 114. 'Die Demokratische Staatsidee und die jüdische Nationalbewegung'.

57 Eduard Bernstein, *Von den Aufgaben der Juden im Weltkriege* (Berlin, 1917), 7 ff. Also E. Bernstein, *Entwicklungsgang eines Sozialisten.*, 49.

58 Eduard Bernstein, *Von den Aufgaben der Juden, in Weltkriege*, 30–2.

59 See *Bernstein Nachlass* (I.I.S.H.) Correspondence with Joseph Bloch [D. 61] and pacifism [E. I]. Also, *Das Kriegestagebuch des Reichstagsabgeordneten Eduard David 1914 bis 1918* (Düsseldorf, 1966), edited by Erich Matthias and Suzanne Miller, 210. (21st November 1916) for a number of antisemitically tinged comments about the pacifism of Bernstein and other Jews in the SPD during the First World War. Eduard David (who was not Jewish) had been one of Bernstein's strongest supporters before 1914.

60 Eduard Bernstein, *Von den Aufgaben der Juden im Weltkriege* 24.

61 Ibid, 27 ff. See also Eva G. Reichmann, 'Der Bewusstseinswandel der Deutschen Juden', in *Deutsches Judentum in Krieg und Revolution 1916–1923* (Tübingen, 1971), edited by Werner E. Mosse and Arnold Paucker, 511–612. This is a masterly analysis of the subtle shift in German-Jewish self-consciousness during this period.

62 Eduard Bernstein, *Von den Aufgaben der Juden im Weltkriege*, 32.

63 Eduard Bernstein, 'Wie ich als Jude in der Diaspora augwuchs' in *Der Jude* II (1917–18), 187.

64 See *Bernstein Nachlass* (I.I.S.H.), A. 23 Salman Rubashow (Shazar), 7. Also Zalman Shazar, *Or Ishîm* (Tel-Aviv, 1955). 19 ff. [in Hebrew.]

65 Ibid. For another assessment from a non-Zionist standpoint of Bernstein's return to Jewry, see Eva Reichmann-Jungmann, 'Trotz allem Jude—Zu Eduard Bernsteins Tod', in *Central Verein Zeitung* 23rd November 1932, XI Jg., No. 52.

66 Zalman Shazar, op. cit., 20.

67 Kautsky had already espoused this view in his *Rasse und Judentum* (Berlin, 1921) [2nd. ed.] See the English translation *Are the Jews a Race?* (London, 1926), 207–10.

68 See *Bernstein Nachlass* (I.I.S.H.), B. 10, 'Zwei sozialistischen Antworten auf Karl Kautskys Artikel, "Die Aussichten des Zionismus".'

69 *Bernstein Nachlass* (I.I.S.H.) D. 305, Marc Jarblum–Eduard Bernstein, 19th May 1930.

70 For Bernstein's concern with this problem, see *Nachlass*, A. 79, 'Die Ostjuden in Deutschland'.
71 Eduard Bernstein, 'Die Joden in de Dutsche Sociaal-Democratie', in *De Socialistische Gids* (Amsterdam), Jg. VI., No. II (November 1921), 984.
72 See *Nachlass* A. 79.
73 *Nachlass Kautsky* I.I.S.H. (Amsterdam), K. DV 562. Bernstein–Kautsky, 23 January 1932.

ROSA LUXEMBURG

1 See J. P. Nettl, *Rosa Luxemburg* (London, New York, Toronto, 1966) Vol. I, 50–5.
2 Ibid. See also Paul Fröhlich, *Rosa Luxemburg. Gedanke und Tat.* (Frankfurt-am-Mains, 1967) 3rd ed., 16. It should be remembered that only a tiny percentage of Polish Jews at this time spoke Polish, let alone German and Russian. The overwhelming majority were Yiddish-speaking.
3 See the short essay on Rosa Luxemburg, 'Nesher Ha-Mehapkha' (Eagle of the Revolution), in Abraham Bick (Shauli), *Merosh Tszurim* (Jerusalem, 1972), 76–90. This study of socialist thought in Judaism for the first time traces the rabbinical heritage of Rosa though her mother's family tree. Western scholarship has hitherto completely ignored the antecedents of the Löwenstein family.
4 For further details about Jacob Joshua Ben Zvi Hirsch Falk (1680–1756), see the *Encylopaedia Judaica* (1971), Vol. VI, 1155–8.
5 See Abraham Bick, op. cit.
6 Luise Kautsky, *Rosa Luxemburg. Ein Gedenkbuch* (Berlin, 1929), 23, mentions that Lina's brother, Dr Bernhard Löwenstein, was a rabbi in Lemberg. Nettl, who is generally reticent on the Jewish background has nothing much to say on this subject. But see Abraham Bick, op. cit., 76 ff.
7 J. P. Nettl, *Rosa Luxemburg*, op. cit., I, 52.
8 Helmut Hirsch, *Rosa Luxemburg in Selbstzeugnissen und Bilddokumenten* (Hamburg, 1969), 16, suggests that Rosa may have been latently attracted to Christianity, but there is no real evidence for this assertion.
9 Nettl, op, cit., I, 72–82.
10 See Michael Lowy, 'Rosa Luxemburg et la Question nationale', in *Partisans* No. 59–60 (May–August 1971), 62–8.
11 Rosa Luxemburg, *Die industrielle Entwicklung Polens* (Leipzig, 1898). This dissertation is still of interest today to the historian studying economic development in nineteenth-century Poland.
12 R. L., 'Die nationalen Kämpfe in der Turkei und die Sozialdemokratie', in *Sächsische Arbeiter-Zeitung*, 8–10 December 1896; Rosa Luxemburg, 'Der Sozialismus in Polen', in *Sozialistische Monatshefte* (December 1897), No. 10, 547–6. Also Arieh Yaari, 'Rosa Luxemburg ou le nihilisme nationale' in *Les Nouveaux Cahiers* No. 39 (Winter 1974–5), 27–31.
13 See 'Fragment über Krieg, nationale Frage und Revolution: Rosa Luxemburg über die russische Revolution', in *Archiv für die Geschichte des Sozialismus und der Arbeiterbewegung* XIII (1928), 293.
14 Róży Luksemburg, 'Kwestia narodowosciowa i Autonomia', in *Przegląd Socjaldemokratyczny* (August 1908 No. 6), in *Wybór Pism.* Vol. II (Warsaw, 1959), 146–7.

15 Ibid.

16 Ibid., 143–5.

17 See Annie Kriegel, 'La IIe Internationale devant les questions nationales en Europe (1889–1914)' in *Le pain et les roses; jalons pour une histoire des socialismes* (Paris, 1968) 88–9.

18 On the relations between the Bund, the PPS and the SDKPiL, see M. K. Dziewanowski, *The Communist Party of Poland* (Cambridge, Mass., 1959), 37 ff.; M. Rafes, *Ocherki po istorii Bunda* (Moscow, 1923), 45; and Moshe Mishkinsky, *Yesodot Le-Umiyim Be-Hitpatkhutah Shel Tńuat Ha-poalim Ha-Yehudim Be-Rusia*, doctoral dissertation (Jerusalem, 1965), 227 ff.

19 Adolf Warszawski (Warski)–Karl Kautsky. Letter dated 20th May 1903 in *Kautsky Nachlass* D XXIII (Amsterdam). In the same letter Warski, as co-editor with Rosa Luxemburg of *Przegląd Socjaldemokratyczny*, requested an article from Kautsky on the Kishinev pogrom. See Robert S. Wistrich, *Socialism and the Jewish Question* (doctoral dissertation, 1974), 308–11.

20 Warszawski–Kautsky, 20th May 1903.

21 See R. L., 'Krytyka i Bibliografja', in *Przegląd Socjaldemokratyczny* IV (1903) No. 4, 159–63. Review of a pamphlet published in London by the Bund in March 1903, entitled *Polska Partja Socjalistyczna o Żydowskim ruchu robotniczym.* I wish to thank Dr Feliks Tych for confirming Rosa Luxemburg's authorship of this review article.

22 Ibid.

23 Róży Luksemburg, 'Obrachunek Polityczny', in *Czerwony Sztandar*, No. 25, in *Wybór Pism.* Vol. II, 359.

24 R. L., op. cit., 159 ff.

25 Ibid.

26 Ibid.

27 Nettl, *Rosa Luxemburg* Vol. I, 82–3.

28 John Mill, *Pionirn un Boier* (New York, 1946), Vol. I, 167.

29 Ibid., Vol II, 251, for Mill's subsequent disillusion with the SDKPiL leaders, who called for the complete assimilation of Jewish workers to Polish culture. A mark of Rosa Luxemburg's growing hostility to the Bund was her speech at the 1907 London conference of the RSDWP, which even contained an anti-Semitic nuance. She accused one of the Bundist leaders of speculating in the rising and falling prices of sugar. Her speech against the Bund evidently made a great impression on the young Stalin. See J. V. Stalin, *Sochineniya* (Moscow, 1949), Vol. 2, 51–2 Londonskii S'ezd RSDRP.

30 *Młot* 15th October 1910, p. 9 'Odwrót na całej linji'. The authorship of this article was first established by Jadwiga Kaczanowska and Feliks Tych, in *Z Pola Walki* (1962) No. 3 (19), [Bibliografia Pierowodruków Róży Luksemburg], 211.

31 Moshe Mishkinsky, op. cit., 200–1, 209–10, 215.

32 Ibid.

33 L. Jogichesa-Tsyzki '"Nowi towarzysze"—o ruchu rewolucyjnym wśród robotników żydowskich w Rosji', in *Sprawa Robotnicza* in No. 7 (January 1894) Included in *Socjaldemokracja Królestwa Polskiego i Litwyi. Materialy i Dokumenty, Vol. I, Pt. I (1893–1897)* (Warsaw, 1957), 146–52 edited by H. Buczek and F. Tych.

34 *The Four speeches of Jewish workers* made at the May Day Rally of 1892 in

Vilna were first published in Geneva (1893) by Leo Jogiches, probably in collaboration with Rosa Luxemburg. The introduction was written by Boris Krichevskii, a leading Russian social democrat of Jewish origin. For the full text in the original Russian (with parallel Hebrew translation) see *Pervoe Maya 1892 Goda. Chetiri Rechi Evreiski Rabochi* (Jerusalem, 1967), with a preface by Moshe Mishkinsky.

35 L. Jogichesa-Tsyzki, op. cit., 149–50.

36 See I. Ignatieff, 'Russisch-jüdische Arbeiter über die Judenfrage', in *Die Neue Zeit* (1892–3), I, 126 ff., for an almost identical point of view. Ignatieff was the pseudonym of Alexander Israel Helphand (Parvus), the amazing Russian-Jewish revolutionary who became the close collaborator of both Rosa Luxemburg and Trotsky. See Z. A. B. Zeman and W. B. Scharlau, *The Merchant of Revolution: The Life of Alexander Israel Helphand (Parvus) 1867–1924* (London, 1965).

37 Rosa Luxemburg, 'Dyskusja', in *Mlot*, No. 14, 5–7, 5th November 1910. Also reproduced in *Marxisten gegen Antisemitismus*, edited by Iring Fetscher (Hamburg, 1974), 144.

38 Ibid.

39 Ibid., 145.

40 Ibid., 147–8.

41 Ibid., 148.

42 Ibid.

43 Ibid., 149.

44 Andrej Niemojewski, *Myśl Niepodległa* (November 1910), No. 153, 1599 Also Nettl, op. cit., 86.

45 See Julian Unszlicht (Sedecki), *O program Ludu Polskiego: rola socjal-litwactwa w niedawnej rewolucji* (Cracow, 1913).

46 Julian Unszlicht (Sedecki), *Social-litwactwo w Polsce: z teorii i praktyki SDKPiL* (Cracow, n.d.) and *Młot*, 29th October 1910.

47 Rosa Luxemburg, 'Po Pogromie', in: *Młot*, 8th October 1910, Nr. 10.

48 Ibid.

49 Ibid.

50 See the short note by Moshe Mishkinsky in *Soviet Studies*, Vol. XIX, No. 3 (January, 1968), 455–7.

51 Rosa Luxemburg, *Briefe an Karl und Luise Kautsky*, (Hamburg, 1923), 59.

52 See Rosa Luxemburg, *W obronie narodowosci* (Poznan, 1900). She wrote nothing comparable in defence of the Jewish minority in Russia and Poland.

53 Róży Luksemburg, 'Co Dalej?' (Warsaw, 1906) in *Wybór Pism*, Vol. I, 469.

54 Rosa Luxemburg, *Briefe an Freunde* (Hamburg, 1950), 48–9, edited by Benedikt Kautsky, Letter dated 16th February 1917.

55 Nettl, op. cit., 860–2. Also Helmut Hirsch, *Rosa Luxemburg*, 18.

56 Rosa Luxemburg, *Briefe an Freunde* 44–46, Letter dated 28th December 1916.

57 *Sächsische Arbeiterzeitung* (1898) Aus Frankreich, 23rd, 26th, 27th, 28th, 30th July; 4th, 9th, 18th August; 13th, 14th, 18th September. Some of these articles have been collected together in Rosa Luxemburg, *Le Socialisme en France 1898–1912* (Paris, 1971), 50–61.

58 *Sächsische Arbeiterzeitung*, 28th July 1898.

59 See Rosa Luxemburg, 'Die Sozialistische Krise in Frankreich', in *Die Neue*

Zeit (1900–01), I, 495–9, 516–25, 548–58, 619–31, 676–88.

60 'Consultation internationale sur l'affaire Dreyfus et le cas Millerand', in *Cahiers de la Quinzaine,* (Paris, 1899), No. II, 76–82. 'Car dans le cas Dreyfus se sont manifestés quatre facteurs sociaux qui lui donnent directement le cachet d'une question intéressant la lutte de classe, ce sont: militarisme, chauvinisme-nationalisme, antisémitisme et cléricalisme.'

61 For this remark, see the rather misleading introduction by Daniel Guérin to Rosa Luxemburg, *Le Socialisme en France (1898–1912)*, 18.

62 In my view the idea that Rosa Luxemburg was 'impervious' to anti-Semitism should be treated with some scepticism. See J. P. Nettl, *Rosa Luxemburg* Vol. I, 33.

63 Róży Luksemburg, *Listy do Leona Jogichesa-Tsyzki* (Warsaw, 1968), edited by Feliks Tych. Letter dated 27th April 1899.

64 J. P. Nettl, op. cit., Vol. II, 860. I find it rather revealing that Nettl should equate 'pointless stories and too much good food' with a 'Jewish atmosphere' chez Kautsky!

65 *Protokoll über die Verhandlungen des Parteitages der Sozialdemokratischen Partei Deutschlands* (Stuttgart, 3rd–8th October 1898), 99–100, 117–18; *Protokoll* . . . (1899), 171–5, 219, 265–7, 290–1.

66 See Victor Adler, *Briefwechsel mit August Bebel und Karl Kautsky* (Vienna, 1954), 137. Letter dated 4th September 1901.

67 *Protokoll über die Verhandlungen des Parteitages der Sozialdemokratischen Partei Deutschlands* 22nd–28th September 1901 (Berlin, 1901), 191.

68 Ibid.

69 Ibid., 202. See also Robert S. Wistrich, *Socialism and the Jewish Question* 142–8.

70 Rosa Luxemburg, *Briefe an Karl und Luise Kautsky*, 68–9, 3rd October 1901.

71 See Werner Blumberg, 'Einige Briefe Rosa Luxemburgs', in *International Review of Social History* Vol. VIII (1963), 107–8.

72 The one exception I have found is contained in an unsigned article she wrote for *Vorwärts*, 27th September 1910, entitled 'Freidenkertum und Sozialdemokratie.' Significantly, in this polemic against Andrej Niemojewski, Rosa Luxemburg remarked that the vulgarity of Polish 'free-thinking' anti-Semitism made Stöcker and Ahlwardt appear as 'most respectable' (*höchst anständig*) by comparison.

73 See the illuminating article by Gerhard Beier, 'Rosa Luxemburg. Zur Aktualität und Historizität einer umstrittenen Grösse', in *Internationale Wissenschaftliche Korrespondenz* (June 1974) Heft 2, 184–8.

74 Ibid., 188.

75 See Nettl, *Rosa Luxemburg,* Vol. II, 510–13, for an interesting discussion of her Russian orientation.

76 Gustav Noske, *Erlebtes aus Aufstieg und Niedergang einer Demokratie* (Offenbach-am-Main, 1947), 27.

77 Ibid.

78 Isaac Deutscher, *The Non-Jewish Jew and Other Essays* (Oxford, 1968), 34.

79 Ibid., 33–34.

80 Rosa Luxemburg. 'Die Ordnung herrscht in Berlin', in *Rote Fahne*, 14th January 1919, reproduced in *Ich war, ich bin, ich werde sein!* (East Berlin, 1958), 142–3. This formula 'I was, I am, I shall *always* be!' is curiously

reminiscent of Exodus III: 14, where God defines himself to Moses as *Ehyeh asher ehyeh*—I will be what I will be. The divine name was meant to assure the Israelites of their eventual deliverance, though its precise manner was not yet revealed. For Rosa Luxemburg the certainty of the 'final victory of the revolution' is based on the eternal creativity of the masses, though the advent of socialism must pass through a series of inevitable defeats. Her messianism is of course entirely secular in spirit, with the role of Providence rationalized by a voluntarist *theory* of historical dialectics.

VICTOR ADLER

1 'The Jewish Background of Victor and Friedrich Adler', *LBIYB* (1965), X, 266–76.
2 Ibid.
3 Max Ermers, *Victor Adler. Aufstieg und Grösse einer Sozialistischen Partei* (Vienna/Leipzig, 1932), 21.
4 Ibid.
5 Julius Braunthal, *Victor und Friedrich Adler. Zwei Generationen Arbeiterbewegung* (Vienna, 1965), 16.
6 Ibid., 18.
7 Ibid., 21.
8 For Schnitzler's attitude to anti-Semitism, see Robert S. Wistrich, 'Arthur Schnitzler's "Jewish problem"', in *The Jewish Quarterly* (Winter 1975) 27–30.
9 Theodor Billroth, *Über das Lehren und Lernen der Medizinischen Wissenschaften an der Universitäten der Deutschen Nation* (Vienna, 1876), 150–4.
10 Braunthal, op. cit., 19.
11 Ibid.
12 Ibid., p. 330; *Adler Archives*, letter dated Vienna, 7th November 1913, quoted in Braunthal, op. cit., p. 330.
13 *LBIYB* (1965), X, pp. 266 ff.
14 For the case of Karl Kraus, see Robert S. Wistrich, 'Karl Kraus: Jewish prophet or renegade?' in *European Judaism*, No. 2, June 1975.
15 See William J. McGrath, 'Student radicalism in Vienna', in *Journal of Contemporary History* Vol. 2, No. 3 (July 1967), 183–202.
16 See the remarks in Karl Kautsky's memoirs about the cultured pan-German milieu of Jewish artists, doctors, lawyers, journalists and musicians around Victor Adler in the early 1880s. They were 'oppositional, anti-Habsburg, anti-aristocratic and socially liberal in outlook', and at the same time ardent supporters of *Anschluss* with Germany. See *Erinnerungen und Erörterungen von Karl Kautsky*, edited by Benedict Kautsky ('S Gravenhage, 1960), 530–1, also Engelbert Pernerstorfer, 'Aus jungen Tagen', in *Der Ström*, July 1912, II, 98.
17 See Robert S. Wistrich, 'Herzl's "Jews' State" and Israel', in *AJR Information* (January 1975), 6–7; McGrath, op. cit., 184–9.
18 Max Ermers, *Victor Adler*, 105.
19 See Adam Wandruszka, 'Die Drei Lager', in *Geschichte der Republik Österreich* (Vienna, 1954) edited by Heinrich Benedikt, 292 ff.
20 See Robert S. Wistrich, 'Victor Adler: A Viennese Socialist against

Philosemitism', in *The Wiener Library Bulletin* (1974), Vol. XXVII, New Series. No. 32, 26–33.

21 Josef Buttinger, *In the Twilight of Socialism* (New York, 1954), 80–1.

22 Victor Adler, *Briefwechsel mit August Bebel und Karl Kautsky* (Vienna, 1954), 13, Adler–Kautsky, 21st August 1886.

23 Ibid.

24 Ibid, p. 12.

25 Carl E. Schorske, 'Politics in a New Key', in *The Journal of Modern History* (December 1967), XXXIX, No. 4, 345.

26 The quality which his colleagues prized above all in Adler was his capacity to maintain the *unity* of the party. Allied to this was his diligence, knowledge of men, shrewdness and compassion. See *Grosse Gestalten des Sozialismus. Victor Adler aus seinen Reden und Schriften* (Vienna, 1947), edited by Anton Tesarek.

27 Victor Adler, op. cit., p. 15, Adler–Kautsky 21/8/1886.

28 *Arbeiter-Zeitung*, 9th May 1890 (Nr. 19).

29 Leon Trotsky, *Political Profiles*, translated by R. Chappell (London, 1972) p. 45. The original article on Victor and Friedrich Adler appeared in *Novy Mir*, No. 903, 5th February 1917.

30 *Gleichheit* (Equality), 7th May 1887 p. 1.

31 Victor Adler, *Aufsätze, Reden und Briefe* (Vienna 1922–9), Vol. VIII 338, 387.

32 Victor Adler, Der Antisemitismus, *Gleichheit*, 7th May 1887.

33 Ibid.

34 Ibid.

35 *Gleichheit*, 17th September 1887, p. 1.

36 Victor Adler, 'Unser Parteitag und die Presse', in *Gleichheit*, 12th January 1889, p. 2.

37 *Gleichheit*, 31st December 1887, p. 2.

38 Victor Adler, *Gleichheit*, 12th January 1889.

39 *Arbeiter-Zeitung*, 1 November 1889, p. 2.

40 A. Barkai, 'The Austrian Social Democrats and the Jews', in *The Wiener Library Bulletin*, XXIV, No. I (1970), 32.

41 Robert S. Wistrich, 'Victor Adler: A Viennese Socialist against Philosemitism', *ibid.*, 32–3.

42 *Arbeiter-Zeitung*, 25th April 1890, p. 2.

43 Edmund Silberner, *Sozialisten zur Judenfrage* (Berlin, 1962), 234, 279–82.

44 Victor Adler, *Aufsätze, Reden und Briefe*, op. cit. Vol X, 200 'Weder Lueger noch Badeni', 26th December 1896.

45 *Aufsätze*, Ibid., Vol. XI, 106. 'Christliche und jüdische Ausbeutung', 28 February 1897.

46 Ibid.

47 Victor Adler, op. cit., Vol. X, 110–18, 'Die jüdischen Führer', 2nd March 1897.

48 Ibid.

49 *Verhandlungen des sechsten österreichischen Sozialdemokratischen Parteitages, abgehalten zu Wien vom 6 bis einschliesslich 12 Juni 1897* (Vienna, 1897), 87.

50 Ibid.

51 Ibid., 103.

52 Ibid.

53 Ibid, 77. Also Victor Adler, *Aufsätze*, Vol VIII, 375.
54 See Robert S. Wistrich, *Socialism and the Jewish Question in Germany and Austria 1880–1914.* (London Ph. D. thesis, 1974), 553–68.
55 Max Ermers, *Victor Adler*, 230.
56 Jakob Brod–Kautsky, 9th February 1897, previously unpublished letter in *Kautsky Nachlass*, International Institute of Social History [Amsterdam] DVI (Nr. 675): 'Der Adler war immer in der "Judenfragen" befangen.'
57 For a different interpretation by a great friend and admirer of Victor Adler, see Braunthal, op. cit., 144–5. I had two long interviews with Julius Braunthal in 1971 and 1972, but on this point we agreed to differ.
58 *Arbeiter-Zeitung*, 5th January 1898.
59 *Verhandlungen des Parteitages der Deutschen Sozialdemokratie* (Linz, 29th May–1st June 1898), 50–1. Also in Victor Adler, op. cit., Vol. VIII, 390–5.
60 *Verhandlungen des Parteitages der Deutschen Sozialdemokratie*. Ibid., 80.
61 Ibid.
62 Robert S. Wistrich, *Socialism and the Jewish Question in Germany and Austria 1880–1914*, op. cit., 576–84.
63 *Arbeiter-Zeitung*, 4th August 1899, 1–2, 'Antisemitische Untersuchungsrichter'.
64 *Arbeiter-Zeitung*, 19th November 1897, and 8th August 1899, 'Das Ende des Affaire Dreyfus'.
65 Ber Borochov, *Ketavim* (Tel Aviv, 1955), Vol. 3, 198.
66 For a vivid contemporary description of the poverty among East Galician Jews see S. R. Landau, *Unter jüdischen Proletariern* (Vienna, 1898).
67 See Robert S. Wistrich, op. cit., 679–703.
68 See *Arbeiter-Zeitung*, 4 September 1913, 6–7, 'Der Zionistenkongress in Wien'.
69 *Bernstein Nachlass*, IISH., B. 10, for Camille Huysmans's anecdote.

OTTO BAUER

1 See Otto Bauer, *Eine Auswahl aus seinem Lebenswerk* (Vienna, 1961), 9. Introduction by Julius Braunthal.
2 Ibid., 10–11.
3 Ibid., 16.
4 Ibid., 19.
5 See Avraham Barkai, 'The Austrian Social Democrats and the Jews', in *The Wiener Library Bulletin* (1970), Vol. XXIV, No. 2, 16, and Robert S. Wistrich, *Socialism and the Jewish Question in Germany and Austria 1880–1914* (unpublished Ph.D. dissertation, University of London, 1974)., 654–75.
6 See the analysis by A. L. Patkin, *The Origins of the Russian-Jewish Labour Movement* (Melbourne/London, 1947), 164–74.
7 See Markus Ratner, 'Die Nationale Autonomie und das jüdische Proletariat', in *Sozialistische Monatshefte* Jg. XVII (1911), III, 1341, and Mendel Singer, 'Zum Problem der Assimilation der Juden', *Der Kampf* (1928), 295–302, for some telling criticisms.
8 Otto Bauer, *Die Nationalitätenfrage und die Sozialdemokratie* (Vienna, 1907), 371.
9 See my article, 'Marxism and Jewish Nationalism: the theoretical roots of

Confrontation', in *The Jewish Journal of Sociology*, Vol. XVII, No. 1 (June 1975), 43–54.

10 In contrast to Marx and Engels, Bauer in his classic study of 1907 recognized the historic significance of the awakening of the Slav nations in Central Europe and the Balkans. For a summary of some pertinent texts related to the concept of 'historyless peoples', see *Les Marxistes et la question nationale 1848–1914* edited by Georges Haupt, Michael Lowy, Claudie Weill, (Paris, 1974).

11 Otto Bauer, op. cit., 371.

12 Ibid, 379. See also the criticisms of Max(im) (Schatz) Anin, 'Probleme des jüdischen Arbeiterlebens', in *Sozialistiche Monatshefte*, XIII Jg. (1909), 234–5.

13 Robert S. Wistrich, 'Karl Kraus: Jewish Prophet or Renegade?', in *European Judaism*, Vol. 9, No. 2 (Summer 1975), 32–38 for further discussion.

14 *Die Fackel* (July 1899), 5.

15 Otto Bauer, op. cit. 376.

16 Ibid., 378.

17 Ibid., 379.

18 Otto Bauer, 'Sozialismus und Antisemitismus', in *Der Kampf*, Jg. IV (1910–11), 94.

19 See *Les Marxistes et la question nationale* . . . op. cit. 234–256.

20 Otto Bauer, op. cit.

21 Otto Bauer, 'Das Ende des Christlichen Sozialismus', in *Der Kampf*, (1910–11), 395.

22 Ibid. Bauer's comment on Vogelsang was to praise his 'Marxian' anti-Semitism. 'Man hört die Antithese des jungen Marx'.

23 V. I. Lenin, 'Critical Remarks on the National Question', in *Collected Works* Vol. XX (Moscow and London 1964).

24 J. V. Stalin, 'Marksizm i natsionali vopros', *Sochineniya* (Moscow, 1949), II, 297–303.

25 Otto Bauer, *Die Nationalitätenfrage und die Sozial demokratie*, 379.

26 Ibid.

27 Otto Bauer, 'Sozialismus und Antisemitismus', 94.

28 See the interesting remarks of Berl Locker, 'Die Allegemeine Gesetze der Assimilation und die Ostjuden', in *Der Jude*, I (1916–17), 504–29.

29 Otto Bauer, 'Galizische Parteitage', in *Der Kampf* Jg. V, 1st January 1912 (Heft IV), 160.

30 Ibid., 159.

31 See Otto Bauer, 'Die Bedingungen der nationalen Assimilation', in *Der Kampf*, Jg. V March 1912 (Heft IV), 246–63. This essay was written in rebuttal of an earlier article by Ludo M. Hartmann, 'Zur nationalen Debatte', in *Der Kampf*, Jg. V January 1912 (Heft IV), 152–4. Hartmann (who was of Jewish descent) was a pan-German socialist opposed to minority schools. He favoured drastic measures to encourage the rapid assimilation of minorities, an extreme position with which Bauer did not agree.

32 Otto Bauer, ibid. *Der Kampf* (March 1912), 251 ff.

33 Ibid., 249.

34 By 1918 Otto Bauer had ceased to believe in the viability of the Austro-Hungarian Empire, and in his earlier theories of cultural-national autonomy. In its place he proposed union with Germany and self-determination

for the Slav nationalities of the Empire. See his article, 'Der deutschösterreichische Staat', in *Arbeiter-Zeitung*, 13th October 1918.

35 See Susanne Miller, 'Das Ringen um "die einzige grossdeutsche Republik"', in *Archiv für Sozialgeschichte*, Vol. XI (1971), 1–68.

36 Quoted in Braunthal edition of Otto Bauer, *Eine Auswahl aus seinem Lebenswerk*, 33–4.

37 F. L. Carsten, *Revolution in Central Europe 1918–1919* (London, 1972), 293–8.

38 Otto Bauer, 'Nach der Annexion', in *Der Sozialistische Kampf*, Nr. I (Paris) 2nd June 1938, 5. Also Otto Leichter, *Otto Bauer: Tragödie oder Triumph?* (Vienna, 1970), 144–5.

39 See Norbert Leser, *Zwischen Reformismus und Bolshewismus. Der Austromarxismus als Theorie und Praxis* (Vienna/Frankfurt/Zürich, 1968), 282–90, 397–8.

40 Ibid, 233–48. See also his essay, 'Austro-Marxism: A Reappraisal', in *Journal of Contemporary History*, Vol. I, No. 2 (1966).

41 Ernst Fischer, *An Opposing Man* translated by Peter and Betty Ross. (London, 1974), 135.

42 Ibid., 134–5.

43 Quoted in Otto Bauer, *Eine Auswahl aus seinem Lebenswerk*, 277–8.

44 Ibid.

45 Carsten, op. cit., 301.

46 Otto Bauer, 'Der 24 April', in *Der Kampf* (May 1932).

47 Robert S. Wistrich, 'An Austrian Variant on Socialist Antisemitism', in *Patterns of Prejudice*, Vol. 8, No. 4 (July-August 1974), 1–10.

48 See the perceptive analysis by Gerhard Botz, 'Genesis und inhalt der Faschismustheorien Otto Bauers', in *International Review of Social History*, Vol. XIX (1974), Pt. I, 37.

49 See his speech at the 1933 Party Congress, and the discussion of it by Gerhard. Botz, ibid.

50 Otto Bauer, *Zwischen zwei Weltkriegen? Die Krise der Weltwirtschaft, der Demokratie und des Sozialismus* (Bratislava, 1936), 135 ff.

51 Gerhard Botz, 'Genesis und inhalt der Faschismustheorien Otto Bauers, 45–53.

52 Otto Bauer, *Zwischen zwei Weltkriegen*, 188 f.

53 Otto Bauer, *Eine Auswahl aus seinem Lebenswerke*, 100.

54 On the fate of Austrian Jewry, see J. Moser, *Die Judenverfolgung in Österreich 1938–1945* (Vienna, 1966).

BERNARD LAZARE

1 See W. Rabi, 'De l'anarchisme au nationalisme juif', in *L'Esprit Républicain* (Colloque d'Orléans, 4 et 5 Septembre 1970), 385–93, who regards Lazare's anarchism as a secularized Jewish messianism and as the key to his reconciliation of socialist internationalism with national particularism.

2 See the portrait of Bernard Lazare (written by W. Rabi) which serves as an epilogue to the pamphlet *Antisémitisme et Révolution* (1895), reprinted by the Cercle Bernard Lazare.

3 Jean-Maurice Muslak, 'Bernard Lazare', in *Revue des Études Juives* (1946), 39 ff.

4 Ibid.

5 Edouard Drumont, *La France Juive* (Paris, 1886), Vol. I, XVI ff.

6 Bernard Lazare, 'Juifs et Israélites', in *Entretiens politiques et littéraires,* Vol. I (September 1890), 176–9. See also the perceptive analysis by Nelly Jussem Wilson, 'Bernard Lazare's Jewish journey: from being an Israelite to being a Jew, in *Jewish Social Studies* (July, 1964), No. 3, Vol. XXVI, 146–68.

7 Bernard Lazare, 'La Solidarité juive', in *Entretiens politiques et littéraires* (October 1890), 228 ff.

8 Ibid. See also J-M. Muslak, 'Bernard Lazare', 44, who aptly remarks, 'II répresente ici très typiquement le Juif français tel que l'avait fait un siècle d'assimilation'.

9 Bernard Lazare, La Solidarité juive, 231.

10 Ibid.

11 Ibid.

12 Ibid, 230.

13 See Bernard Lazare, *Le Miroir des Légendes* (Paris, 1892), 232, which contains a significant passage that perhaps explains Lazare's hostility to his co-religionists: 'Je reproche à ce peuple une fâcheuse inconséquence, une contradiction manifeste, qui consiste à repousser âprement la réalisation des idées qui de tout temps furent ses directrices.' This collection of stories based on Greek, Christian and Jewish myths shows the poetic side of Lazare's historical imagination, but also his ignorance of Judaism at the time when it was written.

14 See Muslak, op. cit., 42 and the comprehensive study by Zeev Sternhell, *Maurice Barrès et le Nationalisme Français* (Paris, 1972).

15 Bernard Lazare, *L'Antisémitisme, Son Histoire et Ses Causes* (Paris, 1969), II. Significantly this work is still much admired in nationalist, anti-Semitic circles today, which have ensured its reissue edition in France and England.

16 Ibid., 12.

17 Ibid., 143–4.

18 Ibid., 148.

19 Ibid., 149.

20 Ibid., 114.

21 Ibid., 168–9.

22 See Gougenot des Mousseaux, *Le Juif, le judaïsme et la judaïsation des peuples chrétiens* (Paris, 1869), XXV, and Bernard Lazare, 'L'esprit révolutionnaire dans le judaïsme, in *Revue bleue,* 20 May 1893.

23 Bernard Lazare, *L'Antisémitisme, Son Histoire et Ses Causes,* 152–3.

24 Ibid., 154.

25 Ibid., 157.

26 Ibid., 192.

27 Ibid., 166.

28 Ibid., 170, 'Ils n'en ont pas moins subi, ataviquement et éducativement, l'influence nationale juive'.

29 Ibid., 176.

30 Ibid., 179–80.

31 Ibid., 198.
32 Ibid., 199.
33 As late as 31st December 1894 Lazare could still praise Drumont in *L'Écho de Paris* for his 'Jewish' (!) prophetism in denouncing the rich. 'C'est un homme doué d'une violente et excellente haine instinctive; il est animé d'un vif desir de justice, et agité d'une horreur toute évangelique et toute juive des riches—je dis juive, car nul plus que les prophétistes et les psalmistes n'a attaqué la richesse, et on trouve dans l'Évangile l'écho de ses colères.'
34 Edouard Drumont, *La Libre Parole*, 10th January 1895, p. 1 'C'est un livre fort nourri de faits et dominé d'un boût à l'autre, par un bel effort d'impartialité. . .'
35 Edouard Drumont, *La Libre Parole*, 22 October 1895 and Bernard Lazare, *Contre L'Antisémitisme* (Paris, 1896), 25–6, letter to *La Libre Parole* dated 23rd October 1895.
36 Bernard Lazare, *La Justice*, 17th November 1894.
37 Bernard Lazare, Lettres Proletariennes . . . *Antisémitisme et Révolution* (Paris, 1895), 12.
38 Bernard Lazare, *Contre l'Antisémitisme,* 8, a collection of polemical articles which originally appeared in *Le Voltaire* during May–June 1896.
39 Ibid., 6.
40 Bernard Lazare, *Une erreur judiciaire: la vérité sur l'affaire Dreyfus* (Bruxelles, 1896), 9.
41 Alexandre Zévaès, 'Une apologie de Dreyfus', in *la Petite République,* 10th November 1896.
42 Ibid.
43 See Harvey Goldberg, 'Jean Jaurès and the Jewish Question', in *Jewish Social Studies,* Vol. XX, No. 2 (April 1958), 67–94, and Robert S. Wistrich, 'French Socialism and the Dreyfus Affair', in *The Wiener Library Bulletin* (1975), Vol. XXVIII, New Series, Nos. 35–36.
44 Bernard Lazare, 'Lettre Ouverte à M. Trarieux', in *L'Aurore*, 7th June 1899.
45 Ibid.
46 Bernard Lazare, 'Le Nationalisme et Émancipation juive', in *L'Écho Sioniste* 20th March–5th April 1901, Nos. 9–10, 134 (lecture delivered in the winter of 1899).
47 *L'Écho Sioniste,* 20th April 1901, No. XI, 150–1. 'En effet, quand le Juif eut rompu les barrières qui le separaient du monde, il se déjudaïsa lentement et de plus, . . . il se corrompit au contact de la société chrétienne; il perdit ses vertus propres, et ne gagna que les vices de ceux qui l'entouraient.'
48 Arthur Hertzberg, *The Zionist Idea, A Historical Analysis and Reader*, (New York, 1959), 473.
49 Bernard Lazare, 'Nationalisme et Émancipation', in *Kadimah* (15 August 1898), 2–3.
50 Lecture delivered on 6th March 1897 by Bernard Lazare to the Association of Russian-Jewish students in Paris. Reproduced in *Job's Dungheap* (New York, 1948), 70.
51 Ibid., 73.
52 *The Zionist Idea,* edited by Arthur Hertzberg, 475.
53 Bernard Lazare, *L'Écho Sioniste* (March–April 1901), 135.

54 Ibid.
55 Ibid., May 1901 Nos. 12–13, 168.
56 Ibid., March–April 1901, 134.
57 Ibid., April 1901, No. XI, 152.
58 Charles Péguy, *Notre Jeunesse* (Paris, 1957), 117.
59 Ibid., 97–98. 'Quand on faisait des pourparlers pour créer un grand quotidien . . . et qu'on demandait de l'argent aux juifs . . . les capitalistes, les commanditaires juifs n'y mettaient guère qu'une condition: c'était que Bernard-Lazare n'y écrivit pas.'
60 Bernard Lazare, *L'Écho Sioniste,* 20th April 1901, 152. See also his vitriolic article entitled 'Capitalisme juif et Démocratie', in *L'Aurore* 20th May 1901, which attacked the Jewish bourgeoisie of France—'la pire de toutes', for their indifference to their persecuted brethren.
61 Bernard Lazare, *L'Aurore,* 7th June 1899.
62 The correspondence between Herzl and Lazare in the Zionist Central Archives (Jerusalem) is reproduced in Edmund Silberner's important article, 'Bernard Lazare and Zionism', in *Shivat Zion* (Jerusalem, 1953), 350–61. On 14th May 1897 Lazare wrote to Herzl: 'Je crois plus que jamais à la force de la nation juive, plus que jamais à la nécessité de la voir s'affirmer en tant que telle et j'y aiderai de toute ma force.'
63 Lazare–Herzl, ibid., 360, letter dated 24th March 1899.
64 Ibid.
65 Lazare-Herzl, ibid., 359. 'Vous avez su remuer les profondeurs d'Israël, vous lui avez apporté votre amour et votre vie, vous l'aurez reveillé. . .'
66 Ibid., 360.
67 Lazare-Herzl, ibid., 357–60, letter dated 4th February 1899.
68 Ibid.
69 Ibid., 358.
70 See J-M Muslak, 'Bernard Lazare', 62, and Hannah Arendt, 'From the Dreyfus Affair to France Today', in *Jewish Social Studies* (1946), 173–217. Given Lazare's anarchist background and his profound hatred for authoritarian centralism, it is scarcely surprising that he rejected Herzl's concept of the State.
71 Muslak, ibid., 52. 'Tribun du peuple dispersé, il est reçu comme un sauveur.' The Jews of Rumania were especially grateful for his constant intercessions on their behalf. See Bernard Lazare, 'Les Juifs en Roumanie', in *Cahiers de la Quinzaine,* Series III, No. 8 (Paris, 1902).
72 Charles Péguy, *Notre Jeunesse,* 101.
73 Ibid., 102.
74 Ibid., 108–9. 'Bernard-Lazare s'opposait de tout ce qu'il avait encore de force à la dénegation, à la déviation du dreyfusisme en politique, en démagogie combiste.' See Bernard Lazare, 'Pour et Contre les Congrégations', in *Cahiers de la Quinzaine,* Series III, No. 21 (Paris, 1902).
75 See Jacques Viard, 'Péguy et la mort de Bernard-Lazare', in *Les Nouveaux Cahiers,* No. 21 (Summer 1970); 45–8.
76 Michael A. Marrus, *The Politics of Assimilation: A Study of the French Jewish community at the time of the Dreyfus Affair.* (Oxford, 1971), 249–51.
77 *Lettre des ouvriers juifs de Paris au parti socialiste français* (Paris, 1898). Quoted in E. Tcherski, Die Dreyfus-Affare, die Arbeter-Immigranten, un die französische-yiddische Firers, in *Yidn in Frankraich* (New York, 1942)

edited by E. Tcherikower, 2 vols. 165–8. See also Henry Bulawko, 'Les Socialistes et l'Affaire', in *Les Nouveaux Cahiers* (1971–2), No. 27, 26–30.

78 *Lettre des ouvriers juifs de Paris au parti socialiste Français*, 17–18.

79 In his 1897 lecture on nationalism and Jewish emancipation, (see *L'Écho Sioniste*, May 1901, Nos. 12–13, 167) Lazare observed that 'Drumont s'appuie sur Proudhon, sur Fourier, sur Toussenel et il peut invoquer Bakounine qui ne parlait jamais de Marx qu'en l'appelant le Juif allemand'.

80 Bernard Lazare, 'Judaism's Social Concept and the Jewish People, in *Job's Dungheap*, 109. This essay was a reply not only to Jean Jaurès but also to Lazare's anarchist colleague, Augustin Hamon, whose writings were antisemitically tinged. Hamon had published a French translation of Karl Marx's 'Zur Judenfrage' in *L'Humanité Nouvelle* (1898), 580–5.

81 See Jean Jaurès, 'L'Embarass de M. Drumont', in *La Petite République*, 13th December 1898, for the original source.

82 Ibid.

83 Bernard Lazare, *Job's Dungheap*, 109–10. For Jaurès's reaction to the charge that he had flirted with antisemitism, see Marc Jarblum, 'Démocratie, question nationale et sionisme en Europe centrale: qu'en pensait Jaurès', in *Le Mouvement Social* (July–September 1965), No. 52, 85–97. Jaurès also made an interesting comment about Zionism in connection with Lazare: 'Je n'ai connu qu'un Juif français qui ait défendu cette cause: Bernard Lazare. Mais il était seul ou presque. Il s'est heurté à une opposition violente de la totalité des intellectuels juifs, bourgeois aussi bien que socialistes.'

84 Bernard Lazare, *Job's Dungheap*, 113.

85 Ibid., 121–2.

86 Ibid., 128.

87 Ibid., 41.

88 Ibid. See also Bernard Lazare, 'Capitalisme juif et Démocratie', in *L'Aurore*, 20th May 1901.

89 Muslak, op. cit., 56, described *Le Fumier de Job* as '*le* livre du reveil juif en France, la confession, le récit du juif revenu au judaisme'.

90 Bernard Lazare's wife, Isabelle Grumbach, whom he married in Paris on 18th June 1892, may have played an important role in his return to Judaism. Born in Buenos Aires in 1865, she lived until 1960, and according to one testimony she was 'une très bonne juive', even a Zionist. In 1910 she wrote a moving letter to Charles Péguy, warmly thanking him for his portrait of Bernard Lazare in *Notre Jeunesse*, and quoted from a letter addressed to her by her husband: 'Tu as fait s'insurger en moi le vieux sang des prophètes'. See Jacques Viard, *Les Nouveaux Cahiers* (Summer 1970), op. cit., 45 ff.

91 Charles Péguy, *Notre Jeunesse*, 147.

LÉON BLUM

1 See André Blumel, *Léon Blum. Juif et Sioniste.* (Paris, 1951), 4. Also Marc Vishniac, *Léon Blum* (Paris, 1937), 7; and Geoffrey Fraser/Thadée Natanson, *Léon Blum: Man and Statesman* (London, 1937).

2 Vishniac, Ibid., 25.
3 Fraser/Natanson, op. cit., 10 ff; Louis Lévy, *Comment ils sont devenus Socialistes* (Paris, 1932), 18.
4 Michael A. Marrus, *The Politics of Assimilation: A Study of the French Jewish Community at the time of the Dreyfus Affair* (Oxford, 1971), 91 ff. See also Julien Benda, *La jeunesse d'un clerc* (Paris, 1936), 33–41, on republican patriotism among middle-class French Jews. The most important early influence on Léon Blum's republicanism had been his maternal grandmother, known as 'La Communarde' because of her sympathies for the Paris Commune.
5 See the speech of Léon Blum on 15th May 1936 in *L'Exercice du Pouvoir: discours prononcés de mai 1936 à janvier 1937* (Paris, 1937), 128. 'J'appartiens à une race qui doit à la Révolution francaise d'avoir acquis le droit à la liberté humaine et à l'égalité et c'est une chose inoubliable.'
6 Gilbert Ziebura, *Léon Blum et le Parti Socialiste 1872–1934* (Paris, 1967), 18–23; Fraser/Natanson, op. cit., 41 ff.
7 See the interesting study by A. B. Jackson, *La Revue Blanche 1889–1903: Origine, influence, bibliographie.* (Paris, 1960).
8 Léon Blum, *Souvenirs sur l'Affaire* (Paris, 1935), 86–88. Describing his rupture with Maurice Barrès over the Dreyfus case, Blum wrote: 'Quelque chose était brisé, fini: une des avenues de ma jeunesse était close.'
9 A. B. Jackson, op. cit.
10 Blum concluded that 'The future in France belongs not to Socialism but to anarchy'. See Léon Blum, 'Le Progrès de l'apolitique en France, 25 July 1892', in *La Revue Blanche* Nr. 10, 10–21.
11 Fraser/Natanson, op. cit., 52; Léon Blum, *Souvenirs sur l'Affaire,* 28.
12 *Souvenirs,* 17, 28. Also Hubert Bourgin, *De Jaurès à Léon Blum: L'École Normale et la Politique* (Paris, 1938), 104–32, and Charles Andler, *Vie de Lucien Herr* (Paris, 1932), 95 ff.
13 See James Joll, *Intellectuals in Politics: Three Biographical Essays* (London, 1960), 3–59, for a perceptive and concise evaluation of Blum's intellectual approach to politics. Also Alexander Werth, *The Destiny of France* (London, 1937) on Blum's relationship to the socialist rank and file.
14 Fraser/Natanson, op. cit., 53 ff.; Louise Elliott Dalby, *Léon Blum, Evolution of a Socialist* (New York/London, 1963), 166 ff.
15 Léon Blum, *Souvenirs sur l'Affaire,* 19.
16 Ibid.
17 Un juriste [Blum]: 'Le Procès', in *La Revue Blanche,* Vol. XV (15 March 1898) 401–14.
18 Léon Blum, op. cit., 25.
19 Marrus, op. cit., 196.
20 Léon Blum, op. cit., 25–6.
21 Ibid., 27.
22 Ibid., 43 ff.
23 Gilbert Ziebura, *Léon Blum et le Parti Socialiste,* 43.
24 *L'Oeuvre de Léon Blum. Nouvelles Conversations de Goethe avec Eckermann* placency vis à vis antisemitism was a prevailing tendency among French Jews. Émile Durkheim also viewed the French brand of antisemitism as a 'superficial symptom' of social malaise rather than a chronic disease as in Russia, Germany and Austria.

25 *Nouvelles Conversations de Goethe avec Eckermann,* 262–3, 11th April 1899. Blum seemed relatively unperturbed by discrimination against Jewish officers in the French Army. 'Si ces messieurs souhaitent d'être considérés selon leur valeur individuelle, ils n'avaient qu'à choisir un autre milieu et une autre vie.'
26 Ibid., 267–8.
27 Ibid.
28 Colette Audry, *Léon Blum ou la politique du Juste* (Paris, 1970) 29–30; Ziebura, op. cit.
29 Ibid.
30 Louise Elliott Dalby, op. cit., 101 ff.
31 *Nouvelles Conversations de Goethe avec Eckermann,* 266.
32 Ibid. See also his review of *Israël*, a play by Henry Bernstein, in Léon Blum, *Au theâtre: réflexions Critiques* (Paris, 1906–11), Vol. II, 205–6.
33 *Nouvelles Conversations de Goethe avec Eckermann,* 267.
34 Ibid.
35 Ibid.
36 Ibid.
37 Ibid. See also my chapter on Bernard Lazare for a more extreme formulation of this idea.
38 Léon Blum, *Souvenirs* op. cit., 25 ff. 'Un juif moyen, tel que je l'étais, inconsciemment soumis à l'équilibre de la famille et des fréquentations ordinaires, n'avait pas de vocation plus marquée que tout autre à recevoir la grâce dreyfusarde.'
39 See Felicien Challaye, *Péguy Socialiste* (Paris, 1954) 87–106 and Jules Isaac, *Expériences de ma Vie*, Vol. I (Paris, 1959) 133–54.
40 See Léon Daudet. *Au temps de Judas* (Paris, 1920) 122. It was also Daudet who caricatured Blum as 'la révolution en gants gris perle' Ibid., 123. Hubert Bourgin. *De Jaurès à Léon Blum* . . . op. cit., 515. '. . . le sémitisme est à l'origine de tous les mouvements révolutionnaires.' This was a standard refrain of the Maurrassian right in inter-war France.
41 Ziebura, op. cit., 38–41.
42 Léon Blum, *Les Congrès Ouvriers et socialistes français* (1876–1900) 2 vols. (Paris, 1901)
43 On Blum's mediating role in obtaining funds for *L'Humanité*, see Harvey Goldberg. *The Life of Jean Jaurès*. (Madison, Wisconsin, 1962), 319.
44 Léon Blum in: *Le Populaire* 6 December 1929. 'Mais c'est de Jaurès que je tiens tout ce que je pense et tout ce que je suis.' See also Ziebura, op. cit., 95–99.
45 André Gide, *Journal 1889–1939* (Paris, 1941) 396–8. Entry dated 24 January 1914.
46 Ibid. 'Un temps viendra, pense-t-il, qui sera le temps du Juif; et dès à présent, il importe de reconnaître et d'établir sa superiorité dans tous les ordres, dans tous les domaines, dans toutes les branches de l'art du savoir et de l'industrie.'
47 *Nouvelles Conversations* op. cit., 265.
48 Ibid.
49 Ibid., 266.
50 Ibid., 263–4 'L'état du fonctionnaire s'adaptait mal aux caractères fondamentaux de leur race.'

51 Ibid., 264.
52 André Gide, *Journal 1939–1949* (Paris, 1954), 24th January 1914.
53 André Gide, *Journal*, op. cit., 320. Entry dated 9th January 1948.
54 Ibid., 30. 'Curieux de constater ici que, entre juif et chrétien, c'est de son côté que l'on peut trouver et reconnaître l'Espérance et la Foi. Mais j'ai rarement rencontré chez un chrétien pareil désintéressement personnel et pareil noblesse . . .'
55 Ziebura, op. cit., 98.
56 Ibid., 156–67.
57 Parti Socialiste, *Compte Rendu sténographique*. Congrès National XVIII, 25th–30th December 1920 (Paris, 1921); Speech of Léon Blum, 27th Dec. 1920, 101–36, in Annie Kriegel, *Le Congrès de Tours. Naissance du Parti Communiste Français* (Paris, 1964).
58 Jacques Fauvet, *Histoire du Parti Communiste Français*. (Paris, 1964), Vol. I, 134–7, 142–3.
59 Annie Kriegel, 'Un phenomène de haine fratricide: Léon Blum vu par les Communistes', in: *Le Pain et les Roses* (Paris, 1968), 235–55.
60 André Marty, 'Lettre ouverte à M. Léon Blum, directeur du "Populaire"', in: *Les Cahiers du Bolshevisme* (Paris, 1951), 43–47. Preface by A. Rossi. Marty's article contained a delirious exaltation of Stalin.
61 Maurice Thorez, 'Portrait (Blum tel qu'il est)', in: *Oeuvres de Maurice Thorez* Bk. V, Vol. 19 (October 1939–July 1944), Paris 1959, 28–53. This vicious diatribe first appeared in *L'Internationale Communiste* in February 1940. Thorez described Blum among other things as an 'agent of the bourgeoisie', a 'juggler with ideas' (32), a '*rusé politicien*' (38), a '*Tartuffe immonde*' (40) and a repugnant personality stained in blood '*qui tâche à jamais ses mains aux doigts longs et crochus*'. With his alleged '*instincts féroces de bourgeois exploiteur*', Blum was for Thorez a defender of Capital and a slanderer of the USSR. Among other grossly offensive epithets Thorez characterized him as a '*canaille politique*', '*reptile répugnant*' and '*vil laquais des banquiers de Londres*' (48). See Annie Kriegel op. cit., 244–55 for a discussion of the profound differences of polititical style between the two men.
62 See *Le Populaire*. 28th December 1922. Also *Journal Officiel, Débats Parlementaires à la Chambre,* 11th January 1923.
63 Ibid.
64 Blumel, op. cit., 7.
65 Even a sophisticated observer like Georges Suarez in *Nos Seigneurs et Maîtres* (Paris, 1937), 11–18, characterized Blum as an evil genius and fomenter of disorder and chaos. According to Suarez, Blum was 'un homme sans joie, sans indulgence, sans humanité', an intransigent, 'rootless' doctrinaire whose success was built on French ruin. See also the much more scurrilous and anti-Semitic portraits of Gustave Tery, *La Vie de Monsieur Blum* (Paris, 1936) and Laurent Viguier, *Lew Juifs à travers Léon Blum: leur incapacité historique de diriger un état* (Paris, 1938).
66 *Journal Officiel,* 6th June 1936.
67 Action Française more or less openly called for his murder, and on 13th February 1936, a royalist mob dragged Blum out of a car off the Boulevard Saint Germain, and would have battered him to death had not the police and some bystanders intervened. See Alexander Werth, *The Destiny of France,* 281.

68 See David H. Weinberg, *Les Juifs à Paris de 1933 à 1939* (Paris, 1974), 112–13, and A. Blumel, op. cit., 8–9, who points out that the Chief Rabbi of France and other officials in the French Jewish community were far from enthusiastic at Blum's victory in 1936. Blumel notes that Blum received 'un très large lot de lettres injurieuses, outrageantes ou tout simplement viles' from his co-religionists.

69 *Compte rendu sténographique. Congrès National 14–17 July 1933* (Paris, 1933). See also John T. Marcus, *French Socialism in the Crisis Years 1933 to 1936: Fascism and the French Left* (New York, 1958).

70 *Le Populaire* 19th July 1933; *La Vie Socialiste,* 24th July 1933.

71 Ziebura, *Léon Blum et le Parti Socialiste*, 257.

72 See James Joll, 'The Front Populaire After Thirty Years', in *Journal of Contemporary History,* Vol. 2 (1966), 27–42.

73 Blumel, op. cit., 8.

74 David H. Weinberg, op. cit. This was the position of the Chief Rabbi Julien Weill on the immigration into France of persecuted German Jews. Blum was indignant at this attitude, though conscious of a possible contradiction between his sympathies for the German Jews and his own position as French Premier.

75 These tactics were to no avail. Despite their evident patriotism, French Jewry were increasingly accused in 1938 of being 'war-mongers' who adopted a hard line against Hitler for 'racial' reasons. See Weinberg, op. cit., 227.

76 The full text of this speech delivered at the IX Congrès National of the LICA can be found in *Léon Blum contre le racisme* (Paris, 1938).

77 Blum's concern for the fate of his co-religionists, his socialist convictions and the fact that he did not conceal his origins made him much admired by the large Jewish immigrant population in the Parisian ghettoes of the 1930s. The immigrants of the Pletzl saw in him 'un Juif authentique qui a un coeur juif et une mentalité juive. . .'. They also applauded his firm attitude to fascism and the abrogation by the Popular Front regime of the laws against foreigners previously adopted by the Laval government. See Weinberg, op. cit., 139, 176.

78 See L. Elliott Dalby, op. cit., 89. During his stay at Bordeaux in 1940 Blum felt desperately lonely, and aware that his Jewishness created a barrier between himself and many of his compatriots.

79 Ibid., 323.

80 Blumel, op. cit., 8.

81 *L'Oeuvre de Léon Blum* (1940–45). *La Prison, Le Procès, La Déportation* (Paris, 1955), 513.

82 Blum attended the XVI Zionist Congress in Zürich (28th July–14th August 1929) as one of three French delegates who did not belong to Zionist organizations.

83 Blumel, op. cit., 11. Blum consistently defended the view that one could at the same time be a good Jew and good Frenchman. Articles of his on Zionism later appeared in the Parisian Yiddish press—e.g. *Parizer Haint,* 28–30 June 135). See Weinberg, 139.

84 Blumel, ibid.

85 Léon Blum, 'Jude und Franzose', in *Der Jude* (*Sonderheft: Antisemitismus und jüdisches Volksthum*) 1925, 85.

86 Ibid., 86.
87 Ibid.
88 Ibid., 87.
89 Ibid., 90.
90 Blumel, op. cit., 12.
91 See *L'Oeuvre de Léon Blum,* Vol. VII 1947–50 (Paris, 1963) 'Hommage à Weizmann', 1 February 1950, 442.
92 Ibid.
93 See the excellent study by David Lazar, *L'Opinion française et la naissance de l'État d'Israël 1945–1949* (Paris, 1972) for further details.
94 See *Le Populaire,* 21st August 1946.
95 *Le Populaire,* 6th July 1946.
96 Ibid.
97 See Lazar, op. cit., 157.
98 *L'Oeuvre de Léon Blum,* Vol. VII, 442.

JULIUS MARTOV

1 For details about Alexander Zederbaum (1816–9) a pioneer of Jewish journalism in Russia and an enthusiastic supporter of the Hovevei-Zion movement, see the *Encyclopaedia Judaica* (Jerusalem, 1971), Vol. XVI, 964–5.
2 Israel Getzler, *Martov: A Political Biography of a Russian Social Democrat* (Cambridge, 1967), 9–20 gives a vivid picture of Martov's family background.
3 Leopold H. Haimson, *The Russian Marxists and the Origins of Bolshevism* (Cambridge, Mass., 1955), 62.
4 Y. Martov, *Zapiski Sotsial-Demokrata* (Berlin/Petersburg/Moscow 1922), 16. Even Leon Trotsky in *Young Lenin* (London, 1972), 79, [translated by Max Eastman] observed that the anti-Jewish pogroms determined the political orientation of Martov.
5 Y. Martov, *Zapiski,* ibid., 19.
6 Ibid.
7 Ibid., also 21, 27, 32 for further references to Martov's humiliating experiences of anti-Semitism in Russian schools.
8 Ibid., 27.
9 The right of Jews to reside in St Petersburg was extremely restricted in Alexander III's reign, See *Zapiski* ibid., 41–4.
10 Haimson, op. cit., 60–1.
11 See Y. Martov, *Zapiski,* 227–32.
12 See Ezra Mendelsohn, 'The Russian Jewish labor Movements and others', in *Yivo Annual of Jewish Social Science,* vol. XIV (N.Y., 1969), 88. Also Moshe Mishkinsky, 'Regional Factors in the Formation of the Jewish Labor Movement in Czarist Russia', in *Yivo Annual,* ibid., 29–30, 42–3, 45–6.
13 Ezra Mendelsohn, *Class Struggle in the Pale* (Cambridge, 1970), 32 ff.
14 Y. Martov, *Zapiski,* 225.
15 Ibid., 184–5.

16 Koppel S. Pinson, 'Arkady Kremer, Vladimir Medem and the Ideology of the Jewish 'Bund',' in *Jewish Social Studies* (July 1945), No. 3, Vol. III, 237–8.
17 'A briv tsu di agitatorn', in *Yivo Historische Shriftn* (Vilna-Paris) Vol. III, 628–48, [edited by A. Tscherikower]; A. Kremer, *Ob Agitatsii* (Geneva, 1896), edited by Y. Martov, with a conclusion by Paul Axelrod. Also Y. Martov, *Zapiski,* 234.
18 Pinson, op. cit., 242–4.
19 Mishkinsky, 'Regional Factors', in *Yivo Annual,* 27–52.
20 Y. Martov, op. cit., 210.
21 V. Jabotinsky, *Bund i sionizm* (Odessa, 1906), 6.
22 See I. Getzler, op. cit., 56.
23 Martov's speech was, to his great embarrassment, subsequently published by the Bund as a pamphlet entitled *Povorotnyi Punkt v Istorii Evreiskogo Dvizhenia* (Geneva, 1900), 17 ff.
24 Ibid., 19.
25 Ibid.
26 Y. Martov, *Evreiskie Rabochie protiv evreiskikh Kapitalistov, Rabotnik* (Geneva, 1896), 86, Nr. 1 and 2.
27 Ibid.
28 Bertram D. Wolfe, *Three who made a Revolution* (rev. ed., London, 1966), 145–6.
29 Getzler, op. cit., 50–6.
30 Haimson, op. cit., 129–31.
31 Y. Martov, 'Vpered ili nazad?', in *Iskra,* No. 69, 10th July 1904.
32 On the factors which influenced the emergence of a Jewish national programme of the Bund see Moshe Mishkinsky, *National Elements in the Development of the Jewish Labour Movement in Russia* (Jerusalem, 1965, unpublished Ph.D thesis) [in Hebrew] 177–86, 227–40; Y. Martov, 'Chetvertyi S'ezd Bunda', in *Iskra* No. 7, (August 1901).
33 Y. Martov, 'Edinaia russkaia sotsialdemokratiia i interesy evreiskogo proletariata', in *Iskra,* No. 36, 15th March 1903.
34 Y. O. Martov, 'Mobilizatsiia reaktsionnyikh sil i nashi zadachi', in *Iskra,* No. 41 (June 1903). In this article Martov attacked Zionist propaganda after the Kishinev pogrom (April 1903), for preaching political indifference towards the Tsarist regime. For a similar view see Karl Kautsky, 'Das Massaker von Kishineff und die Judenfrage', in *Die Neue Zeit* (1902–3), II, 303–9.
35 *Vtoroi S'ezd RSDRP* (Moscow, 1959), 57.
36 Getzler, op. cit., 71.
37 Ibid., 101.
38 Bertram D. Wolfe, op. cit., 581–9.
39 Getzler, op. cit., 28.
40 L. O. Dan, *Martov i ego Blizkie* (New York, 1959), 26. Martov was deeply impressed by his grandfather's view that it was despicable for a Russian Jew to accept baptism, since this involved deserting 'the camp of the persecuted' and allying oneself with the persecutors.
41 Getzler, op. cit., 150 ff.
42 Ibid., 165.
43 L. D. Trotsky *History of the Russian Revolution* (London, 1934), III, 1156.

44 Getzler, op. cit., 170, 177.
45 Ibid., 181 ff.
46 Ibid., 191.
47 Quoted in E. Wilson, *To the Finland Station* (London, 1962), 404–5.
48 Ibid., 218.
49 L. Trotsky, 'Martov' in *Political Profiles* (London, 1972), translated by R. Chappell, 97.
50 Ibid., 98.
51 For an interesting picture of Martov's personality, see N. N. Sukhanov, *The Russian Revolution, 1917*. Edited and translated by J. Carmichael (London, 1955), 352–6.

LEON TROTSKY

1 See Vladimir Medem, *Fun mein Lebn* (New York, 1923), Vol. II, 9. Also [Leon Trotsky, 'A Social Democrat Only',] in *The Golden Tradition,* edited by Lucy S. Dawidowicz (London, 1967)., 441.
2 Leon Trotsky, *My Life* (New York, 1930), 6.
3 Ibid., 5–6.
4 Ibid., 18. According to Trotsky, his father spoke only a broken mixture of Russian and Ukrainian, but his father came from Poltava, and must almost certainly have known some Yiddish.
5 Ibid., 84.
6 See Joseph Nedava, *Trotsky and the Jews* (Philadelphia, 1972), 35, and Joel Carmichael, *Trotsky: An Appreciation of His Life* (London, 1975), 17. Both regard this claim as part of Trotsky's affected indifference to Jewishness.
7 Bertram D. Wolfe, *Three Who Made a Revolution* (London, 1966), 205–6.
8 Leon Trotsky, *My Life,* 86.
9 Ibid., 85.
10 Ibid., 86–7.
11 Ibid., 81–4.
12 Ibid., 340–1.
13 Ibid., 86–7.
14 Ibid., 110–11.
15 *The Age of Permanent Revolution: A Trotsky Anthology* (New York, 1964), 64.
16 See Henry J. Tobias, 'The Bund and Lenin until 1903', in *The Russian Review,* Vol. XXIX, No. 4 (October 1961); *Vtoroi s'ezd RSDRP Protokoly.* (Moscow, 1959), 50–123.
17 R. Abramovich, *In Tsvei Revolutsies* (New York, 1944), Vol. I, 115. 'The contention between Iskra and the Bund was to a certain extent struggle between assimilationists and national-Yiddishists within the Jewish people itself. The struggle revolved around the question of whether the Jewish people in Russia would assimilate or not.'
18 *Vtoroi S'ezd RSDRP Protokoly,* 57.
19 Ibid.
20 *Vtoroi S'ezd RSDRP Protokoly, Otchet Sibirkoi Delegatsii* (Geneva, 1903) 9–10.
21 Chaim Weizmann, *Trial and Error* (Philadelphia, 1949), 50.
22 V. I. Lenin, 'Polozhenie Bunda v Partii', in *Iskra,* No. 51, 22nd October 1903.

23 Leon Trotsky, 'Razlozhenie Sionizma i ego vozmozhnye preemniki', in *Iskra* 1st January, 1904.

24 See Vladimir Medem, *Shestoi Sionistichesky Kongress v Bazele* (London, 1903), 29–30. 'One thing is clear to us: political Zionism is bankrupt . . . the liquidation of Zionism has begun.' Also Medem, *Fun mein Leben,* Vol. II, 33 ff.

25 Leon Trotsky, Razlozhenie Sionizma . . . op. cit.

26 Ibid.

27 Vladimir Medem, *Fun mein Lebn* II, 8–9.

28 Joseph Nedava, *Trotsky and the Jews,* 54–7.

29 Ibid., 61.

30 Ibid., 66.

31 Ibid., 75–77. Berlis was eventually released after a world-wide public outcry.

32 Leon Trotsky and C. Rakovsky, *Ocherki Politicheskii Ruminii* (Moscow-Petrograd, 1923), Chapter IX, 82 (Evreiskii Vopros, 17th–21st August 1913, *Kievskaia* Mysl Nos. 226, 229, 230).

33 Leon Trotsky, Evreiskii Vopros, 83. Vladimir Purishkevich (1870–1920) was a co-founder of the Black-Hundred anti-Semitic organization in 1905, whose name became synonymous with the pogromist policy of Tsarism.

34 Ibid., 84.

35 Ibid., 85–8.

36 *The Age of Permanent Revolution,* 74.

37 Ibid.

38 See Joel Carmichael, *Trotsky*, 148–84.

39 Nedava, op. cit., 199–200. Trotsky took little interest in the activities of the Yevsektsiia.

40 Leon Trotsky, *Nashi Politicheskie Zadachi* (Geneva, 1904), 95.

41 Ibid.

42 E. H. Carr, *Socialism in One Country* (New York, 1958), Vol. I, 139–52, notes that Trotsky was the most Westernized and Stalin the least European among the Bolshevik leaders. He points out that Trotsky emphasized with special zest 'the nullity of the Russian contribution to civilization.'

43 Leon Trotsky, *The Permanent Revolution* (New York, 1962), 6–10.

44 Leon Trotsky, *My Life*. op. cit., 341.

45 Ibid., 340. Lenin's angry reply, as recorded by Trotsky, was to say: 'We are having a great international revolution; of what importance are such trifles?'

46 Ibid., 361.

47 Ibid.

48 Avrahm Yarmolinsky, *The Jews and Other Minorities under the Soviets* (New York, 1928), 50. See also Zvi Y. Gitelman, *Jewish Nationality and Soviet Politics* (Princeton, 1972), 117–18.

49 E. Tchevikover, *Antisemitizm un Pogromen in Ukraine 1917–18* (Berlin, 1923), 103–4 See also Nedava, op. cit., 156.

50 Leon Trotsky, *The Trotsky Papers Vol. I* (1917–1919), edited by Jan M. Meijer (The Hague, 1964) 361–363. This statement appeared in a cable dispatched by Trotsky as head of the Military Revolutionary Committee, on 10th May 1919. It was in response to requests by Poale Zion

was sabotaged by the Yevsektsiia. On Trotsky's general attitude to Jewish recruits in the Red Army, see Nedava, op. cit., 110–15.

51 See G. A. Ziv, *Trotsky-Kharakteristika po Lichnym Vospominiam* (New York, 1921), 46. Also the *Jewish Chronicle,* 28th December 1917, p. 7. The Chief Rabbi of Petrograd quoted Trotsky as saying to him just after the Balfour Declaration, 'I am not a Jew; I am an internationalist'.
52 Leon Trotsky, *My Life*. 20.
53 Nedava, *Trotsky and the Jews,* 112–13.
54 Isaac Deutscher, *The Prophet Unarmed. Trotsky: 1921–1929* (London/Oxford/New York, 1970), 259, 286–88).
55 J. V. Stalin, *Works* (Moscow 1953–55), Vol. VI, 350–2; Robert C. Tucker, *Stalin as Revolutionary 1879–1929* (London, 1974), 380–90.
56 Leon Trotsky, *Stalin* (New York, 1958) 393–4. L. Trotsky, *The Revolution Betrayed* (New York, 1945), 277.
57 Winston Churchill, *Great Contemporaries* (London, 1937), 202.
58 Quoted in Isaac Deutscher, *The Prophet Unarmed,* 258.
59 'Leon Trotsky, Thermidor und Antisemitismus 22nd February 1937', in *Marxisten gegen Antisemitismus*, edited by Iring Fetscher (Hamburg, 1974) 179–88.
60 See Leon Trotsky, *On the Jewish Question* (New York, 1970), 14–15. The letter referred to here was written by Trotsky from Prinkipo (Turkey) and published in May 1930, in *Klorkeit* No. 3. Its subject was 'The Role of the Jewish Workers' Movement within the General Workers Movement in France'.
61 Leon Trotsky, *On the Jewish Question,* 15.
62 Ibid., 16. From a letter of 9th May 1932 to *Unser Kamf,* a Trotskyist Yiddish-language paper in New York.
63 Ibid., 18. Letter of 7th August 1932 to Lazar Kling, editor of *Unser Kamf.*
64 Ibid.
65 Ibid.
66 Ibid.
67 Ibid.
68 Ibid., 19.
69 Ibid.
70 See *Writings of Leon Trotsky (1932–33)* (New York, 1972), 133–6, 246–57. Also Isaac Deutscher, *The Prophet Outcast. Trotsky: 1929–1940* (London/Oxford/New York, 1970) 132–54 for Trotsky's general interpretation of Nazism.
71 Leon Trotsky, *On the Jewish Question,* 20. From the interview given in Mexico on 18th January 1937 which appeared in the Yiddish socialist paper *Forverts,* 24th January 1937.
72 *On the Jewish Question,* 21.
73 Ibid.
74 Ibid.
75 Ibid.
76 *Der Tog,* 26th January 1937, quoted in Nedava, op. cit., 186.
77 'Leo Trotzki, Thermidor und Antisemitismus', in *Marxisten gegen Antisemitismen,* 179.
78 Ibid.
79 Ibid., 180.

80 Ibid., 181.
81 Ibid.
82 Ibid., 184.
83 Ibid., 185.
84 Ibid., 183–4.
85 Leon Trotsky, *On the Jewish Question,* 29.
86 Ibid., 28.
87 Leon Trotsky, 'An Appeal to American Jews, menaced by Fascism and Anti-Semitism', written on 22nd December 1938 and printed in *Fourth International* (December 1945).
88 Ibid.
89 Ibid.
90 Ibid.
91 Extract from a manifesto of the Emergency Conference of the Fourth International held in May 1940. Reprinted in *Writings of Leon Trotsky* (1939–1940) (New York, 1969) and Fetscher (ed.) 'Leo Trotzki, Imperialismus und Antisemitismus', op. cit., 189–190.
92 Ibid.
93 Quoted in Leon Trotsky, *On the Jewish Question,* 12.
94 *The Age of Permanent Revolution,* 15.
95 Ibid.

Select Bibliography

The primary material used in this study, including newspapers and periodicals, printed documents, memoirs, and manuscript sources dispersed in various libraries and archives, have already been extensively listed in the notes. The select bibliography which follows contains only the more important secondary works and published correspondence consulted while preparing this book.

ABRAMOVICH, R.: *In Tsvei Revolutsies* (New York, 1944).

ADLER, F. (ed): *Victor Adler. Briefwechsel mit August Bebel und Karl Kautsky* (Vienna, 1954).

ADLER, V.: *Aufsätze, Reden und Briefe* (Vienna, 1922–9), 11 vols.

ANGEL, P.: *Eduard Bernstein et l'évolution du Socialisme Allemand* (Paris, 1961).

ARENDT, H.: *The Origins of Totalitarianism* (New York, 1966).
Men in Dark Times (London, 1970).

BERNSTEIN, E. (ed): *Ferdinand Lassalle. Gesammelte Reden und Schriften* (Berlin, 1919), 12 vols.

BICK, A.: *Merosh Tszurim* (Jerusalem, 1972).

BLUM, L.: *Souvenirs sur l'Affaire* (Paris, 1935).

BLUMEL, A.: *Léon Blum. Juif et Sioniste* (Paris, 1951).

BLUMENBERG, W.: *Karl Marx* (Hamburg, 1962).

BOTTOMORE, T. (ed.): *Karl Marx. Early Writings* (London, 1963).

BOURDET, Y. (ed.): *Otto Bauer et la Révolution* (Paris, 1968).

BRAUNTHAL, J. (ed.): *Otto Bauer. Eine Auswahl aus Seinem Lebenswerk* (Vienna, 1961).
Victor und Friedrich Adler. Zwei Generationen Arbeiterbewegung (Vienna, 1965).

BUCZEK, H. and TYCH, F. (eds.): *Socjaldemokracja Krolėstwa Polskiego i Litwy. Materialy i Dokumenty* (Warsaw, 1957), Vol. I.

BUNZL, J.: *Klassenkampf in der Diaspora. Zur Geschichte der jüdischen Arbeiterbewegung* (Vienna, 1975).

CARMICHAEL, J.: *Trotsky. An Appreciation of His Life* (London, 1975).

CARSTEN, F.: *Revolution in Central Europe 1918–19* (London, 1972).

DAN, L.: *Martov i ego Blizkie* (New York, 1959).

DAVIDOWICZ, L. (ed.): *The Golden Tradition* (London, 1967).

DEUTSCHER, I.: *The Prophet Armed* (London/New York, 1954), Vol. I.
The Prophet Unarmed (London/New York, 1959), Vol. II.
The Prophet Outcast (London/New York, 1963), Vol. III.
The Non-Jewish Jew and Other Essays (Oxford, 1968).

DIMANSTEIN, S. (ed.): *Revolutsionnoe dvizhenie sredi evreev* (Moscow, 1930).

DZIEWANOWSKI, M.: *The Communist Party of Poland* (Cambridge, Mass., 1959).

FEJTÖ, F.: *Les Juifs et L'Antisémitisme dans les Pays Communistes* (Paris, 1960).

FETSCHER, I. (ed.): *Marxisten gegen Antisemitismus* (Hamburg, 1974).

FISCHER, E.: *An Opposing Man* (London, 1974).

FRAENKEL, J. (ed.): *The Jews of Austria* (London, 1967).

GERLACH, A.: *Der Einfluss der Juden in der Österreichischen Sozialdemokratie* (Vienna/Leipzig, 1939).

GETZLER, I.: *Martov: A Political Biography* (Cambridge, 1967).

GITELMAN, Z.: *Jewish Nationality and Soviet Politics* (Princeton, 1972).

HAMBURGER, E.: *Juden im öffentlichen Leben Deutschlands. Regierungsmitglieder, Beamte und Parliamentarier in der Monarchischen Zeit 1848–1918* (Tübingen, 1968).

HERTZBERG, A.: *The French Enlightenment and the Jews* (New York, 1968).

HIRSCH, H. (ed): *Eduard Bernsteins Briefwechsel mit Friedrich Engels* (Assen, 1970).

JOHNSTON, W.: *The Austrian Mind. An Intellectual and Social History 1848–1938* (Berkeley, 1972).

JOLL, J.: *Intellectuals in Politics. Three Biographical Essays* (London, 1960).

KAMPMANN, W.: *Deutsche und Juden* (Heidelberg, 1963).

KAUTSKY, B. (ed): *Rosa Luxemburg. Briefe an Freunde* (Hamburg, 1950).

KAUTSKY, K.: *Rasse und Judentum* (Berlin, 1914).

KAUTSKY, L. (ed): *Rosa Luxemburg. Briefe an Karl und Luise Kautsky* (Berlin, 1922).

KNÜTTER, H.: *Die Juden und die Deutsche Linke in der Weimarer Republik* (Düsseldorf, 1971).

KOCHAN, L. (ed.): *The Jews in Soviet Russia since 1917* (Oxford, 1970).

KRIEGEL, A.: *Le Pain et les Roses. Jalons pour une histoire des socialismes* (Paris, 1968).

KÜNZLI, A.: *Karl Marx. Eine Psychographie* (Vienna, 1966).

LAQUEUR, W.: *Out of the Ruins of Europe* (New York, 1971).
A History of Zionism (London, 1972).

LAZARE, B.: *Job's Dungheap* (New York, 1948).
L'Antisémitisme. Son Histoire et Ses Causes (Paris, 1969).

LEICHTER, O.: *Otto Bauer. Tragödie oder Triumph?* (Vienna, 1970).

LENDVAI, P.: *Anti-Semitism in Eastern Europe* (London, 1972).
LÉON, A.: *La Conception Matérialiste de la Question Juive* (Paris, 1968).
LENIN, V. I.: *Sochineniya* (Moscow, 1929), 2nd. ed., Vols. 19 and 20.
LESSING, T.: *Der Jüdische Selbsthass* (Berlin, 1930).
LUXEMBURG, R.: *Internationalismus und Klassenkampf* (Neuwied/Berlin, 1971).
Le Socialisme en France 1898–1912 (Paris, 1971).

MAOR, Y.: *The Jewish Question in the Russian Liberal and Revolutionary Movement 1890–1914* (Jerusalem, 1964) in Hebrew. [Ph.D. thesis].
MARIENSTRAS, R.: *Être un peuple en diaspora* (Paris, 1975).
MARRUS, M.: *The Politics of Assimilation* (Oxford, 1971).
MARTOV, J.: *Zapiski Sotsial-Demokrata* (Berlin/Petersburg/Moscow, 1922).
MARX, K. and ENGELS, F.: *Marx–Engels Werke* (East Berlin, 1956–68), 41 vols.
MARX, K.: *La Question Juive* (Paris, 1968).
MASSICZEK, A.: *Karl Marx's Jüdischer Humanismus* (Vienna, 1968).
MASSING, P.: *Rehearsal for Destruction. A Study of Political Antisemitism in Imperial Germany* (New York, 1949).
MAYER, G. (ed.): *Ferdinand Lassalle. Nachgelassene Briefe und Schriften* (Stuttgart/Berlin, 1921–6).
McLELLAN, D. (ed.): *Karl Marx. Early Texts* (Oxford, 1971).
The Young Hegelians and Karl Marx (London, 1969).
MEDEM, V.: *Fun mein Leben* (New York, 1923) 2 vols.
MENDELSOHN, E.: *Class Struggle in the Pale* (Cambridge, 1970).
MICHELS, R.: *Political Parties* (New York, 1959), 2nd. ed.
MILL, J.: *Pioniern un boier* (New York, 1946–49), 2 vols.
MISHKINSKY, M.: *Yesodot Le-umiim be Hitpatchutah shel t'nuat ha poalim ha yehudim be Rusia* (Jerusalem, 1965) [Ph.D. thesis].
MISRAHI, R.: *Marx et la Question Juive* (Paris, 1972).
MOSSE, G.: *Germans and Jews* (New York, 1970).
MOSSE, W. and PAUCKER, A. (eds) *Deutsches Judentum im Krieg und Revolution 1916–1923* (Tübingen, 1971).

NA'AMAN, S.: *Ferdinand Lassalle, Deutscher und Jude* (Hanover, 1968).
Lassalle (Hanover, 1970).
NEDAVA, J.: *Trotsky and the Jews* (Philadelphia, 1972).
NETTL, P.: *Rosa Luxemburg* (Oxford, 1966), 2 vols.
NIEWYK, D.: *Socialist, Antisemite and Jew: German Social-Democracy confronts the problem of Antisemitism 1918–1933* (Baton Rouge, 1971).

PATKIN, A.: *The Origins of the Russian-Jewish Labour Movement* (Melbourne, 1947).
PÉGUY, C.: *Notre Jeunesse* (Paris, 1969).

PULZER, P.: *The Rise of Political Anti-Semitism in Germany and Austria* (New York, 1964).

REICHMANN, E.: *Flucht in den Hass* (Frankfurt a. M n.d.).
RENNAP, I.: *Anti-Semitism and the Jewish Question* (London, 1942).

SARTRE, J. P: *Reflêxions sur la Question juive* (Paris, 1954).
SILBERNER, E.: *Sozialisten zur Judenfrage* (Berlin, 1962).
STERNHELL, Z.: *Maurice Barrès et le Nationalisme Français* (Paris, 1972).

TALMON, J.: *Israel among the Nations* (London, 1970).
TOBIAS, H.: *The Jewish Bund in Russia. From its Origins to 1905* (Stanford, 1972).
TOURY, J.: *Die Politische Orientierungen der Juden in Deutschland* (Tübingen, 1966).
TROTSKY, L.: *My Life* (New York, 1930).
On the Jewish Question (New York, 1970).
Political Profiles (London, 1972).
TYCH, F. (ed): *Rôży Luksemburg. Listy do Leona Jogischesa-Tsyzki* (Warsaw, 1968), 2 vols.

WEINBERG, D.: *Les Juifs à Paris de 1933 à 1939* (Paris, 1974).
WEINSTOCK, N.: *Le Sionisme contre Israël* (Paris, 1969).
WEIZMANN, C.: *Trial and Error* (London, 1949).
WISTRICH, R.: *Socialism and the Jewish Question in Germany and Austria 1880–1914* (London, 1974). [Ph.D. thesis.]
WOLFE, B.: *Three Who Made a Revolution* (New York, 1948).

ZEMAN, Z., and SCHARLAU, W.: *The Merchant of Revolution: The Life of Alexander Israel Helphand* [Parvus] (London/New York, 1965).
ZIEBURA, G.: *Léon Blum et le Parti Socialiste 1872–1934* (Paris, 1967).

Index